Grandparenting

I0799613

Also by Terri Apter

Altered Loves: Mothers and Adolescent daughters

Secret Paths: Women in the New Midlife

The Confident Child: Raising Children to Believe in Themselves

Best Friends: The Pleasures and Perils of Girls and Women's Friendships (co-author Ruthellen Josselson)

The Myth of Maturity: What Teenagers Need to Become Adults

You Don't Really Know Me!: Why Mothers and Daughters fight and How Both Can Win

The Sister Knot: Why We Fight, Why We're Jealous, and Why We'll Love Each Other No Matter What

What Do You Want From Me? Learning to Get Along With Our In-laws

Difficult Mothers: Understanding and Overcoming Their Power

Passing Judgment: Praise and Blame in Everyday Life

The Teen Interpreter: A Guide to the Challenges and Joys of Raising Adolescents

'*Grandparenting* is a long-awaited, well-informed, personal and well-researched insight into what it means to be a grandparent. Terri Apter is brilliant, warm, human and wise... A wonderful book'

Julia Samuel, author of
Every Family Has a Story

'In tones of good humour and rare sanity, *Grandparenting* seamlessly weaves together sage practical counsel, granular observation of intergenerational relationships and relevant context from psychology, neurology and anthropology. An invaluable resource for grandparents and parents alike'

Josh Cohen, author of
All the Rage

'Wise, deep, illuminating and so compassionate – for mothers, daughters, children, everyone who makes a family. I've recommended it to many friends, both mums of young children, like myself, who are trying to understand their shifting relationships, and friends who are now at the grandmothering stage. I know it's a book I'll return to as time passes'

Liz Berry, author of
The Republic of Motherhood

'Perceptive, wide-ranging, lively, and astute, this book is a must-read for grandparents and parents alike'

Lisa Appignanesi, author of
Everyday Madness: On Grief, Anger, Loss and Love

'A magnificent book, written by one of the most impressive experts on family psychology, Dr Terri Apter has created a highly readable and deeply honest investigation of the joys, the burdens, and the complexities of becoming a grandmother or grandfather. A work of deep emotional sensitivity, Apter has helped us to understand the true interactions among three intimate generations: babies, parents, and grandparents'

Professor Brett Kahr, Tavistock Institute of Medical Psychology, and Freud Museum London

Grandparenting

On Love and Relationships Across Generations

TERRI APTER

s
epte
m
b
er

Grandparenting is a general resource for grandparents and parents. The names and details of the participants presented in the book have been changed. This book is not a substitute for individualised professional advice. Standards of clinical practice and protocol change over time, and no technique or recommendation is guaranteed to be effective in all circumstances. For concerns about legal issues you should seek professional advice and support.

First published in the United Kingdom by September Publishing in 2025

September Publishing, an imprint of Duckworth Books Ltd
1 Golden Court, Richmond, TW9 1EU, United Kingdom
www.septemberpublishing.org

© Terri Apter, 2025

All rights reserved. No part of this publication may be reproduced, stored in a retrieval system, or transmitted, in any form or by any means electronic, mechanical, photocopying, recording or otherwise, without the prior permission of the publisher.

The right of Terri Apter to be identified as the Author of this Work has been asserted by her in accordance with the Copyright, Designs and Patents Act 1988.

A catalogue record for this book is available from the British Library

Book design by Danny Lyle

Printed and bound in Great Britain by Clays Ltd, Elcograf S.p.A.

1 3 5 7 9 10 8 6 4 2

Trade paperback ISBN: 9780715655740
eISBN: 9780715655764

The authorised representative in the EEA is Easy Access System Europe, Mustamäe tee 50, 10621 Tallinn, Estonia.

MIX
Paper | Supporting responsible forestry
FSC® C018072

To my brilliant daughters Julia and Miranda
who gave me everything
and then gave me grandchildren

Contents

Introduction

The power of grandparenting took me by surprise. It was not only the love – though there was plenty of that – or the new set of worries and cares. What struck me most, and motivated this book, was the radical transformation of our family and everyone's position in it. As a young generation joined us, I expected my input to diminish; instead I found that the importance of each member was magnified. I was now a different kind of mother: the mother of a child who was a parent, and a very new grandmother, without any idea what that entailed. The image I once had of grandparents as tangential to younger generations became stranger each day. Cross-generational bonds were now central to my way of thinking, feeling and breathing, as I knew they were for others, particularly for the one in every three people over the age of fifty who is a grandparent. I could find no platform, in book or blog, that did justice to this new chapter of love, so I set out to explore it more widely.

This book brings the crucial role of grandparenting into the limelight. It celebrates the love between generations while acknowledging how difficult it sometimes is to enact and engage positively. It explores the psychological forces that bring generations together – and those that set barriers between them. It examines the social and historical pressures that shape intergenerational relationships today, and also looks back at how grandparenting shaped human evolution. It shows how the bond between grandparents and their grandchildren remains strong, even as the nature of the relationship shifts all over our ever-changing world.

Experiences of grandparenting are central to the human experience. They should be part of every conversation, whether personal or political, on family connections and dynamics. The input of grandparents in the family is relevant to every family member – and in writing this book, I had in mind *all* readers interested in maintaining cross-generational love and understanding families.

Many grandparents feel alienated, as I did, by the image of a sedentary, benign old person, who plays nothing more than a passive role within the wider family. To understand the lived experience of modern grandparenting we need to reassess the stereotypical Western model of 'family' as consisting of only two generations, parents and their children, and introduce a revolution in thinking about families, ageing and attachment that addresses the following topics:

- The special nature of love for grandchildren.
- The impact of becoming a grandparent on our identity.
- The need to relearn ways of parenting our adult children.
- How grandparents protect a child from life's knocks and setbacks.

- The role of grandparents in human evolution.
- The tricky triangulation of attachment and authority – grandparents, parents, grandchildren.
- Navigating relationships with in-laws – and our own adult children.
- Childcare and grandparents' contributions to parents' careers.
- Supporting grandchildren through parental divorce.
- The changing nature of grandparents' family involvement throughout the world.

Like any long-term, intimate relationship, cross-generational bonds involve elemental passions – love, belonging and protectiveness, but also fear of loss, exclusion, lack of control, diminished authority and influence. The full story cannot be told, nor guidance offered, without looking squarely at the sometimes messy aspects of intimate relationships, with inevitable tensions between belonging and individuality, between generosity and selfishness. There should be shelves of books to address these issues, but since grandparenting is seen as neither a primary nor complex relationship, the challenges families have in working out grandparenting roles remain invisible.

Although this topic is underexplored in our wider culture, it is far from absent in our personal experiences. Individually, as parents or grandparents, we puzzle over how we can benefit from the love and care that can be present across generations without losing our privacy or autonomy. Yet so engrained is the idea that families are nuclear and that ties across generations are marginal, that this big conversation has not made its way into mainstream discussions about families and their relationships – until now.

Grandparenthood Re-imagined

The cultural sidelining of grandparents results partly from ageism – one of the last acceptable prejudices. Becoming a grandparent is seen as an icing on the cake of life, the slices of which have mostly been eaten. The word 'elderly' itself conjures up the idea of someone whose vision has narrowed to their small personal comforts and irritations. A holiday in the sun is a special source of excitement but, supposedly, their interest is more usually on heating bills and gammy knees. 'Grandparent' is linked to a sitting-down and inward-looking image that is badly out of date.

Grandparents today are unlike any other generation of grandparents. Many, in younger adulthood, spearheaded shifts in female identity, challenging the customary gendered division of labour in the home and extending women's identities far beyond the domestic sphere. They live longer, and are often healthier and more active than their parents at the same age; many are still working, focused on their careers and driven by ambition, financial need, eagerness for adventure and engagement with the wider community.

This strong, outward-looking cohort anticipated a later midlife where that tricky tension between competing desires and duties would ease. But instead of the empty nest imagined by so many middle-aged people in the US and Europe, grandparents today have to engage with their adult children's need for support – support that often involves travel and money, and always involves high expenditure of energy. Across the world, contemporary grandparents – 90 per cent of them – play a role in caring for and influencing and supporting the next generation.[1] More than two-thirds of grandparents routinely provide essential childcare for overstretched working parents. While some childcare is ad hoc – taking grandkids to buy shoes or get their eyes tested – 20 per cent of grandmothers regularly provide up to ten hours of help every week.[2]

The younger generation – the new parents – have demanding working lives. They also have very high standards for monitoring and enriching their children's development. They are overstretched and stressed, and turn to a grandparent as the source of an extra pair of hands. When grandparents step up to these requests, they discover they take a step *down* in status; from being the parental authority, they are now the parental aid; from the instigator of decisions about children's well-being, education and health, to being the bystander; from the person with primary rights to beloved children to being the person dependent on the parents for their right of access. This shift in status also holds around the world, even in countries such as China and India, where grandparents once felt assured of their continuing authority over adult children who become parents. Across the globe, new parents are determined to secure their mobility and independence, even as they draw on the practical, emotional and often financial resources of grandparents.

Beyond the joy of welcoming a new person into the family lies a maze of shifting relationships with their own children and children-in-law as they become parents, and also with their children-in-laws' parents who have an equal, but often very different, emotional interest in their grandchildren. With so much at stake, where – as Barbara Graham puzzled in the preface to *Eye of My Heart*, her edited book of personal grandparenting essays – can we see people 'grappling with the role itself?'[3]

Past Perceptions – and New Understanding

Research about grandparents was nonexistent until the 1930s, when it was skewed by misogyny and ageism. Grandparents were described as strict, rigid and locked into archaic assumptions about childrearing.[4] They were seen as hell-bent on interfering with the new mother's child-rearing efforts. Young mothers were following the new enlightened advice of the day, while grandmothers barked out old-fashioned and dogmatic views. Disgruntled, slow, and set in her outdated ways, grandmothers were seen as unsuitable custodians of young children. Two decades later, clinicians' views were equally critical, focusing on the 'disliked grandmother' who was unable to adjust to change and was 'unpleasantly aggressive' towards both parents and grandchildren.

This book offers an essential new perspective on grandparents, examining research showing that regular contact with grandchildren contributes positively to children's mental health, resilience and social skills. My own experience of the unexpected and overwhelming emotions of grandparenting informs much of this book, but also showcased are the voices of many different grandparents, parents and children as they navigate, struggle and delight in love between family generations. I draw, too, on work I have done over the past thirty-five years on family dynamics, particularly those between parents and children of all ages – from infancy to midlife – and between families brought together by marriage and ripped apart by divorce.

The aim of this book is threefold. Firstly, it explores the vital but neglected complexity of intergenerational family relationships. Secondly, it takes a new look at how grandparenting impacts identity, priorities and values. Thirdly, it offers guidelines for those who seek to navigate new family puzzles, new emotions, new needs and new compromises. The guidelines at the end of each chapter can be seen as a version of piecemeal engineering. They suggest simple step-by-step adjustments that can be tried, modified, then tried again, as you explore what works and what does not in your individual family. This flexible, personalised approach allows important intergenerational bonds to thrive.

My recent work, supported by Newnham College, Cambridge, involves close observations and in-depth interviews with seventy-two grandparents from thirty-two families in the US and the UK. All the grandparents were – or had been – part of a heterosexual couple, and only two of the parents were part of a same sex couple, but, as will emerge within the case histories, the families came from a wide variety of religious and ethnic backgrounds. They were observed at occasions of interaction, from casual babysitting to large formal gatherings at religious and secular ceremonies or birthdays.[5] Their experiences of being a grandparent are explored – how the reality differs from their expectations, whether this role affects choices they make about where to live and how to spend their time, how grandparenting affects the experience of parenting adult children, how it changes personal identity, ambition and meanings of ageing, and how it impacts on overall satisfaction.

Because women are more likely to take a larger active part in shaping and sustaining intergenerational relationships, 65 per cent of the participants whose voices are presented are grandmothers, though distinctive roles and relational styles of grandfathers are also presented. The voices of these grandparents and their families are put in the context of the few but valuable large data sets looking at the impact of grandparents on the well-being of children, their parents and on the grandparents themselves.[6]

My hope is that readers who are grandparents will find soulmates in the book's case histories, companions and guides throughout the shifts and expansion of family relationships. I hope readers who are parents will understand how the upheavals of parenthood may render them both more dependent on and less tolerant of their parents and parents-in-law. When I envisage readers as grandchildren, I think of my own, and hope that they will read the message so many grandparents want to convey: 'This is the quality and character of my love; hold it close for support, confidence and comfort, in all that lies ahead.'

One
The Birth of a Grandparent
'I didn't expect to feel all this'

When I was a young woman, parenthood loomed before me as a desirable but terrifying future. I knew that becoming a parent would threaten the freedom I associated with youth. It would disturb the uncertain but exciting ambitions and identity I believed were central to my existence. Having a child would bring responsibilities, demands and emotions that I could neither anticipate nor control. But, as I struggled with the prospect of becoming a mother, never once did I reflect on a time I might become a grandparent. And in this omission, I am not alone.[1]

Whether becoming a grandparent takes us by surprise, or whether it is a role we have long yearned for, it is a transition into the unknown. The new attachment brings joy, but requires significant adjustments to our position in a family and our relationships with our children and their partners. When we become a grandparent, we find our core emotional identity in flux. It is as though we have walked onto the set of a new family drama without a script to guide us.

Love at First Sight

When Faye's daughter, Chrisy, gave birth to her first child, the new grandmother experienced what she calls an 'explosion of love'. The sight of any newborn child, packed with their own character and already expressing needs and interacting with the world, brings with it a jolt of wonder. Combine this with a realisation that the infant belongs to you, and you are flooded with much higher levels of wonder and love.

'I couldn't keep my eyes off him,' Faye explains. 'My son-in-law was talking to me, but I barely heard him. When I got back into the here and now, my daughter was laughing at me.'

'Grandma swoon,' Chrisy teases gently.

Love, whether romantic, parental or grandparental is, scientifically speaking, a total eclipse of the brain. Though each category of love has its own set of brain chemicals,[2] the two primary hormones involved in loving attachments are oxytocin and vasopressin. It is widely known that high levels of oxytocin – known as 'the cuddle hormone' – are found in most new mothers in the 'golden hour' after giving birth and when breastfeeding; less well-known is how these chemicals also surge in fathers and in grandparents who engage with their grandchildren. So, yes, the grandparent swoon is real. But this new love is only one piece in the expanded family configuration.

Chrisy, still recovering from an emergency Caesarean, is absorbed in her baby and discovers a new depth in family connection. 'I see how important families are,' she explains. 'My mother used to say, "You won't appreciate me until you have children of your own." I hated hearing that. I felt she was saying either I didn't properly love her now, or I would come to regret my criticisms of her later. But now I get it. There's this connection you never want to break. It's overwhelming because you'd do anything for your child. And she had the same feelings when she had me. I get it now, how important the bloodline is.'

Faye watches her daughter croon over the infant and is also overwhelmed with a new kind of love. 'Seeing your own kid being a parent, it's falling in love with her all over again, too.' As the author and journalist Anna Quindlen reflects, 'There are many thrilling things about being a grandmother… but for me, one of the most thrilling is watching my eldest child be a first-rate parent.'[3] The transition to parenthood strengthens the bonds between mother and daughter, just as it forges a new link with grandparent and grandchild.

Different Paths to Love

Many grandparents who are devoted to their grandchildren do not experience that chemical 'grandmother swoon' the first time they hold the baby. My own response was more along the lines of, 'Phew, he's got his fingers, toes, functioning bodily organs and reflexes.' I was still more mother than grandmother, relieved for my daughter's sake that she had such a stunning baby. My impulse to hover and help was only partly to stake a claim on my grandson. His birth revived memories of the isolation and bewilderment that accompanied my own introduction to motherhood. My mother was dying at the time my first daughter – now a new mother herself – was born, and in those far off days before iPhone cameras or email, we raced to take, develop and send photos of her first grandchild. She was too weak to hold them herself, but my father positioned them so that they were in her sightline when she opened her eyes.

As with many new grandmothers I discovered that my 'altruistic' offers of help sometimes misfired. A phone call interrupted the new mother's much-needed sleep. Bringing dinner along with my visit seemed to generate a great deal of work, with the setting out of plates and cutlery and sauces. I discovered early on that I should expect more criticism of my input than gratitude for my motives. But I remained available to sit with my grandson for a few hours while my daughter went to the gym, and to be an extra pair of hands while she did her best to impose some order on her newly disrupted life. And every time I offered this kind of 'cover', I remembered the early days of being a mother, when, in the rare times I had someone else to mind the baby, I was able to retrieve aspects of my pre-maternal life. I recalled the pleasure of walking with suddenly strange but once familiar freedom, my hands unoccupied, my mind wandering where it would, and my breath easy. I wanted to offer my daughter such precious periods of reprieve.

I cannot remember at what point my focus shifted from 'doing this for my daughter' to realising that a connection between my grandson and me had opened up a new, unexpected vein of joy. My daughter's maternity leave came to an end, and I was on hand when their childminder had her own family emergency. Using my daughter's old buggy (which the parents disapproved of, because it fell below the standards of today's far more expensive baby paraphernalia) I walked him to parks and shops and doctor's appointments. He was learning to talk and he would repeat phrases I used, tensing his brow, deeply preoccupied as he articulated. I felt in direct contact with his mental efforts, seated on a special perch just inside that soft, concentrating head. Sometimes I listened to music while we played with blocks or cars; suddenly I noticed him watching me and swaying, imitating the movements I was making but of which I had been unaware. I was abashed, but also deeply flattered.

Soon he was a proper toddler, and I held his hand as we walked. Small though it was, his hand – or the sensation of his hand in mine – filled my mind. When I took him to his first dental appointment, he drew back when instructed to sit in the large brown reclining chair. I offered to sit first, so he could lie on top of me, and all was well. 'Your feet are a triangle,' he observed, because all he saw were the tips of my feet forming an apex above the base formed by the chair. He held his own feet like mine, and said, 'There are now two triangles.' I fluttered with pleasure on my perch within the centre of his brow, sharing his vision. On the way back to the car, the pavement was blocked and we were directed to a pedestrian detour. I momentarily lost my sense of direction. 'We go that way,' he said as I hesitated, and when I thanked him and explained I had been in 'a muddle', he said, 'I can help you when you are in a muddle.' With that precise repetition of a phrase I used, now accompanied by an awareness of his own agency, I tightened my grip on his hand. There must be a specific grandparent heartbeat that accompanies such intimate interactions.

Later, when he started pre-school, I picked him up once a week and took him to a swimming class. When he came out of the pool, shivering and hungry, I wrapped a towel around him, sat him on my lap and opened the snacks I had prepared. The rhythm of his chewing and the wriggling of his body on my lap filled me with peace and pleasure. While the parents around me were chivvying their children to 'stop fooling around, get dressed, we have to get on', I was in a zone outside of time. It's not that parents don't enjoy the sensations and smells and sounds of their children's bodies. They do, but they are also on a schedule, with hundreds of other things to focus on. Grandparents can be more in the moment precisely because they are less likely to captain the military precision needed for domestic life today.

The walk back to his home provided opportunity for a variety of games. He would run ahead to hide, and delight in my make-believe worry that I had lost him. He would make 'dinner' out of leaves, to which he would then invite me as his guest. A shortcut became a setting for adventure where we were explorers lost in the forest. I slipped easily into 'let's pretend', as grandparents do, and elaborated on the scenarios he initiated. He took these additions to the game – what other people might be coming to the 'dinner' or what country we were exploring – very seriously. For me, this was the ultimate experience in imaginative intimacy.

When we arrived home, he would always ask, 'Do you want to come in and build a train track?' He was enticing me to stay with what he supposed was my favourite activity. I became very good at building train tracks from both wood and plastic sets. They ran from the sitting room into the hall, and then around the corner to the kitchen. He soon outstripped me with constructions of multidirectional points systems and double tracks; but though I was now banned as design engineer, he was happy to issue instructions or have me watch him and listen as he carefully explained what he was doing. It was becoming harder to take up that perch inside his intense gaze, but any success came with a burst of delighted surprise.

Claudine Attias-Donfut, a French academic writing about intergenerational relationships, reflected that 'by being drawn into [her grandson's] small world, and becoming an important part of it, I have begun to step back from the active adult universe in which I had been enclosed since my children left home … I am passing into a new phase of life."[4] Psychologist (and grandmother) Alison Gopnik writes with both imagination and scientific rigour about the development of children's minds. She shows the myriad ways that the child's mind is tuned to learn, whereas older people – the age group most likely to be a grandparent – find it much harder to learn or question or revise and re-imagine the world.[5] This is not merely the difficulty that old dogs may have in learning new tricks, it is because older people do not tend to play in the same imaginative way that children do. Entertainment can be enriching, such as talking to friends, reading, watching films and plays and listening to music, but fluid engagement in fresh, inventive play is rare – except with grandchildren. The pleasure it brings is like a shot of cocaine, generating gratitude and love for our delightful teacher and visionary.

Of course parents also thrill to their children's surprising, original ways of seeing the world. But grandparents, whose brains are generally less plastic (in the sense of adaptable, or absorbent), find an increased benefit in stimulating intimacy with grandchildren. Walking with a two-year-old, Alison Gopnik observes, is like going for a walk with William Blake. It takes much longer to get from point A to point B, because your grandchild is rarely focused on the destination, but on details of the journey.[6]

This is perfect for my eighty-year-old husband and our nine-year-old granddaughter. She points out the smells and sounds and sights along their path. Her grandfather's now slow pace allows her to do what a child does – take in information from everything around her. Instead of focusing on one thing or another, her attention spreads out in front of her and scans the scene like a lantern shedding light on anything that might be important, or pleasing or curious.[7] As Anna Quindlen says, 'Talking with a small child is like talking to yourself – yourself before you forgot to notice things.'[8]

This explains research showing that grandparents who take care of grandchildren one day a week have a significantly reduced risk of developing dementia compared to those in their age group who do not participate in the lives of younger generations.[9] Intimate imaginative engagement with grandchildren stimulates greater mental agility and improved problem-solving skills, as Claudine Attias-Donfut discovered. In engaging with her grandson's imaginative world, she felt 'a change in [her] emotions. Problems encountered in [her] professional life seem to weigh less heavily and are brought into a new perspective.'[10] And, as a grandparent is led into an imaginative place they never thought they would inhabit again, their grandchild learns that they have a person eager to listen to them with warmth and curiosity, laying down a special trust that has a remarkable and lasting effect.[11]

The Emergence of New Complexities

Whether it comes via the 'grandparent swoon' or is more incremental, love is only the beginning. Grandparents' new-found attachment generates many additional needs: that of developing a long-term relationship with a child, the reassurance of mutual connection, and of involvement in the child's life. Love for the new child carries with it a desire for tactile interaction and the rewards of infant-to-carer gaze, so grandparents often seek opportunities to participate in the intimate tasks of holding, soothing, cleaning and feeding. But the needs of the grandparent have to be mediated via the parents.

To understand the intricacy and variation of grandparents' experience, we need to see how it hinges on a number of other relationships: the relationship between each new parent and their parents; between the nexus of wider relatives, such as siblings, aunts and uncles, step-relatives from both sides of the family; and on the notoriously uneasy space that both separates and joins new parents and grandparents with their in-laws.

New parenthood and new grandparenthood take place in a context of intense and, as yet, uncharted emotions. The new parents' day-to-day life is unrecognisable. Whatever joy and love they feel are likely to be accompanied by confusion, anxiety and fatigue. In this context, their sensitivity to one another is heightened, both for good and for ill. There is greater appreciation for warmth and connection, but tempers are shorter, and grandparents should prepare for quick-firing irritability and readiness to take offence. Sometimes these storms pass quickly, but they can inflict lingering wounds, particularly among in-laws.

Chrisy's mother-in-law, Aisha, is also a grandmother. She, too, is overwhelmed by a new love and is proud to see her son take on the role of parent. But Aisha feels uneasy holding the infant with her daughter-in-law watching so closely. She explains, 'I feel the new baby is really mine, even though I know he's not. And when I leave him, I keep thinking I've lost something. When I left them, I felt like I was leaving part of myself behind.'

Aisha's emotional system is hijacked, as so often happens in grandparenting, by her attachment to the infant. This attachment generates an urgent desire for involvement. But she worries whether her involvement will be welcome. 'I walk on eggshells when I'm with my daughter-in-law. She's polite enough, but I have to be careful. I say something and I can tell, you know, just by the way she moves her head, that I've said the wrong thing.'

This unspoken wariness increases during her visit to her new grandson. 'I try to help when he's crying or fussing. But it's like I'm offending her. I don't know what it is. Whether she thinks I'm trying to take the baby away? But that's only to give her a rest. Or maybe she thinks I'm showing her up? I ask my son, but he just says, "It's early days, Ma. Let her be." I guess he doesn't want to hear me out.'

A common theme in the voices of grandparents is that of a *his and hers* story: paternal grandparents versus maternal grandparents. 'There's so much to do as a new mother,' Aisha remarks. 'I just want to help out. I know I welcomed help when each of my children was born. I thought my daughter-in-law would be grateful.'

That makes perfect sense – doesn't it?

Alas, we are complicated, touchy beings. 'Help' has many different meanings, depending on who is providing it and in what context.

Which Mother Knows Best?

While advice for grandparents is sparse, parents are deluged by it. At each step, they are primed to think everything they do might have lifelong consequences, either good or bad. It is not surprising that so many new parents are insecure about their ability to parent. 'Am I doing it right?' and, 'If the baby is crying or won't sleep or feed, am I doing something wrong?' The standards of being 'a good parent' are high, and the standards of being 'a good mother' are higher.

Not knowing how to interact with a new baby, for a father, is acceptable. 'After all, he'll learn,' people say. Not being a naturally 'good mother', on the other hand, seems like a deep moral failing. Most new mothers resist old ideals of the 'good mother' – or at least they try to. But *knowing* that the ideal of the ever-present, always-effective mother is sexist and controlling, does not always protect a mother from *feeling* that she should meet that impossible standard.

So, when both new mother and grandmother hear the baby's cries, and each sees a different need, competition arises. Whose gut response is better? And whatever the answer, the worry is that the real question being asked is, 'Who is the better mother?'

The cries of an infant are unignorable. The brain processes these sounds so that they grab our attention in a way that few other noises do. Even before our brain logs what is going on – the baby is crying – it tags this sound as 'important'. The cries quickly prime both parent and grandparent to act.[12] This ensures our prompt response and willingness to do just about anything to stop the baby's wails.

When Aisha responds to the baby's cries by picking him up, Chrisy tells me tearfully that she feels Aisha is showing her how this or that should be done. 'Like she has to teach me, because I don't know anything.' She turns her face away, but her shaking shoulders reveal she is weeping, however silently. 'And I don't,' she admits after a few moments. 'There's so much I don't know. But she doesn't know either. She doesn't see that I don't want to give him formula even if he's not sleeping, let alone from a plastic bottle!' After a pause, Chrisy adds, now weeping openly, 'And she annoys me.'

Maternal sensitivity and weepiness after birth are so common that they have a name: 'the three-day blues' or 'the new-baby blues.' This label can be reassuring because it carries the message: 'This is normal,' and, 'This will pass.' But the term should not be used to dismiss a new mother's responses. Even when distress is driven by postnatal hormonal surges, it is not 'just' hormones talking.

The misfiring of messages between the new mother and grandmother hearken back to ancient tensions between mother-in-law and daughter-in-law. These often emerge in the early years of marriage or partnership, when a mother-in-law is used to being the dominant woman in her family, the expert on many domestic things, particularly on servicing her son's needs and influencing his behaviour. The new wife, however, wants to be the woman in charge in her new family and resents a mother-in-law's presumption of authority. But, as she tries to convey the importance of her status within this new family unit, and works on setting boundaries, the mother-in-law feels threatened: 'Am I no longer of any use?' and, 'Am I losing my status in the family?' and, 'Will I be humiliated, or even worse, cast out by the new couple-dynamics that change my one-to-one relationship with my son?' A mother-in-law's anxiety about being excluded may lead her to be more persistent and more intrusive as she tries to secure a foothold in the newly configured family. In response to her mother-in-law's search for security and reassurance, the daughter-in-law doubles down in her efforts to set boundaries.

While these tensions tend to work themselves out as the two generations learn new rhythms of interaction, they often re-emerge after the birth of a first child. The grandmother is the more experienced mother, and to her it seems right and proper that she should show the new mother the ropes. But the new mother feels the ultimate and direct burden of responsibility for this new precious human. The weight of cultural norms about mothering bare down upon her: *I have to get this right.* Expectations about what she should feel towards her baby and how her baby should respond to her are likely to be challenged by her actual experiences, riven as these are with the fatigue brought on by disturbed sleep, the abrupt changes in routine and the brutal new restrictions on even the most simple personal freedoms. Common ways of managing her mood or comforting herself – such as going for a walk, taking a nap, reading a book or talking to a friend, or even using the toilet – are blocked by a myriad of urgent infant-related tasks. Help with these is sometimes welcomed, but offers of help can also be seen by a new mother as an accusation, 'You're not coping,' or, 'You're not good at mothering.' She may read the mother-in-law as saying, 'You need my help because you're not doing this well.'

A grandmother whose daughter-in-law is *not* irked by her sense of possessiveness is fortunate. Anna Quindlen describes her relief and sense of good luck when she asked her daughter-in-law, 'Can I pick him up?' and her daughter-in-law replied easily, 'Yes. Of course.'[13] That great relief comes from an expectation of what a paternal grandmother might experience: guarded, uneasy responses from a daughter-in-law. And Chrisy, at this stage, is too uncertain of her own skill in meeting her baby's needs to sit back and watch her mother-in-law croon and sway the fretting infant to sleep. So why is the paternal grandmother particularly 'lucky' when the new mother says, 'Yes, of course you can pick him up?'

Maternal versus Paternal Grandmother: Learning the Differing Dynamics

So different are the issues for maternal and paternal grandmother that in Chinese languages there is no common word 'grandmother' but two distinct words for the maternal grandmother and the paternal grandmother.[14] In societies such as India, Pakistan, several African tribes and China, the maternal grandparents, until recent decades, had marginal influence on the new parents and their children, while the paternal grandmother wielded authority over them both. But in contemporary Western families, new mothers usually retain the practice of kin-keeping – arranging visits, and implicitly or explicitly giving priority to one rather than the other side of the family. As a result, paternal grandparents are dependent on a daughter-in-law's goodwill for easy access to their grandchildren.[15]

Most daughters-in-law do not want to exclude any grandparent from engaging with grandchildren. Chrisy does not 'like herself,' she tells me, 'for resenting her mother-in-law for just being here,' but in searching for an explanation, the simple admission that reduces Chrisy to tears of frustration and shame is, 'She annoys me.'

I know all too well what she means. I experienced a similar mood implosion as my well-meaning mother-in-law 'annoyed me'. I saw her determination to 'help' as a means of showing off her expertise. I felt she was positioning me as novice, when I needed to become, rapidly, an expert. I understand what a terrible place Chrisy is in, where she knows she is being unfair but cannot, at this point, see a way to be fair. I sympathise, too, with her mother-in-law's pain and confusion: 'What on earth am I doing wrong?' Aisha must ask herself. Of course Aisha has done nothing *wrong*; it's just that the new mother's fatigue, anxiety and passionate desire to get things right, transform Aisha's well-intentioned efforts – in her daughter-in-law's eyes – into acts of intrusion and hubris.

Why is this a particular issue with paternal grandmothers and less so with maternal grandmothers? After all, there are few women who do not find their own mothers very annoying, at least some of the time. And grandmothers, whether maternal or paternal, have a habit of speaking with a cavalier authority: 'She's tired. She needs a nap,' or, 'You need to feed her for a bit longer.' At this early mothering stage, shouldn't that annoyance be equally shared between the two grandmothers?

The difference for Chrisy, and for many new mothers, is that when her mother annoys her, she can snap openly, rather than bottle it up and seethe. 'I can tell Mum to butt out. I can inform her that her way is no longer the recommended way. You don't put babies down to sleep on their stomachs. You don't wrap them up so they are too warm. I tell her, and she makes a face, but then it's over. We tussle as we go.'

The new mother and her mother have had a lot of practice 'tussling' in their past. In fact, a mother and her adolescent daughter are likely to engage in some kind of quarrel every two and a half days.[16] As awful as those quarrels seem at the time, they lay the groundwork for negotiating and repairing conflicts. The teen girl and her mother oppose one another over issues of parental control ('No you can't stay out that late/go there/with those people' or, 'Yes you do have to clean your room/do your homework/look after your little brother') or goals and values ('This seems important to you now, but it's really a waste of time' or, 'Stop caring what your friends think) without breaking the bond between them.

Whether or not the teenager is right about how much she has learned or how responsible she is, she and her mother are used to negotiating positions via argument. Most mother/

teenage daughter pairs learn that showing impatience and taking offence does not kill the relationship. Along the way they learn to shift from rupture – anger, hurt or defiance and self-righteousness – to repair, where once again they are friends, trusted, loving, working towards mutual understanding. In fact, such quarrels often serve as a means of revitalising that bond, as the outspoken teenager gets the message across to her slow-learning parents: 'I'm not the little kid you think you know. I have changed and matured, and learned to be responsible.'

These exercises ease the transition from mother/daughter to grandmother/new mother. The new mother can scold, shout or sigh when the new grandmother offends her with bossy authority or presumption of her own maternal wisdom. The new grandmother draws on past experience with her daughter. The irritability and opposition are familiar, and not too frightening, because the grandmother already knows that conflict with her daughter is part of the relational package.

Of course, not all mother/daughter pairs learn these difficult relational dance steps. Some people tell me that, for them, the mother-in-law/mother dynamic is reversed. It is their own mother who annoys them or who makes comments that 'pull me down' and 'remind me I'm not coping as well as my sister'. Some find there is less negative history with a mother-in-law and fewer triggers for quarrels.

Quarrelling, however, is not the only symptom of tension. Many new parent/grandparent pairs who find their relationship stressful do not quarrel. Caught in what I call *good behaviour syndrome* they avoid open argument.[17] They are both too worried about quarrelling to criticise, complain or explain openly. Instead, the tension in their lips, the tenor of their voice and the rhythm of their breathing send clear but silent signals of discontent, impatience and offence.

We saw how Aisha tries to manage her daughter-in-law's confusing responses by 'walking on eggshells' and trying to 'help'. Surely, by showing her willingness to learn, she will placate whatever inner storms she rouses in her daughter-in-law? That, at least, is her assumption, but her tense politeness actually makes matters worse.

In the grip of good behaviour syndrome, neither grandmother nor new mother can engage in easy, open and genuine conversation. Aisha fears anything she says will cause offence, and Chrisy feels bad for being 'awful' or 'unfair'. Fear of 'not getting along' makes the reality of getting on impossible.

Over and over, grandparents – whether paternal and maternal – talk about the need to 'keep my mouth shut'. They are advised not to voice their views about discipline or diet, toilet training or sleeping arrangements. Whatever change there has been over the past decades in gender roles, these issues still largely remain under the purview of women, so the directive to 'bite your tongue' is usually addressed to the grandmother. Even the normally outspoken writer Ann Roiphe says, reflecting on her experience as a grandmother, 'My poor tongue is sore from being bitten,' and similar jokes about grandmothers' sore tongues regularly appear in conversations and chat rooms.[18]

Such self-silencing exacts a high cost. In a ten-year study, women who said they did not speak out during family conflict were four times more likely to die in the course of the next decade than women who described themselves as 'outspoken'. Keeping quiet and swallowing their complaints impacted badly not only on their mental well-being but also on their physical health.[19] A different solution to cross-generational conflicts is essential.

New Fathers and Paternal Grandmothers: Leaning In and Leaning Out

Where there is tension between a mother-in-law, as a new grandmother, and her daughter-in-law, as a new mother, the person whose intervention could be most effective is the new father. He is best placed to support both women and resolve their opposing perspectives. His position, in principle, allows him to sympathise with each woman's motives and remind them how powerfully the other responds to the new child, and how vulnerable that makes them to each other.

Unfortunately, few new fathers do step in. Instead, like Aisha's son Vijay, they try to calm a wife by saying, 'She's doing her best. That's how she is. There's no point in trying to change her.' He tries to soothe his mother by saying, 'She's just tired. She doesn't mean anything by it.' Vijay is trying to defuse Chrisy's complaints about his mother, but she hears, 'Your feelings are unreasonable.' She sees this as betrayal: he is on his mother's side, not hers. In the cauldron of post-birth sensitivities, these small missteps can generate huge divisions.

I try to avoid easy generalisations about 'what women do' versus 'what men do', but sometimes it is helpful to highlight patterns we more often see in either men or women. What follows is an example of behaviour that I, and many others, have observed in men when caught in the midst of family tensions.[20]

A familiar generalisation, with only very limited truth, is that men are more comfortable with conflict than women.

Conflict is often woven into their games, starting with rough play in early childhood. With their buddies, they compete and then crow over their success while remaining friends. Girls and women, it is said, aim for harmony and do their best to avoid competition.[21] But things are very different when men and women are dealing with cross-generational tensions.

Girls' competitive spirit is equal to that of boys, but *seems* less pronounced because they gild their one-upmanship with complaints about an adversary's personality such as, 'She thinks she's better than everyone else,' or, 'She's a snob.' Because their interpersonal competition is less open and often enacted behind each other's backs, girls are hyper-alert to any put-down, however well disguised, whether in a friendship group or in a family.

Men, more accustomed to overt conflict, are often oblivious to low-grade, indirect conflict between the women in the family. New mother Chrisy interprets her mother-in-law's 'involvement performance' as a kind of competition, while Aisha picks up on her daughter-in-law's discomfort and hostility. She does not know what to make of Chrisy's response because she herself 'means well'. Perhaps she is hoping that Chrisy will appreciate her store of maternal knowledge, but even so, her primary aim is to be involved, not to put Chrisy down. Aisha's son, Vijay, like many men, does not register the force of these uneasy interactions, and his efforts to calm Chrisy only upset her further.

All too often, efforts to lower interpersonal tension actually increase it. Someone who tries to soothe us by saying, in effect, 'You're upset about nothing,' adds fuel to our anger. Dismissing someone's uncomfortable or negative feelings, when they are turning to you for understanding, makes interactions *more* fragile – not less – at least for women.

For men, the cost of self-silencing seems to be much lower than it is for women. The same ten-year study that found a correlation between women 'keeping quiet' and their poor mental and physical health, found no such correlation in men.[22] In fact, looking at men's behaviour, one might conclude that, for them, ignoring family conflict has many benefits.

Of course, the new father wants to be both a good partner and a good son. However, he does not know how to support both women. An adult son is less likely to have that adolescent history of face-to-face argument with his mother as teenage girls do. Teenage boys do quarrel with their mothers, of course, but such quarrels are less frequent and more likely to fizzle out because the issue is 'not worth an argument', because 'the mood changed', or because the teen boy simply withdraws from the fray.[23]

The tendency of some men to step away from interpersonal arguments may be linked to their physiological responses. A series of studies over several decades involved close and detailed observations of couples quarrelling. During these quarrels, each partner's blood pressure, heart rate and perspiration were measured. Men's heart rate, blood pressure and adrenaline levels increased much earlier in a quarrel than women's and were much slower to return to normal after a quarrel. So, while a woman was breathing easily, and she was able to turn away from the quarrel to think of other things, her male partner's body remained on high alert: his stomach tense, his mind awhirl, his legs braced with a sense of 'danger'.[24]

With his own internal responses to a quarrel putting him in flight or fight mode, a man's withdrawal from an argument – fleeing rather than fighting – can be seen as a good outcome for everyone. The downside of 'fleeing', though, is that it can present as 'stonewalling' – shutting down so that he doesn't respond to anything, turning mind and body into a stone wall. Going blank, leaving the room, and refusing to talk are all acts that defend us against the flood of emotions that rise up when we fight with people we love. The new father ducks out of the fray rather than engage with either the new grandmother's pain or the new mother's distress. In backing away from the challenge of being mediator, he protects himself from terrible stress, but misses an opportunity to support both new mother and grandmother, leaving both women feeling aggrieved.

The point of identifying this common occurrence is not to complain or mock a male pattern of behaviour. Anyone can be coached out of a stonewalling response if they see the potential for positive effect. At the end of this chapter I have included guidance for the new father who believes he is in a no-win situation, for the new mother who feels let down and unsupported, and for the grandmother who wants to understand why her best motives are constantly distorted.

Toddler Tantrums and Intergenerational Tensions

Leaving behind the flashpoints of a new birth, we come to early childhood's 'terrible twos' to see another common point of contention between grandparent and parent. This is less about practical concerns such as diet, feeding schedule or potty training; these can be a cause for disagreement, but the resulting conflicts are fairly easily resolved. The more fiery issues are about behaviour and, in particular, how to deal with a toddler's tantrums.

A downside to children's constantly active and brilliant brains is that the prefrontal cortex, the brain's so-called executive controller, is inefficient in messaging more excitable parts of the brain. 'You can't have it now but you can have it later', 'You need to choose one or the other' or a simple 'No' can trigger explosive protests.

In 2006, an exhibition of photographs showed faces of very young children in distress.[25] Each image showed a toddler in a state of apparent grief and despair. Entitled *End Times*, the images were intended to express the photographer's frustration with the political landscape. Understandably, viewers thought the background stories would involve war, famine or abandonment. How else would the photographer have access to such poignant images?

It turns out these images were captured when the photographer gave the children, and then took away, a lollipop or cell phone. But that explanation did not silence accusations of child cruelty. Knowing the backstory – that the children were reacting to a minor disappointment or denial – could not overcome some viewers' responses to such consummate expressions of sadness. The heated debate over the photographer's 'cruelty' continues to this day.

Young children's brains do not contain a damage-limitation advisor; there is no internal monitor that reassures them, 'It's really not so bad'. In the moment, they experience tiny disappointments just as they would major tragedies. When your child or your grandchild is falling apart, then you, in empathy and exasperation, are likely to feel that you, too, are coming apart. The heightened tension is contagious and everyone's anxiety levels rise. The urge to put a stop to the tantrum propels a grandparent to step in, even when they know better.

Whether they step in to distract or soothe or scold or shout, a parent is likely to protest, 'Let me handle this!' A disgruntled grandparent complies, but thinks, 'My way would be better.'

At the beginning of this chapter we saw Chrisy and her mother Faye in a state of contented intimacy as they shared their delight in Chrisy's newborn son. Faye cherished her daughter's new state of motherhood and Chrisy valued this more extensive connection between generations. Two years on, the grandchild remains a source of deep, warm excitement. Mother and grandmother share delight as he discovers uses for objects, all of which are new to him; and so, seeing through his eyes, become new to them. But he, Sonny, is also frustrated when something does not do precisely what he wants it to do, or when he goes to the freezer and proudly opens it, only for someone to shut the door, taking away his agency and his hope of ice cream. In such a state, he not only cries, his face crumpled with a toddler's distinctive rage and despair, but also hits or bites or tells the people he loves that he 'hates' them.

Adults can wear themselves out trying to reason a child out of a tantrum: 'You can have ice cream another day. There are lots of things you can have instead. You are making a fuss over nothing. You've already had lots of treats today. You can't always have what you want. That kind of behaviour will get you nowhere. You're wasting your time.'

When none of these arguments has any effect, adults can find themselves in a tantrum-like state too. 'You've had everything you want this morning. We went to the park. We played games. You can't just have everything you want.' Chrisy works herself into what she calls 'a pickle', as her reasonable arguments go unheeded. When her mother steps in, hugs

Sonny and says, 'Let's look at the new Lego I brought. And here are some raisins,' Chrisy shouts bitterly at her mother, 'That's right. Reward his awful behaviour.'

Each adult is trying to bring the child's mood back to equilibrium. Focused on ending the tantrum, Faye takes her grandson to another room and crouches on the floor, looking directly into his eyes. Eventually his attention shifts away from his inner sorrow to the raisins and the Lego. In a few moments he is building something with his grandmother and the tantrum recedes as though to a distant past. But Chrisy is still shaken, both by her helplessness in face of her son's tantrum and by her anger at her mother's intrusive management. After spending some time trying to calm herself, she watches her son and mother working on their project. After a beat, she observes plaintively, 'You were never this patient with me.'

Afterwards Faye tells me how her heart sank at her daughter's rebuke. The shared bond with the boy, which brought mother and grandmother closer, now brings up memories that set them apart. The child's tantrum passes, the mood of both mother and son improves, but Faye has not got over the shock of her daughter's accusation. Has Chrisy always harboured such resentments against her mother? Will these complaints, that seem to come out of nowhere, set up barriers between mother and grandmother, and between grandmother and grandson?

When grandparents talk about their experiences of grandparenting, they usually say how wonderful it is. And of course it is, particularly when we focus on the grandparent/grandchild pair. But this dyad is embedded in a network of relationships that require delicate navigation. Many grandparents are slow to speak about the darker side of their love. They are sometimes reluctant even to consider how dependent they are on the parents' goodwill for access to grandchildren.

There are many reasons why grandparents do not see their grandchildren as much as they would like. The most common barrier is distance, living too far apart from each other. However, one in seven grandparents is prevented from seeing their grandchild at all, frozen out by their own daughter or son or, more commonly, by an in-law.[26] Those grandparents who are excluded from seeing their grandchildren talk about 'a living bereavement', and I will explore this all-too-common experience in detail in Chapters Six and Seven. But even grandparents who enjoy good relationships with the parents and easy access to grandchildren, are shadowed by fear of potential exclusion. When both grandparents and parents understand the complicated dynamics of grandparenting, they are better placed to preserve love across all three generations.

The Foundational Rule: Respect the New Parents' Status

Grandparents talk about a visceral need to hold a grandchild, to see them develop and to feature in their lives. Sometimes this need for physical closeness takes them by surprise, and heightens anxiety as to whether the parents will allow them their 'fix' – their infusion of pleasure in being with their grandchild. Every generation benefits from grandparent attachment, but the performance or expression of grandparent love sometimes demands tolerance, understanding and monitoring in response to the different needs of the new parents. New parents' needs and grandparents' needs are both met when grandparents accept their new status as the non-experts of this child's care.

Even when a grandparent talks the talk – 'Of course I respect the new parent's authority. They are the child's *parents*' – they do not always behave accordingly. Grandparents know they have more experience than the new parents, but childcare guidelines change. Should a child sleep on their stomach, back or side? What does crying mean and what is a reasonable response? How important is scheduled feeding versus feeding on demand? What's the best way to encourage a child to sleep through the night? Answers to these questions today are different from those of twenty-five years ago. Sometimes these changes are responses to new evidence; sometimes they are shifts in fashion. In either case, wise grandparents take the lead from the new parents.

Guidelines

Watch how you frame your suggestions

Grandparents, as veterans of parenthood, often use a distinctive commanding tone in giving advice. 'You need to feed her.' 'It's time to put him down.' 'She's over-stimulated.' If grandparents frame their suggestions and comments as questions to be put to the expert parent, they are more likely to be welcomed. As Anna Quindlen notes: 'Be warned: those who make their opinions sound like the Ten Commandments see their grandchildren only on major holidays and in photographs.'[27]

Be sensitive to different needs at different times

Accept that there may be times when the new parents want your company, input and help and times when they don't. This is just how people are; it is not a rejection and it is counterproductive to take offence. We will explore more about new parents' special sensitivity to grandparents' involvement in Chapter Four.

Does your help cause others more work?

Sometimes a grandparent's visit generates extra work for the new parents. Consider whether you are expecting them to prepare your meals or ensure a bed is ready for you. It is helpful to both grandparent and parent if expectations are set out and steps taken to ease the burden of a visit. 'I will bring my own linen. And can I bring food?' Wanting to be helpful is not enough; you have to make an effort to discover what is helpful.

Be reassured: over time your help gains value

Keep in mind that it will probably be easier to offer help for a second – and certainly third – child. The new parents have, by then, established their expertise and the grandparent can be the older child's person, thereby easing the stress on parents, and showing special attention to the older sibling who is likely to be uneasy in sharing the family stage with a newcomer.

How can new parents help grandparents be less annoying?

New parents can help grandparents accept their lesser status without humiliating them. By highlighting what a grandparent can usefully do ('Could you choose his outfit while I feed him?') and assuring the grandparent they are involved ('He's interested in your face'), the parent takes some control over the grandparent's input without criticism or rejection. A grandparent who is reassured of their involvement is less likely to step in when they are not wanted.

BOTH new parents can help

We saw in this chapter how difficult it can be for one parent to mediate between their partner and parent. Men often worry that they are being disloyal to their mother by voicing their partner's complaints. They may try to soothe both grandmother and new mother by avoiding the real issues between them. This is unfortunate, because one or the other – grandparent or new mother – is then very likely to feel the new father is 'siding' with the other.

Simply acknowledging what everyone feels, and recognising the problem, can go a long way towards assuring the grandparent, or the partner, that they are supported. The explanations can be clear, simple and true: 'She's really overwhelmed at the moment, and needs some space,' can always be followed by the reassurance of a subsequent visit: 'But we would love to see you later this week.' It is much easier to persuade someone to respect boundaries if they are not anxious about being excluded.

Sometimes the mediating parent needs a reminder from their partner that they can set boundaries without being disloyal. So instead of saying, 'You should support me, not your mother,' a new parent could explain to their partner, 'We can have a stronger relationship with her if we are all clear about our boundaries.'

Some new problems are deeply embedded, but even these can be managed

Sometimes old resentments re-emerge as new parents watch grandparents interact with grandchildren. 'You were never that loving/patient/attentive with me,' they say. These complaints often seem, to the grandparent, to come out of nowhere. Adolescent storms are long over, but suddenly a grandparent is presented with a litany of accusations.

Jumping to your own defence – 'I never shouted at you,' or, 'I was always patient' – is counterproductive. Instead, express sympathy for the feelings underlying the complaint. 'I didn't realise how much you took in. I did often find it hard to keep it together. I am amazed how well you do it.' After all, there is no shame in saying to the new parents, 'You'll be even better parents than I was.'

Another effective response is to invite the new parent to say more rather than less about their complaints. 'I'm sorry,' or 'I didn't realise that,' or 'That must have been hard for you,' spoken without rancour or defensiveness, can open a genuine conversation that is more likely to bring you closer together, even if what you hear is upsetting. Long-term family relationships are not always plain sailing, but occasional bad weather does not make them bad relationships. You can take a deep breath and wait for the storm clouds to clear.

Can grandparents avoid 'spoiling' grandchildren?

The risk that a grandparent will 'spoil' a grandchild is a common and very heated topic between grandparent and parent.

It is fruitless to try to set out clearly what counts as 'spoiling' and what doesn't, but a register of considerations could help both grandparents and new parents. Children learn to distinguish a parent's rules from those of a grandparent, so parents can be reassured that the grandparents' indulgences are unlikely to set general expectations. However, if there are specific things – such as toys, gadgets or food – the new parents do not want the grandparents to give the child, these should be clearly identified, and grandparents would be wise to comply.

Parents might also accept that grandparents often see *them* as 'too indulgent'. I heard grandparents complain that a parent tolerates tantrums that, in their view, should be ignored or shut down. I witnessed grandparents' disapproval as a parent stood patiently by while a child engages in delaying tactics when leaving the house – 'I just need to do/get/finish something.' Grandparents note that parents give in to pester power and buy some useless things that have momentary appeal. Grandparents worry that parents allow children sweets and ice cream that they themselves would forbid. Such examples might remind parents that 'spoiling' is not something only grandparents do.

Is 'bite your tongue' good advice for grandparents?

In every discussion I have come across about grandparenting, there is a directive to 'bite your tongue' and 'wear beige': shut up, be neutral, and don't stand out. Grandparents are warned, 'Don't give advice unless specifically asked,' and, 'Don't comment on the new parents' childcare arrangements, beliefs or practices.' But, as we have seen, silencing is not good for one's health – especially if you are a woman. Since the theme of silencing oneself, along with parents' sensitivity to what grandparents say, are such prominent themes in grandparenting, I will return to them in later chapters. For now, I suggest that the ideal solution is to speak out with as much tact as possible, even if it leads to argument. Across generations, arguments can be effective routes to negotiation and understanding. So, instead of advising grandparents to bite their tongue, I suggest they try out different ways of framing their thoughts, learning what is less likely to trigger a protest. Then thicken your skin, and practise repairing any ensuing damage to the relationship.

Two

Grandmothering: Feminist, Radical and Subversive

'How does being a grandparent shape my identity?'

Becoming a grandparent is a jolt to one's identity as significant as turning thirty, forty, fifty or whatever age it is that signals, 'You are now different and there is no going back.' The narrator in Margaret Atwood's *Bodily Harm* prayed that she 'wouldn't live long enough to get like [her] grandmother'; though this extreme negativity is rare, every woman I have spoken to does, at some time, battle with being 'an old granny', both in how they are seen by others and in how they see themselves.

Most people are relatively young when they become grandparents. The average age to become a grandparent is a mere fifty years old. Many others feel young at sixty and seventy. They look in the mirror and see a young-enough face. They continue to feel pleasure in the aesthetics of grooming and self-presentation, either as 'fun' or as 'social armour' or as signals of competence and status. Their sense of self remains that of a familiar youngish persona: fit, active and intellectually sharp.

Our bodies, however, do change. Our skin, our hands, our knees and our hair are unlike those of the grandchildren we cuddle, and grandkids are quick to point out these differences – though their take is not always negative. As my granddaughter plays with my hand, she points to each age spot, and says, 'I hope I get these when I am older.' Of course she will probably change her mind as she absorbs social cues about ageing, but the immediacy of her current acceptance transforms the meaning of those marks of age. Even when her four-year-old cousin asks, 'What are those green things on your hands?' and his seven-year-old sister explains, 'They're veins. They stick out when you get *old*,' I continue to see a kindly tolerance, both from my grandchildren and within myself. Grandchildren seldom soften their clear-eyed observations of the signs of age, but do not devalue grandparents on that account.

Of course age is not only about appearance. The increased risk to health and capability in later life was highlighted by the Covid-19 pandemic, during which various lockdowns separated grandparents from grandchildren, while the new parents, in spite of their greatly increased need for extra support and additional childcare, enforced the separation for fear of, as the UK government warned, 'killing granny'. In fact, the enforced separation from grandchildren during lockdown had hugely negative consequences on grandparents' mental health.[1] They missed their grandchildren; they regretted their inability to alleviate the burden of lockdown on parents, and they resented being treated by their government as 'old biddies'. They were deeply concerned, too, that this government-enforced protection put such huge burdens on their grandchildren, particularly through school closures.

Each of us receives our own tailor-made reminders of ageing, as hips ache climbing the stairs, knees buckle lifting a child from a climbing frame, as our breath shortens with the strides we take to keep up with an escaping toddler. Young people, looking ahead to the frailties of age, say (as grandparents did in their own youth), 'It would be *awful* to be old like that.' But research shows that even major physical setbacks, such as being confined to a wheelchair or impeded by Parkinsonian shaking, only impacts a person's baseline level of happiness for a limited time. Remarkably, within six months of their accident or the onset of their illness, people are likely to revert to their usual levels of contentment, and most disabilities still allow older people to engage with and support grandchildren.[2]

There is a distinctive his/hers divide in how becoming a grandparent impacts our identity. Women's self-confidence, self-appraisal and identity show far more change over the course of their lives than do men's.[3] Women are still more sensitive to – and victims of – stereotypes of ageing. As they negotiate this transition, they think back to paths taken in their past, and to what they see as their unfinished business in achieving satisfaction. Did they comply with traditional female norms in their youth, and now hope to spread their wings? Did they challenge the status quo, but now wonder about the costs? These exacting questions are more salient for women, and I therefore focus on grandmothers as I look at how this highly personal turning point shapes identity.

Every grandmother I spoke to was determined to engage proactively with her grandchildren. But how each grandmother enacted this new role depended on her personal history, what personal goals she had fulfilled and what she had missed, what she hoped for – or feared – in her future, and that of her children and grandchildren.

By the time we become a grandparent, we live within a network of wider obligations, both personal and professional. I spoke to grandparents who held demanding jobs while caring for a very elderly parent, but still had adolescent or young adult children living with them. Nevertheless, by the time they became grandparents, they had access to what Anna Quindlen calls the 'MeMe place' – restorative pockets of time during which they withdraw from the demands of family, tend to their own thoughts and explore private interests and goals. Becoming a grandparent jeopardised the security of this treasured space.

In enacting their new identity, three distinct categories emerged among grandmothers: feminist, radical and subversive. Feminist grandmothers often (but not necessarily) describe themselves as feminists, and many grandmothers who describe themselves as feminists may not be a feminist grandparent: what characterises someone as a feminist grandparent is the urgency with which they respond to the threats parenting places on a daughter's or daughter-in-law's career. Paradoxically, these feminist grandparents often take on traditional caring roles to protect the new parents' professional progress. Radical grandmothers, on the other hand, resist what they see as the danger of being subsumed by traditional caring roles. Having put many aspects of their lives on hold while they cared for their young children, they do not want their time, energy and care to be taken for granted again, at this later life stage. Subversive grandmothers tend to be fully engaged in their own interests. They focus more on what they can teach their grandchildren than on easing the new parents' burdens. Their primary role, subversive grandmothers believe, is to induct their grandchildren into values and priorities that are generally sidelined and to introduce their grandchildren into ways of thinking that others might suppress.

The Paradox of Feminist Grandmothering

Feminist grandmothers took part in the social revolution that drew female identity into a brave new world. In their youth, anything seemed possible, including equal opportunities for women in every career, and perfectly fair division of work within the home. They guarded against the domesticity that confined their own mothers. No space would carry the sign, 'No women allowed'. Women's work would be whatever each woman wanted it to be.

In their young adulthood, they would have been dismayed by how much energy their future selves would devote to taking on childcare as grandparents. This apparent paradox – resistance to traditional roles in youth and adoption of these roles as grandmothers – does not signal a reversal of values, nor is it a backward slide to 1950s female roles. It is a way of protecting their feminist legacy.

For many new mothers, grandparent care is crucial to their careers.[4] Feminist grandmothers' readiness to provide support and care arises from their investment in and respect for their daughter or daughter-in-law's success. They want to protect new mothers from the very hard choices they themselves confronted as mothers of young children. Lisa, now seventy-two years old, worked initially as a senior theatre nurse in a large hospital, later becoming manager of the surgical ward. 'I know how damn difficult it is to manage childcare and career. I see that with my son and daughter-in-law. My son is there for his wife and kids, and does his share, I think – I hope. But from what I see, it's still the mother who is doing the, you know, the lioness's share. I feel mightily invested in her successful career. And that means I have to do what I can to protect it.'

The emotional absorption, responsibility and commitment of motherhood remain sticking points in women's career progression. In spite of positive changes since the grandmothers of today were mothers of young children themselves, a woman's career still risks stalling during the period when she becomes a mother.[5] This is sometimes referred to as a 'broken rung' in the ladder of women's progress, but there is also a 'sticky floor' in lower-paid jobs; these are jobs that are used as a springboard to advancement, but which those with childcaring responsibilities struggle to progress beyond.[6,7] When a new mother's career stutters and a new father's career progresses, the old-fashioned model of career versus carer comes into effect. As economist Claudia Goldin explains, the retrofit seems rational: 'To maximize the family's income but still keep the children alive, it's logical for one parent to take an intensive job and the other to take a less demanding one… It just so happens that in most couples, if there's a woman and a man, the woman takes the back seat.'[8] A grandmother's fierce protectiveness towards her adult daughter or daughter-in-law's career propels her to step in.

Gabriela is a senior legal counsel for a national newspaper. At sixty-eight years old, she has two grandchildren, a boy aged three and a girl aged three months. Her daughter Jessica is head of talent at a technology company. Gabriela raises a finger as she lists each hectic step. 'She wakes up at 6 to leave the house at 6.40, so she can be at work by 7.45. She doesn't come home until 7.30 when all her attention is on the children for ninety minutes and then sits down to prepare for the next day's work until 11.' She pauses: just thinking about their schedule makes her breathless.

As a result, Gabriela explains, 'There's a whole generation of older women who are going back to childcare. And the reason we're putting ourselves out so much is that we are the feminist generation. We're putting ourselves out way above what we expected. But that's the only way we can help these young mothers.'

The grandmothers of today are pretty sure that pre-birth, new parents are unrealistic about management of childcare, particularly about how childcare will be shared with their partner. When they try to prepare their daughters for the professional blowback of motherhood, their warnings fall on deaf ears. Their daughters 'don't listen' or 'don't want to hear' or 'have no idea'. Lisa told me, 'You should've heard Stacy go on about how things had changed. "Don't judge my life according to your outdated expectations," she'd say. But her reality wasn't much different to mine when I was a new mother.'

A recent collaborative project took me back to that fraught time of early motherhood, career precarity and difficult choices. Alongside education charity The Female Lead, I spent eight months talking to women who were intent on career progression and, at the same time, were planning to be mothers. I came to understand that women who set out to combine career ambition with motherhood were not resistant to warnings from others about the difficulties because of optimism, but from fear.

For someone whose identity is welded to her career, motherhood is a scary and strange place. It upends women's day-to-day lives, but even more bewildering is the way it transforms their values. How can they predict what they will want to do, when they have no idea who they will be? Their mothers' efforts to alert them to the future clashes between work demands and baby demands did little to help them plan, and only increased their self-doubt.[9]

I first spoke to Gabriela's daughter Jessica when she was pregnant. 'You're always second-guessing yourself,' she reflected. 'What if your brain all of a sudden turns to mush? You don't know how you're going to react. You don't know how you are going to feel. You don't know, you might want to come back after two weeks. You might want to take a whole year off.' Looking so far ahead gave her 'a headache… I don't know what will happen when I'm off and what anything will look like when I get back, because there aren't really any reassurances around that.'

She is ambivalent about own mother's model of parenthood and professional success. 'I know mum found it difficult when [my brother and I] were little. I thought she was pretty ruthless. I mean, she didn't spend a lot of time with us. But there wasn't maternity leave or flexible working, and to keep on track she had to sort of pretend she didn't have children.'

Today's new mothers believe their own mother's difficult choices took place 'a long time ago' and that her experiences do not provide a roadmap for their own career. Instead, new mothers look to other mothers in their workplace to assess their own possible futures. Jessica explains, 'There are people I work with who have children and I [see] them not faring particularly well in the face of any restructuring and redundancy. Even if people are trying very hard, the business moves quickly. If they are [on maternity leave for] the whole year, the business looks entirely different after that whole year and

I just don't feel like they have had a fair shot... So when I think about taking maternity leave, I worry I won't know how to cope with that. I am excited by change, but if change plus maternity means I'm pushed down or out, I don't know how I'd cope with that. I sometimes see that happening to other women, which is what I mean when I say they're not faring well. In my view they're not being given a fair chance.'

While new mothers see grandmothers' experience as very different from their own, feminist grandmothers have travelled paths all too similar to those their daughters are about to embark on. They know the hurdles and dangers. They have decades of experience trying to achieve an even division of labour in the home. They raised their sons to do their fair share as fathers. And they often succeeded. But they observe that even where a new father is taking on a large share of the myriad of tasks involved in childcare, the mental load of domestic organisation is usually borne by the mother. Whether or not they know the *statistics* that show women's careers stalling at the mid-stage point (in their thirties and early forties) while men's careers follow an upward trajectory, feminist grandparents anticipate the risks to new mothers' careers. Alert to the setbacks from stepping out, cutting down or working flexibly, they offer their services as 'wife' to the daughter, providing support within the family that allows a young mother's career to be consistent with good childcare, and the well-being of both parent and child. As Gabriela explains, 'I found leaving my babies so hard. I often felt like crying on my way to work. But staying home was not an option. It would have made me into someone different, who I didn't want to be. I would have loved to leave my children with someone who loved them as much as I did. And that's what I offer Jessica.'

The Rising Costs of Childcare

Many older women believe that today's new parents 'don't realise their luck. They complain about bias. They complain about harassment. They have no idea what we went through and how much better things are for them.'

This is such a common narrative – older women musing over younger women's lack of appreciation for the battles they fought – that I was amazed to hear older women, *as grandmothers*, reflect on how much harder things are for younger mothers today. They note the high cost of childcare that can waylay a daughter's professional goals. According to *Mumsnet* founder Justine Roberts, 'We [in the UK] have the highest childcare costs in the developed world: parents are paying on average 29 per cent of their income on childcare… Four out of ten [of the people – mostly mothers of young children] say they couldn't afford their childcare without either using their savings, going into debt or *using family members*.'[10]

The financial burden of childcare continues to rise. As I write in 2024, the annual average cost of a full-time nursery place for a child under the age of two in London is nearly £15,000, or 50 per cent of the average salary; elsewhere in Britain costs may be lower but are still between 42 and 45 per cent of the average salary. Without a grandmother's support, a mother's career would be stopped in its tracks.

Irena, now seventy, was a single parent from the time her youngest daughter was five years old, but she also believes, 'It's much harder for these professional women today than it was when I was an academic in my thirties. I mean, at first I had a childminder and the baby went to her house. Then I shared a nanny with two neighbours. Then I had a live-in English girl who somehow got some childcare qualifications. And then

I got an au pair who lived in, all the way until the children were fourteen. These arrangements weren't perfect and none of the girls were super nannies but things worked out.'

Such assorted childcare was possible partly because there was more relaxed legislation over childminders and their employment. The restrictions on visas that came into effect in the UK after Brexit made hosting au pairs extremely difficult. But above all, Irena reflects, 'There was capacity because even as a single parent I could afford a house with an extra bedroom. My daughter, my daughter's friends, no young woman I know now can live in one of the prime cities and afford an extra bedroom.'

In response to these conditions a feminist grandmother uses whatever funds she has available to shore up their daughter's career. 'I told my daughter, "The only way you're going survive this career is to build up or out. You've got to extend." So then I had to fund the attic build and then a renovation so they could get live-in help, and it cost a fortune.'

Counting the Costs and Making Amends

Most grandparents who help with costs such as funding attic renovations that 'cost a fortune' are not wealthy. Funding the loft conversation that will accommodate the helper her daughter needs is difficult for Irena. 'I'll never be as comfortable, moneywise, as I once hoped, so it means I have to think in a different way about how I want to live and whether I can travel, let alone manage the costs of whatever infirmities are ahead of me. So I've given her enough. We can draw a line under it. I just hope I remember that, and stick to that when she next needs a load of dosh. She has an important job, but it's not well paid. Things are really tough on this generation.'

One third of working mothers in the UK rely on grandparents for childcare.[11] This childcare is usually unpaid, but contributes over £7 billion to the UK economy, with the saving to families in childcare costs estimated at £96 billion; however, the cost to grandparents themselves has no official estimate.[12,13,14] Some grandparents travel regularly to care for grandchildren while they themselves are still working. Some have additional caring responsibilities, tending an infirm spouse or very elderly parent. Costs to grandparents come in many forms – money, their own careers, their perceived obligations to others as well as their personal energy and pleasures. But when I asked them about the costs, they focused on the *relative* costs. Giving financial support or allocating their own time to an adult child to ease the burden of childcare is, they reason, a lesser hit to them than paid childcare would be to their daughter. Spending their time as childminder is less hard on them than having a strange babysitter would be on their grandchild. Giving up career opportunities has less impact on them than on the new parent in mid-career. Irena, who remains a research-active academic, explains, 'I've given a lot as granny in terms of childcare, even while I still do a lot in post here, but I don't think it eats into my career in the way it would have at [the] earlier stage [that] my daughter is at now.'

Fang, sixty-eight, travels every other week to spend three days caring for her grandchildren, with the alternate week covered by the paternal grandmother. Travel and childcare mean less time for her new successful career as a graphic artist, less time with her husband, and less time 'doing the little things I love, such as walking and binge-watching. But I want to save Lily from the choices I had to make. I left her and her sister in after-school clubs and playgroups. They survived, sure, but I could see how hard it was at the time. Now the cost of childcare is prohibitive, even if you're willing to put up with the formality and the stress of that. Well, I can do something to help. I've thought about that, you know, and how much money I could give and whether that would be the way to help. But what I want most to offer, what I think matters most, is someone to care for the children who's family and who loves them. You know, someone with a real stake in them. My daughter can go to work and not worry whether she's leaving her children with a carer who doesn't really care.'

Television journalist Lesley Stahl was still working in her spectacularly demanding career when, as a grandmother, she made a similar decision. She looks back, as Fang does, on what Stahl calls her 'cold choices' as a mother of a young child. When her newborn granddaughter's nurse did not show up and her daughter had to go to work, Stahl embraced the joyful 'fix' of being with 'her' new baby; in addition, she seized 'an opportunity to atone for the choices [she] made as a mother.'[15]

Even as we see our children grow into high-functioning adults, we worry over what we did not give them as children and look for ways to make amends. Both Fang and Lesley Stahl suggest a two-pronged approach. They provide 'within family' care to the grandchildren, making up for the formal care they arranged for their own children; and they protect their daughters from having to look back, when they are grandmothers, with regret for the care they provided.

Feminist paternal grandmothers can be equally protective of a daughter-in-law's career. Muriel is the 'other' grandmother to Fang's grandchildren, doing three days' childcare on alternate weeks. 'I feel enormous solidarity with my daughter-in-law, a real woman-to-woman thing. I raised my son to be aware of how much work goes into domestic stuff (my husband was clueless) and he's great – but great for a guy. His need for his "me time" is cut in stone, where I see my daughter-in-law kind of weighing things up and wondering whether she can ask for her free time, so I'm sort of making up for my son's deficit while also getting a fix of my yummy grandkids.'

Uneasy Compromises

Like all gifts and exchanges within a family, the mission to protect their adult daughters' careers is not simple. Gabriela admits that 'among [my friends who are grandmothers] we're constantly talking about how much we do. Like how much our daughters and daughters-in-law ask of us. One of my girls is super-grateful. Another is more hard-nosed. When she needs my help, I have to drive up to her, which is tougher for me than taking a train. At first she took me for granted, and I told her so, and now she says, "You can come next week to cover Tuesday, but maybe you want to save the journey for when you're really needed. I can try to find local cover if that helps." I like that because she acknowledges a kind of bank where she can save or spend my time. But even my sweet, grateful one needs to be reminded that if I'm covering on Monday and Tuesday, it's a bit too much to ask me to come on Thursday as well.'

While Gabriela feels uneasy about being taken for granted, her daughter Jessica is taken aback when I ask her about her experience of her mother's input as grandmother. 'Maybe I ask a lot, but, you know, what strikes me is how easy it was for her to say, when I was a child, "I can't be there," or "You can't do this because I can't organise it." Her life was taken up by [a series of long-running legal cases] and I came second. So I know she can say "no" when I ask for her help. I don't have to worry that she'll do more than she wants.'

Yet for a grandmother committed to supporting her daughter's career, refusing requests for help is uncomfortable. Gabriela admits that the demands of childcare sometimes push her 'into an uncomfortable place. When she phones me, and I hear that tone of voice signalling, "I'm in a fix," my heart starts pounding. I'm thinking of her and what she needs and I'm also thinking about my schedule here, and my mind starts doing a kind of sudoku puzzle as to how everything's going to fit in, and what I have to change to go to help her. I always want to do it because I remember how difficult it was, and I think of all the things I gave up because arrangements were just too complicated. I felt less anxious giving up something myself than cobbling together some ad hoc childcare. Changing my plans, for myself, is far less complicated than it is for Jessica. That's how it is with motherhood and career. You're always asking what will be forgiven, and what will make the difference between getting the next promotion or not?'

The thorny issue of domestic labour – who does what in the planning and execution of caring for kids – impacts on all family relationships. Though grandfathers engage with their grandchildren's care far more today than they did thirty years ago, feminist grandmothers recall how hard it was to get a partner to pull his weight when they were going through those intensive stages of parenting.[16] Facing similar demands now can revive old resentments. 'It's much easier if he comes too,' Fang explains. 'He can stay with one child when I take another swimming. He's retired now, so I'm much more vocal about him pitching in. I wish I'd done that thirty years ago. I'm grateful for what he does now, but my heart sinks when I think back to how hard it was when I was a young mum.' It is perhaps not surprising that feminist grandparents critically assess whether a son-in-law pulls his weight as a parent. While a father is 'doing a lot by old standards', he may not be a 'good organiser, and can't be relied on just to do the job without being given a checklist'.

As feminist grandmothers protect their adult children from the difficult choices they made as young mothers themselves, they confront all over again uneasy questions about helping others versus pleasing themselves. They ruminate over distinctive female questions about selfishness versus selflessness, about gender division of childcare, and whether it is an insult or compliment to be taken for granted. In the process, they confront their own resentments at their formerly unsupportive partner, while their adult children may recall their childhood resentment at competing with a parent's career.

Radical Grandmothers: Identity, Resistance and Care

The transition to 'being grandma' comes in midlife, when we are already reflecting on the demands and choices that shaped our lives so far, and considering whether and how we might follow new paths in the future. Radical grandmothers are women who are still actively exploring their identities. They resist assumptions they may once have accepted – assumptions about who they are and who they should be. As parents, they took on the role of full-time carer. Any employment or career was secondary to their identity, and mainly a means of paying some bills. Thinking about personal development, on their own terms, was not an option in early adulthood. Midlife offers an exciting reprieve, wherein they might take advantage of any financial and material comfort that they have accrued. Freedom to consider their own wishes, and to put themselves first, is a radical change from their previous mindset. Becoming a grandmother casts a shadow over that freedom.

Jacqui was forty-nine when her first grandchild was born. Her husband had just retired from a senior diplomatic position that she, without job description or payment, supported by managing a new home and finding new schools in the half a dozen different countries in which he was posted. She hosted grand parties and intimate lunches, while settling her own children into a new country and its customs. Though she describes herself as 'exhausted', her energy fills the room, and she declares with bravado, 'I will love this new grandchild and then I will leave him. I have been there and done that and I am finished. I am ready for something new.'

She recalls how her own grandmother never questioned her role as 'carer, cleaner, domestic organiser, second parent. By the time I was a teenager, her knees hurt and she was breathless, and I don't think she ever found a pair of really comfortable shoes. But there were little ones much younger than me, and there she was – her whole life taken over by childcare. I do not want this to be me.'[17]

Stating a position firmly, however, is very different from sticking to it. When I meet Jacqui again eighteen months later, she is struggling with the tension between what she wants for herself, what she feels as a grandmother and her sympathy for her son and daughter-in-law. 'There's just no slack in their lives. They are a modern two-income family, not because they're greedy or spendthrift but because that's how things have to be today. So I let them bring the kids here when they need cover – I'm not going to make that journey to them, I'm clear on that. I know I've got to do this, it would be too tough on them and pricey, because they already pay for a lot of childcare. Compared to some, I don't do so much, but it sometimes feels too much for me.'

I know it must be tough for Jacqui, with her strong persona, to expose her vulnerability, but perhaps she sees the resonance her words have with me. There's an immediacy and physicality to looking after young children that goes beyond 'tiring'. Some grandmothers believe it is harder on them now because they are older, and that it was easier when they were younger. In fact, I think it was just as hard on me as a younger parent, and that is one thing that propels me to help my own daughters. I know how a full day in the presence of young children can suck away your soul. Every line of thought about your own interests gets tangled up with endless interruptions and uncompleted projects. Building a castle, even one with cannons and swords, engages my four-year-old grandson for about six minutes. A complicated game with dolls with a six-year-old is abandoned after ten minutes, followed by a puzzle or drawing. They want to watch TV or play on my iPad, but I am under instructions from their parents to limit screen time. There is love and joy, and there is also mind-numbing boredom and a lot of clock-watching. If I can offer my daughters relief from this, I want to; Jacqui wants this too, though she tries to do so on her own terms.

Stipulating that her son or daughter-in-law bring the children to her if they want her to care for them saves Jacqui a journey, but not the changed geography of her home. She says she 'doesn't like mess'. The scattered toys make her feel anxious. Jacqui takes me on a tour. A tent made of cushions is blocking an upstairs landing. Under the dining table lies a 'cafe' of plastic plates and wooden pieces of sandwich, a toy coffee set filled with water, and a few pieces of sliced cheese. Lego boats grace the garden pond, some floating, others half immersed. Jacqui's laughter expresses more stress than pleasure. 'It isn't that I don't supervise them,' she explains, 'but when they're so wrapped up in playing, I let them have what they need for their game. I'm engaged at the time, but the aftermath is hard. It will take me as long to clear up as it takes my daughter-in-law to make the trip home.'

I remember how upset my own grandmother was when my younger cousins visited her apartment. There was plenty of space, but it was indoors. The boys, who must have been five and seven years at the time, thrilled at the novelty of their surroundings, beige, neat and spare. After their forty-five-minute car journey, they used their pent-up energy tussling with each other. They rolled on the floor, squealing with the fun of it. The overturned floor lamp in their path was of no concern to them, and the game was only stopped when they smashed into the leg of a coffee table so thick and weighty that the glasses it supported barely trembled. A welt appeared on the older boy's forehead, and the room filled with piercing cries. 'They're like a tornado,' my grandmother declared. 'She [their mother, my aunt, her daughter-in-law] can't control them. I could trip over them and break my neck. They could kill themselves. I can't be responsible for that. I won't have them here again.'

I recall her shaky voice, predicting disaster, while her fingers picked nervously at the belt buckle around her waist. The image I have is of an old woman, but at that time she must have been ten years younger than I am now. Grandparents today are both younger and older than our own grandparents. We are often older in years when we become grandparents, but younger, generally, in terms of energy and outlook. We are also more likely to express our connection to grandchildren – and our continuing connection to our own children – through active care and support. For the most part, grandmothers would call this a free choice, but few would claim it is an easy one, or that it comes without costs. The radical grandmother who tries to set firm boundaries around her time and energy is rarely completely successful.

Selfishness versus the Radical Notion of Self-care

Radical grandmothers who set strict limits on the time they devote to grandchildren often face public criticism. *Gransnet* and *Mumsnet*, online forums for sharing thoughts, advice and complaints about grandparenting and motherhood respectively, frequently feature discussions about disengaged grandmothers. In one thread, a mother complains that her own mother 'has been singularly unhelpful as a grandparent'. This grandmother, her daughter believes, is 'hands off' and 'uninterested'. She explains that while she does not expect her mother to 'drop everything or give up her own activities', having some help, from time to time, would be 'so nice' and mother's refusal to help is 'hurtful'.

On *Mumsnet*, replies to such posts invite condemnation of the 'selfish' grandmother, on the one hand, and reminders that the mother should thank her lucky stars on the other, because the grandmother is not invading the mother's space, or sidelining her. On *Gransnet*, however, we have the most pertinent reply to the daughter's complaint: 'There is no job description for grandparenting'.

Drawing a line between 'reasonable' versus excessive requests for childcare poses a particular challenge to radical grandparents who have spent so much of their lives attuned to others' needs at the expense of their own. Their desire, in later adulthood, to take control of their time and energy is easily overshadowed by internalised norms about what a grandmother should do.

Lucia will be fifty-five on her next birthday, and her daughter has just had her second child. 'I tell her, "I'm here for you, but I'm not here to step in your shoes. I can help, but I'm not your mainstay." I'm still working on my own life. I need to focus on me, too.' Lucia pauses. Her gaze is steady and I feel I am being assessed. 'You think I'm selfish.' It is part statement, part question. But I know that really she is defending herself from an inner voice telling her, 'It's your job to care for others, thinking about yourself is selfish.'

Throughout her life she has worked in jobs that paid the bills rather than provided satisfaction. She had three children by the time she was twenty-one, and was a single parent for twelve years. She dreads being sucked back into those roles, where she is constantly at the mercy of others' needs.

Her own mother provided regular childcare, just as her grandmother had done, until she died when Lucia was only twenty-eight and her children were ten, nine and seven. She tells me that she had a lot of fun during those years, but 'after a few drinks and a wild night, I was back on the treadmill. These were my endless thoughts: get enough work to look after the kids, make sure the work fits in with looking after the kids, have a few treats so I keep sane so I can work and look after the kids.' By the time she was in her late forties, her children were 'grown and pretty much looking after themselves. Not that they'd left home – I still have two at home, but we all look after ourselves.'

She knows it would be very easy to take up the same role her mother did. Her daughter, who lives nearby, is still young and fun-loving. A full-time granny nanny would suit her. Lucia is devoted to her grandchildren, but is also determined to set limits. After all, she explains, it was 'my daughter who did what she did and became a mother. Up to that point she could have all the relationships and the fun and whatever she wants, but when it comes to your kids, you have to be the one to manage things. I worry about her, but I'm not going to step in and fix everything. I see it in my friends. They're always going to see the grandchildren. They check when school holidays are on before they make their own appointments. Just like we all did when we were mothers ourselves. Now, because of my life experience (with my partner leaving even before my youngest was born, and my mother dying), and now having a great partner and seeing my kids grown into good people, and for the first time in my life not worrying so much about money, my view of children and marriage and life is that whatever happens, happens. I fixed things for my kids when they were kids. I can't keep doing it now.'

But as with most grandmothers, the firm line Lucia tries to draw bends and twists. She admits that 'the goalposts keep changing. I can't deny her help, but I make it clear: if you're working or out looking for work then yes, I'll take the kids, but not regularly. You work to pay for that. But I'm not taking them when you're just swanning around or on a night out. I gave up plenty of that stuff for you. We're quits on that score.'

Like many grandmothers, whether feminist or radical, Lucia worries that setting limits is 'selfish'. She also feels that pull of affection towards her grandchildren and wants to be with them. As Lucia says, 'They're such sweeties, and always give me a smile when they see me. So I look at them and think, "I could stare at them forever." And then I say, "No, no, no." I've been down this road. I'm doing other things now.'

Ebru, now forty-seven, had a more comfortable life than Lucia, but for her, too, others' needs always came before her own. She was married at nineteen and was 'lucky that [her husband] allowed [her] to go to college' but, before the end of her first year, she was pregnant, and she knew her life was changed forever. Recently, however, she has gone back to college. Her husband has a range of interests and obligations in the community, and their trust and respect for one another allow her 'a whole lot of freedom.' Her initial response to becoming a grandmother was 'overwhelming, and I was there for my daughter. The birth – for her, for me… Well, when your daughter gives birth, a mother has to come. I definitely have the view that you spend the first ten days looking after your daughter and they've gotta be able to lie in bed and have lovely food brought to them. Clean sheets, too, washed all the time, which husbands won't do, they won't make it lovely. They'll help, but they won't make it lovely and it's so special. And so I was there and I was doing everything for her, the first child particularly, and that really helped her. She had quite a lot of trouble breastfeeding. She stuck to it, but she did have trouble. So that was where her mother was really important, because you've been through it yourself and you know how exhausting it is. So after that, it was more like, there are some things you can still teach these very overeducated daughters.'

But Ebru is wary of being submerged by grandparenting. 'It was good, being a mother, and a good member of the community, and being the kind of woman people point to and say to their daughters, "She's a good woman," but it's really hard – it was really hard for me at times, and I can't go back there. My daughter has to find her own way. At the birth, you know, there is so much joy, but a whirlpool of other things, too. You can't really say these things, and I don't know how to say them either; and I wouldn't even say these things to my closest friends, but it knocked me over, and I thought, "I'll make this time special for her, and as easy as it can be," but I can't be that woman they'll nod at and say, "Good woman, always helping her daughters." I want to be another kind of person now.'

Radical grandmothers wrestle with what the psychologist Dana Crowley Jack calls the 'Over-Eye' – an internal observer condemning them if they fail to comply with the norms of being a 'good woman'.[18] The list of 'shoulds' includes attention to others' needs and denial of one's own. In pursuing their own needs, they worry that they are 'in the wrong' and adhering to their own preferences makes them 'bad'. The radical grandmothers we see here – Lucia and Ebru and Jacqui – resist, with some success, the Over-Eye's authority, but the transition to grandparent reminds them of the power of this internal judge. All grandparents will internally wrestle with the dialogue between an internal Over-Eye and the 'I' they want to preserve; for radical grandparents this dialogue has a special force and requires courageous resistance.

Subversive Grandmothers

Subversive grandmothers can be enormous fun for grandchildren, but present a challenge to parents. In Salley Vickers' novel *Grandmothers*, Nan, a wonderful depiction of a subversive grandmother, is 'on a mission to teach Billy how to lie'. He needs this skill, she argues, not to encourage him to deceive, but 'for self-protection. Sometimes you have to say or do things to look after yourself'. She reminds him, 'You are the only person truly entrusted to care for yourself.'[19]

The aim of a subversive grandmother is to induct a grandchild into a store of unofficial knowledge; this knowledge is ignored or denied by those who teach a child that they should be 'getting on with people', 'do well in school' and 'obey your parents'. Subversive grandmothers come in all guises, but they are likely to share certain traits. They defy many commonly accepted norms. They are likely to be bound up in their own projects that challenge conventional views and lifestyles. They are generally busy, and since they see their work as important, they do not give up work time in exchange for contact with grandchildren. Instead, childcare involves roping their grandchildren into their own activities. Grandchildren are not taken to Legoland but to public meetings, archaeological digs or political rallies. As Monica White reflects in 'Diary of a Supergran', 'If I'm looking after [my grandchild] I would not stay here doing nothing else, I would take [the baby] along with me.'[20]

Maeve is a local activist determined to instruct the residents of her village to reduce their carbon footprint and any other 'forever waste'. She describes herself as 'an old woman in a hurry' to make up for past carelessness. Phoebe is a politician representing a diverse urban constituency. Charlotte is a psychiatrist who travels wherever there is a crisis that impacts the mental health of children. Whether the war in Ukraine or the devastating earthquake in Turkey, she will go to the epicentre of a crisis to set up places of play, safety and support. My conversation with her is interrupted by phone calls and comings and goings of her staff, which she addresses without losing a beat in our conversation. Each woman is delighted to be a grandmother and describes time spent with a grandchild as 'precious', but each says it is hard to find the time for them – except, both Maeve and Phoebe explain, 'when they tag along with me when I do my work'.

'Tagging along' sounds tedious, but the grandchildren I spoke to found it exciting. 'She's always busy,' Maeve's eleven-year-old granddaughter told me, 'but she doesn't, like, ignore me. We chat in the car about where she is going and why, and we talk about her ideas, and she asks me what I'm doing. I used to just sit in the car seat and tune out, but I really like being with her now, and I can ask her anything.'

The adult children of a subversive grandmother are accustomed to her absences and distractions, and are unlikely to expect much active childcare. Their engagement with a grandchild starts in earnest only 'once he's past the baby stage', Phoebe explains. She likes taking her grandson on trips to wonderful places – Sienna, Delhi and Prague. These are work trips, and she will be in meetings or at a conference much of the day, while her fourteen-year-old grandson fends for himself. Grandmother and grandson dine out together in the evening, sometimes joined by her colleagues, sometimes just the two of them; while her grandson is often anxious in social situations, he takes these in his stride. Phoebe casually accepts her daughter-in-law's disapproval: 'His mother isn't happy with me as a companion for him. She doesn't see me as a "responsible adult", and I can see why. I don't curtail his screen time, and I don't worry that he wanders a little on his own. I could say there's a lot that I don't like about her mothering, either. We disapprove of each other but also accept [each other]. Maybe she lets him come with me because the luxury of five days without a sulky teenage boy is irresistible.'

Subversive grandmothers are a boon to teenage grandchildren because they assume an equal status and take parents' rules 'with a pinch of salt'. Though Maeve insists she would never directly criticise or defy her daughter-in-law, she listens when her grandson 'comes to me in a sulk about something his mum's done or something she won't let him do. Anyone else would say, "You should listen to your mother," and, "She's thinking only of what's best for you," and list all the things she's doing for him and giving him, but I let him stay with his thoughts.'

Subversive grandmothers are thrilling and inspirational. They show a talent for spending long stretches of time with slightly older grandchildren without appearing to be fatigued, because their grandchildren learn quickly to meet them on their terms. Fortunately, many grandparents, whatever their grandparenting identity, have some subversive impulses. The familiar grandparent saying, 'No one will tell you this but me,' opens the door to a special stash of stories, humour and wisdom in which grandchildren delight.

The Essential Grandmother

The three styles of grandparenting we have examined so far are based on the grandmother's choices: feminist grandmothers who do all they can to protect a daughter's career; radical grandmothers who resist an internal judge that might bully them into traditional caring roles; and subversive grandmothers who see their role as a teacher of alternative, unofficial knowledge. But there is another category of grandmother whose style of grandparenting is born out of necessity: when a parent's circumstances require a grandparent to become the de facto parent, or 'essential' grandparent. The alternatives – a grandchild being adopted by another family, fostered or placed in care – are not, for most grandparents, acceptable options.

This essential grandparent is discussed in more detail in Chapter Eight, but it should be noted here that, for these grandparents, a grandchild's need eclipses personal choice. Currently 1 per cent of children live with their grandmothers, separate from their own parents.[21] These grandchildren usually experience disruption and difficulty that do not bode well for their future, but grandchildren living with a grandparent have better outcomes – in terms of health, education, social contribution and adult stability – than those in foster care or other formal placements.[22]

Guidelines for Thinking through Our Grandparenting Style

The first three styles of grandparenting – feminist, radical and subversive – emerge from grandmothers' reflections on their own goals and hopes for their futures, in tandem with the needs of the parents and grandchildren. But sticking to their preferred grandparenting role or identity takes a lot of energy when challenged by others' assumptions (and our own internal voices) that speak to who they, as 'good grandmothers' should be. So grandmothers continue to ponder, just as they did as young mothers, over whether, in setting limits on others' demands, they are being selfish or fair or right.

Most grandmothers have a head start in challenging female ideals. Age and experience are likely to ease concern about others' approval. Yet the powerful internal norms of 'good mother/grandmother' are not easily tamed. The best guidance this book can offer – and the only general guidance possible – is to identify common anxieties in balancing so-called selfishness and self-care.

When anxieties about 'selfishness' arise it is useful to assess selfishness against a number of questions:

'Do I want to do this?'

It is helpful to identify what you want to do yourself. The answer to this might not give you a fixed or final answer, but it sets down a significant point of reference.

'Are my needs and preferences and pleasures less important than those of others?'

It is helpful to challenge the assumption that others' wishes matter more than your own. If people's needs and wishes matter, then so do yours.

'How can I refuse to help without pushing the parent away or discouraging them from asking again?'

The first step involves internal work to challenge the Over-Eye that prioritises others' views over your own, instilling fear that your own preferences are wrong, or that if others see what you really feel, they will reject you. Attend to your responses to the first two questions – 'Do I want to do this?' and, 'Are my needs and preferences and pleasures less important than those of others?' The answer to the latter question is obviously, 'No', and therefore allows you to sit comfortably with the answer to the former question.

The second step is more practical. Preparing templates for refusing requests guards against the 'Yes' that comes too quickly because you cannot think of anything else to say. One template might be:

> I can't do that today. I am available next week on these days, or the following months during these days. Let me know if that's of any use.

Controlling your own anxiety about 'being selfish' paves the way to a more gracious refusal that is far less likely to cause offence. Defensiveness (expressed in an irritable 'No!') comes from your own uncertainty as to whether it is OK to decline. Assure yourself that it's OK to refuse requests from parents, and it's OK to explain your position to them.

Things to keep in mind:

- There is a difference between empathising with the responsibilities of the new parents and being responsible yourself.
- You cannot alleviate all challenges in the new parent's attempt to combine parenthood and career.
- You can make some things a little easier, and just a little reduction in pressure can go a long way in maintaining a parent's equilibrium.

Some things to avoid when you want to decline a request:

- Don't show impatience with your adult child or child-in-law for asking for your help.
- Don't scold them for asking too much of you.
- Don't vent about being too busy.

Some grandparents struggle with questions about payment for babysitting. I cannot give guidance on this, except to remind grandmothers that this is not covered by rules, moral or cultural, but by what is reasonable for you. If the new parents have enough to cover your babysitting costs and you would like the money, then you can discuss it.

Three

Evolutionary Legacies of Grandparenting

'What are grandparents for?'

If a machine were to scan my daily thoughts, it might not register so very many explicit references to my grandchildren. Yet as I focus on other things, I'm aware, always, of the varied lives of my grandchildren. At the sight of a toy or plate they have used, I feel the glow of their faces and warmth of their voices. I worry about life's inevitable misfortunes and how these will affect them. I imagine and loathe possible villains who might dare to mess with the strong sense of self each now shows: they are sassy, proud, and *entitled* – in the best sense of the word. I hope they will retain confidence to voice their needs and to speak their thoughts, knowing they are important to the people around them.

The heft of this protectiveness is as basic to human psychology as the desire to protect one's own children. So, while in the last chapter we looked at the intersection where a grandparent's highly individual identity meets their personal choices about how to be a grandparent, here I examine a more universal aspect of grandparenting, with its ancient legacy of attachment and care imbedded in our genes. This does not mean that all grandparents behave in the same way, but it explains why grandparents are predisposed to feel profoundly connected to their grandchildren, and why the need to be close to them is, as the author Barbara Graham notes, 'so strong, so forceful, that it feels cellular – like an undertow in my blood drawing me towards my grandchild.'[1] This forceful and 'cellular' attachment springs from the evolutionary story in which grandparents are central players.[2]

There are two very common misconceptions of the role of grandparents across human history. The first misconception is that living long enough to be a grandparent is a relatively recent phenomenon. People's greater longevity today, it is claimed, creates an excess role that was historically brief, given the shorter lifespans of the past. While today, a fifth of the population in the UK, and more than 35 million people in the US, are over the age of sixty-five, as recently as the early twentieth century, 95 per cent of the population died before even reaching that age.[3]

However, while all over the world people are living longer today, remaining active and engaged well into their sixties and beyond, in previous centuries people became grandparents at an earlier age, and therefore had the opportunity to be active, engaged and generous within their shorter lifespans. Documents going back to medieval times show that the importance of grandparents, particularly a grandmother (then referred to as *eadlemodor*), has a long history. An eleventh-century will that included an overview of the deceased's life, also singled out a grandmother as someone 'who raised me'. Other Anglo-Saxon documents mention lavish bequests of land and jewels to grandchildren – early examples of grandparents' indulgence and generosity.[4] Going back even further, we have fossil evidence suggesting that early human grandmothers were already 'spoiling' grandchildren with special ground wheat – an ancient version of cookies.[5]

A second very common misconception about grandparents' significance is that it is strictly dependent on culture. It is said that in the US, the UK and throughout Europe, grandparents play a marginal role in family life, compared to China and India where the paternal grandmother is perceived to wield enormous power over the new parents and dominate domestic matters. Yet, just as I show that the 'marginal role theory' of grandparents does not apply to family structures in the West, I will show that the model of supreme authority of the paternal grandmother in the East is out of date. New parents throughout Asia are now likely to live separately from the grandparents. They are likely to choose their own spouse, rather than have a spouse chosen by their parents. They are likely to retain control over the money they earn, rather than contribute to an intergenerational family fund, just as they do throughout Europe and the US. But, though the once socially embedded power of the paternal grandmother is ebbing, the emotional investment of both paternal and maternal grandparents remains as strong as ever.[6] The status, power and expectations of grandparents change as cultures change, but intergenerational bonds are universal and ancient.

With the exception of orcas, humans are the only species in which grandparents play a key role in their grandchildren's lives. This distinctive feature of human grandparenting turns out to be linked to another distinctive feature of humans – menopause. Why is it, evolutionary anthropologists have long wondered, that female humans regularly outlive their reproductive years, often by decades? Why do they remain strong and fit, generally, for so long after menopause?

One theory is that women live longer, healthier lives past the age of fertility as a result of modern diet and medicine. But early human females, too, went through menopause when they were still physically strong and fit. Both humans and chimpanzees experience menopause, but humans are more vigorous and far more likely to survive for many years, even decades, after menopause.[7] Are these older women just freeloaders, taking food from others' mouths and demanding care from the young? Are post-menopausal women a drain on a community's resources? Are they given this extra span of time only to enjoy themselves?

The answer is a resounding 'No': as grandmothers, they made key contributions to feeding, teaching and caring for grandchildren.

Food, Foraging and Grandparents

To understand the importance of post-fertile grandmothers in human evolution, we first need to correct the standard model of early communities as hunter-gatherer societies. This deeply flawed model begins with the 'hunting hypothesis' – the assumption that women gathered bits of seasonal food here and there, while the community was largely sustained by meat that the men hunted throughout the year.

The assumption that hunting provided the primary food supply is not borne out by evidence from animal bones found in sites of early human settlements. These reveal that much of the meat eaten was left over from prey caught and then abandoned by 'primary carnivore predators'.[8] In other words, the lions and tigers of the savannah did the real work, and the men were more likely to bring home the big cats' cast-offs than their own fresh trophies.

Moreover, reliance on the kill of big animals was hit and miss. The amount of meat that hunters could provide – either from their own hunting or from the hunting of larger animals – was far too variable to provide a major source of food. Instead, early humans fed mostly on plants, roots and fungi, with meat as an occasional supplement. Many of these staple plants and roots had to be located, then dug up, which required skill and strength. Hence, early human societies were not so much hunter-gather as *forager* societies, a term suggesting a more active and challenging activity than 'gathering'. And the evidence suggests that the primary foragers in early human societies were women.

But which women?

In the dry climates where our ancestors then lived, the best nutrients were found in hard-cased nuts, seeds and tubers growing underground. Foraging in these conditions was too difficult for young girls, and many young women's energies were taken up by pregnancy and childbirth and breastfeeding. The onset of infertility at an age when women were still strong and active was a necessary solution to this problem. Older women, free from breeding themselves, rich in experience and still physically fit, stepped in as essential providers of food. This new understanding of older women's key role in human family survival is now known as *the grandmother effect*.

Kristen Hawkes, the biological anthropologist who framed the most refined version of the grandmother effect, put together her evolutionary evidence in part by looking at contemporary human behaviour.[9] She and her colleagues observed the work of older women among the Hadza people in northern

Tanzania. They witnessed the strength of the post-menopausal women as they foraged, and noticed that they were as skilled as any of the younger women in extracting the deep-buried tubers that formed the primary starch staple of their diet. But, unlike the younger women who were tending to infants and toddlers, they could forage for longer and bring home more food than they needed themselves. And while the hunters brought home meat from time to time, this was more likely to be shared by the entire community, which gave the successful hunter a special status; by contrast, the older women's more reliable food source was generally distributed to their nearest kin – their daughters and grandchildren.

Infertile themselves, grandmothers channelled their energy to assisting younger generations, allowing these younger generations to thrive. The input from older women is particularly important to humans because human children are dependent on adults for far longer than in any other species.[10] This prolonged childhood is essential to human intelligence, providing a golden opportunity for the young brain to grow complex neural connections, adapt to changing environments and absorb the lessons of others. Their fast-growing, hard-working brains require lots of calories. In the first few months of life, these calories come from the mother's milk, but between the ages of one and five, the child's calories needed to be supplied by the foraging grandmother.[11] By helping their children and their grandchildren, early human grandmothers extended the lifespan of younger generations, and provided the nourishment that allows the development of our unique neural architecture. One could argue that it is this that allowed our species to develop communication, language and culture. Without the contributions of grandmothers, the human species today would surely be very different – and much diminished.

What Does the Grandmother Effect Look Like Today?

While ancient foraging societies are very different from those of today, many families still share aspects of pre-industrial rural societies in which parents worked in the fields from dawn till dusk while grandparents carried out domestic work – particularly childcare.[12] Across the world, 90 per cent of today's grandparents engage with their grandchildren. Nearly two-thirds of grandparents – 63 per cent – with grandchildren under the age of sixteen regularly help with childcare.[13] Throughout Europe, 44 per cent of grandmothers and 42 per cent of grandfathers supply frequent or regular help looking after grandchildren. They collect children from school, help with homework and take them to after-school activities, usually when parents' schedules are too full to leave room for such errands. And many children – 2.75 million in the United States alone – rely on a grandparent, rather than parent, as their primary carer.[14]

The input of grandparents continues to shape economies across the world. Without grandparents who care for grandchildren, China would have had no 'tiger economy'. The roots of China's modern growth harken back to 1949, when the new Communist ruling party declared that all women had to work – all women, that is, under the age of fifty. These younger women often had to leave home to find good jobs, but the system of *hukou*, in which people were deemed to belong to one place and not permitted to relocate permanently, prevented these mother workers from taking their children with them to the cities with the best job opportunities. So 60 million of them left their children to be cared for by their older female relatives, usually their own mothers. These grandmothers stepped in to provide care just as their early human ancestors did.[15]

This pattern of grandparent care can be seen in other parts of the world, too. In Romania, 350,000 children have been 'left behind' by their parents, to be cared for by grandparents, while the parents work in other countries, just as millions of children in the Philippines are cared for by grandparents as the new parents work abroad – often as nannies.[16] In the 1990s, after the dissolution of the Soviet Union and the removal of state support, grandparents looked after their grandchildren when their own children sought employment. When work was scarce, they took the younger generations into their homes and used their modest pensions to provide financial support. Grandparents' engagement had a 'moderation effect', so that when children lived in families with grandparents, they were more likely to weather the social upheaval, poverty and displacement of the immediate post-Soviet era.[17]

Routinely, particularly when resources are scarce, grandparents share whatever they have – shelter, food, time and energy – to help their younger generations of close relatives. And, wherever possible, grandparents share money, even when it is scarce, as Nobel laureate Esther Duflo found when she looked at the economic choices made by impoverished grandmothers in South Africa.[18] In addition, their experience and social wisdom help relieve grandchildren's anxieties and doubts in times of upheaval and poverty.[19]

The measurable impact of the grandmother effect can still be seen today in communities such as rural Gambia where the presence of a grandmother halves the chance of a young child dying.[20] Passing on their knowledge, providing care and supplying additional food, grandparents play a key role in their grandchildren's survival.

While today's grandparents battle against the stereotype of being past their time of usefulness and draining resources from younger generations, in reality they remain key contributors to the family, offering more instrumental and financial support to their grandchildren than they receive from their own adult children.[21]

Self-interest, Altruism and Selfish Genes

Routine decisions about help and support can be seen as modern-day versions of digging for life-sustaining tubers, with grandparents' support making it possible for parents to meet the demands of today. Yet many believe that grandparents' generosity is transactional rather than altruistic. Surely, it is said, grandparents help younger generations so that the younger generation will care for them in their aged infirmity. Isn't the real explanation for grandparental generosity an insurance against future care?

Adult children and older grandchildren *do* often care for their ageing parents and grandparents, either by supporting them directly or by overseeing complicated arrangements for formal paid care. In many cultures, caring for elderly relatives was once the norm, but across the world this is changing. In China and Japan, grandparents are no longer able to count on family care in old age, but their contributions towards their grandchildren have not reduced. In India, too, where grandparents could once depend on the younger generation to provide for them as they aged, urban economics has changed the family structure and now only 16 per cent of family households hold more than two generations – less than the 18 per cent of people in the US who live in households of three or more generations.[22,23]

In fact, grandparents themselves are likely to be the ones offering care to the oldest generation. Nearly two-thirds of people in their fifties have a living parent or parent-in-law, the majority of whom are over eighty. Of this group, a quarter are helping an elderly relative with everyday tasks, and live with the expectation that the care demands will increase in the near future.[24] Fifty-nine per cent of these people expect to provide care for their elderly relative in the next five years, even if they are not currently doing so. Around half of the working caregivers believe that their care responsibilities in the next five years will involve them in having to make changes in their work.[25] In fact, rather than receiving elder care, the majority of today's grandparents are providing it.

Elder Care from the Perspective of Grandparents

My own grandparents did not expect, want or plan for help from younger generations as they grew older. Instead, they moved from their three-storey house to a much smaller flat, which was easier to maintain, and put money away 'in case we need to hire help'. In their minds, they would arrange their own care without recourse to 'burdening you young people'. Yet, when my grandfather died, my mother and her siblings stepped in with daily phone calls to check on her. My grandmother claimed she was fine, but she also complained about loneliness, confusion and anxiety. So, when I was sixteen and had failed to secure what my parents deemed a 'suitable summer job', I was sent to spend the summer with her. I was a very indifferent companion, and my grandmother spent more time worrying about my whereabouts since I was more likely to be gallivanting with friends than helping her with shopping and preparing meals. She bought me clothes, which she then altered to suit me. She was more excited than I was at the prospect of my final year in school. At the end of the summer, my duties discharged, I was relieved; but I also carried within me regret and anxiety, partly for her and partly for me. Had I let her down? Would she be lonely without me? Would she remember to eat without me telling her it was dinnertime?

As I reported back to my mother about what was 'really going on' with her sleeping and eating, my mother pleaded with me, 'Don't let me live to be that old,' as though I had some power over that. My father insisted he would never ask us to look after him. 'You will repay us as parents by looking after your own children, not by looking after us,' he insisted.

The same line was toed by my parents-in-law. My optimistic mother-in-law rarely thought about a future with bad things in it, but when she did, she insisted, 'I don't want you young people to look after me, ever.' But of course we did – or rather my sister-in-law and my husband did. As they navigated the maze of social care, they gave one another support by praising the other's efforts, commiserating when carefully made arrangements fell apart, and consulted one another over problems ranging from heating to health. They exchanged stories in regular evening phone calls that often began, 'Can you believe what she did?' It soon became clear that my mother-in-law's claims to have taken her medication that day, cooked a good supper and gone for a walk were what's called confabulation. Not lying, exactly, but engaging in conversation only to produce an acceptable formula, not a means of conveying information. Her aim was to keep them happy, and maintain the pride she had in managing on her own – even when she wasn't. Like many older people, my mother-in-law would have been physically better off with care from younger generations, but much less happy.[26] The loss of independence, and the belief that they are draining others' resources, is an affront to the fundamental human need to contribute, positively, to the lives of people around us.

Grandparenting is an exercise in *generativity* – working towards the benefit of younger generations. As the great psychologist Erik Erikson tracked the human life cycle, he noted that every stage of life presented its own challenges and motivations. He coined the term 'generativity' to describe the primary developmental task of later adulthood. Here the challenge is to keep stagnation at bay, to continue to grow, to make use of what we have learned, and to extend our vision to a future in which we will not ourselves be active participants.[27] Yet, at a certain point in grandparents' lives, emerging disabilities may require the relationships between the generations to change. They may say, 'It's now time to expect less of me.' But does the possibility that, towards the very end of their lives, they will get help from younger generations prove that grandparents' motives in supporting younger generations are selfish?

Alongside colleagues across Europe, I looked at the scarcity of family-friendly policies that addressed employees' requests to accommodate the demands of elder care.[28] We found that grandparents often could rely on their adult children (primarily aged in their fifties) and grandchildren (often in their late teens or young adulthood) to provide care. We found that 50 per cent of women in midlife were providing some kind of support for their parents. Our work showed that adult children, often grandparents themselves, saw providing elder care as a way of expressing love and gratitude. They wanted to do what they could to mitigate an elderly parent's discomfort or fear or loneliness. They also spoke about duty and decency: 'This is just what you do', 'I can't imagine ignoring it' and 'You just don't stand by when a parent needs you' were some of the general comments made by the women I interviewed. In fact, they often expressed impatience when queried as to their motivations: 'I don't care whether someone else would do it differently' and 'I'm not interested in justifying it'. In addition, three women said that the decision was based on 'gut reaction' and they knew it was 'right for them' or 'right by their book', but they were not interested in 'moralising' on a selfish/unselfish divide.

The need for care is often two-way. My sister-in-law spent so much energy arranging care for her mother and caring for her herself, arranging family birthday celebrations and bringing grandchildren to see her, because *she* needed her mother to have the opportunity to experience things she enjoyed in the past. She was upset when the care home laundered her mother's nice dry-clean-only clothes, not because her mother was still capable of caring, but because *she* wanted to pay tribute to the smartly dressed woman her mother had once been. Every Sunday, when she returned her mother to the care home and made sure she was settled for the night, she herself was comforted and at peace. 'She won't remember she's been here,' her daughter reminded her wryly. 'I don't do it for her,' my sister-in-law explained. 'I do it for me. And I'll remember.'

Adult children often said they 'still needed Mum'. They also need an elderly parent to 'be OK'. They 'couldn't cope at the thought that she was unhappy'. Adult children and older grandchildren provide help to grandparents because *they* need to ease *their* anxiety. Grandparents, on the other hand, hate needing help (however grateful they might be for it).

Optimism that we will remain youthful as we age, and denial of the likelihood that we will need additional support in our later years, are both healthy – because these beliefs maintain our spirits and encourage us to take steps to preserve our health – and unrealistic. When the need for care arises, we are humbled and saddened. We may have planned ahead by installing a walk-in shower or a stairlift. We may have got accustomed to using a personal alarm. But being looked after by our adult children or grandchildren is not part of our life plan.

In fact, there is no convincing evidence to support the theory that engaging with our grandchildren insures us against not having care in our later life.[29] Instead, the evolutionary imperative to protect those who carry our genes shapes our needs and desires *more* than our wish to stay alive beyond our allotted lifespan. The reproductive imperative linked to sexual desire has been given headline status in human psychology, but the protective imperative is equally (if not more) important in shaping our day-to-day behaviour. Our love for our children, our delight in their presence, and the terror we feel when they are in danger, ensure we will do whatever it takes to promote their well-being. When our adult children have children themselves, we seek new ways to support the next generation.

What About Grandfathers?

The evolutionary impact of the grandmother effect has the potential to shape men's emotions and behaviour, just as it does women's. While women's role in gestation and birth and nursing prime her hormonally for that intense connection we call bonding, in the right circumstances, men also develop nurturing impulses and caring priorities.

When the anthropologist Sarah Blaffer Hrdy became a grandparent, she observed her son-in-law providing expert and tender care to the new baby's every need. Blaffer Hrdy had written many books on maternal love, and the caring role of women; now the evidence before her of a male nurturer, who behaved exactly as a female parent would, shook her out of her previous beliefs.[30] Up until this moment, she had bought into traditional theories around evolution, in which females prioritise care for children while men compete for status in order to mate with as many females as possible. According to a crude 'reproductive investment' hypothesis, females invest far more time and energy in bearing (generally) only one child in one year, whereas males can sire hundreds. According to this model, males bank on high numbers of offspring to invest in their genetic legacies, whereas females have to bank on the survival of their existing children.

Her son-in-law's instinctive care of her grandchild refocused Blaffer Hrdy's research. Pivoting away from a female-centred study of infant care, she looked at the fathers and grandfathers across the world who were engaged in infant care. In so doing, she learned that time spent with infants and young children impacted male physiology, flooding their system with distinctive bonding hormones usually associated only with women.[31] She found new evidence, too, that fathers who care for infants experience 'baby brain' exactly as women do. It is the experience of parenting, more than biology, that shapes the human brain, adapting it for care and empathy.[32]

Very little research has been done on grandfathers' attachment to grandchildren, and what is not researched or written about remains unseen; but surely that male capacity for 'instinctive' childcare extends well beyond care of their own newborn infant.[33] Living and working as I do in Cambridge, I come across many distinguished grandfathers, whose experiences as grandparents cast them in a different light. I have heard Nobel Prize-winning grandfathers regale captive audiences with stories about how smart their grandchildren are – not because the younger generations' lifetime achievements will match their own, but because they can operate tech or remember details from past events. I have seen hauteur punctured as someone is interrupted mid-flow, a grandchild's chortle spearing everyone's attention as she cries, 'You sound crazy when you talk like that.' In response to almost anyone else, this grandfather would most likely shrug coldly, and wait to sting his challenger with a clever put-down. But, from a grandchild, this puncture to his vanity is received with the utmost pleasure, as a mark of intelligence, independent and vitality.

The image of a grandfather as 'gruff' and inclined to underplay his attachment is another stereotype that does not survive true observation. The *Financial Times* columnist Martin Wolf, known for his brilliant, acerbic and pessimistic analysis of economic policies, wrote about the pain of separation from his grandchildren during the lockdown of 2020.[34] Like many grandparents who stopped seeing grandchildren during the Covid-19 pandemic, he struggled with the separation.[35] His four-year-old granddaughter and two-year-old grandson lived nearby, but, given the government's message of the day, distance was strictly enforced. Martin waved to the children through a closed window. The young children greeted him with enthusiasm, but turned away ten seconds later, in search of some new activity. Martin mused on the pleasures of having them in his home where he could follow their stop/start bursts of interest and enjoy 'hugging a beloved child's wriggling body'. His craving for physical and mental closeness equals that of any grandmother.

In speaking about grandfathers I draw on stories from my immediate experience because there is little research available. The assumption that grandmothers matter in ways grandfathers do not is so deeply ingrained that the impact of grandfathers has been ignored. It was not until 2016 that a group of scholars explored the experiences and activities and impacts of grandfathering throughout the world.[36] What they found contradicted all expectation.

Grandfathers, it turns out, are often as closely connected to their grandchildren as grandmothers. They describe emotions as 'melting' as the grandmother 'swoon', and are often as eager to engage with grandchildren as the grandmother. They add to the repertoire of games and activities. They help with the drudgery of childcare (and domestic organisation which was also a drain on newer parents) such as fetching and taking to school, preparing meals, and adhering to routines: 'We need to leave the house in five minutes and you need to get your shoes on now.'

Grandchildren returned this love wholeheartedly. Teenage boys, when asked in surveys which family member they got on with best, were likely to name their grandfather.[37] Young boys, sometimes daunted by a grandmother's presumption of close physical contact and probing attention, said they felt 'shy with grandma'. Asked if they also felt 'shy' with their granddad, the answer was a decisive 'No.' I was surprised by this, given the amount of teasing grandfathers do. When my father-in-law teased his grandchildren, I took offence on behalf of my daughters. Even something as simple and silly and obvious as, 'I stole your nose, here it is,' – showing his thumb protruding from his first two fingers in some poor semblance of a nose – tempted me to intervene and reassure them. Why, I wondered, did he engage with them by rattling or confusing them? I have since learned that grandfathers' tendency to tease prompts young children to recognise playful deceits. Not only does this help them distinguish different kinds of discourse (friendly 'joshing' from simple declarative remarks), their unpredictability also stimulates their assessments as to what is going on in another's mind.[38]

Nevertheless, I preferred to watch my daughters engage with their maternal grandfather's special facility in role play. His oldest granddaughter only had to ask to see in his doctor's bag to activate an elaborate and rewarding game. The five-year-old had expected to look in the bag, without touching any of the objects in it. Instead, my father pushed the open bag towards her and asked, 'What are you going to use today? Do you need to look into my ear?' he asked, as he lifted out an otoscope, and held it out to her. 'Or is it my heart you need to check?' and he nodded towards the stethoscope. She lifted it out, gingerly, ready to drop it if he withdrew his assent. 'OK,' he sighed, 'I guess I'd better take off my jacket.' His serious engagement with the role play was so flattering that, in the end, she was too self-conscious to proceed. But that, too, he weaved skilfully into the game. As she returned the stethoscope after only one quick press to his chest, he said, 'You doctors are so busy these days. You have to keep appointments brief.'

The distinctive grandfatherly approach to play is also seen in the stimulation of physical games, particularly tossing a baby in the air and catching them, and in the exaggeration and elaboration of nursery rhymes and songs. Grandfathers are reported to articulate rhymes with funny voices and make up extra verses – another way to surprise a grandchild, while making uncertainty more likely to boost confidence than to provoke anxiety.

Men describe becoming a grandfather as a pivotal event that raises their energy levels and promotes better sleep.[39] It also opens up a new sensitivity and protects them from depression.[40] In her memoir *Becoming Grandma*, Lesley Stahl remarks on the 'new lightness' in the gait of one of her colleagues at the American magazine and news programme *60 Minutes* who for years had battled with what he referred to as 'the dark pit'.[41] Perhaps he, like clinical psychologist Mary Pipher, discovered that a grandchild acts as an antidepressant and teaches more about self-compassion than any cognitive behaviour therapy.[42] Now when Pipher makes a mistake or a poor choice, she no longer spews bitter criticism against herself, but asks, 'What would I say to my grandchild if she did that?' A grandchild's mess-ups and mistakes do not appear as proof of deep personal deficits. Instead, they are just things that happen. Through her love for her grandson, she discovers new paths to self-forgiveness.

The True Meaning of the Grandmother Effect

Evolutionary arguments, particularly about human psychology, are exciting and enlightening, in my view. They remind us of the broad sweep of our shared human development. They show how our emotions and desires, which seem so personal and immediate, are embedded in a very long history of human need. But no evolutionary explanation of our human nature dictates or predicts any individual's experience. So let me be clear:

- The grandmother effect does not mean that all grandmothers want to care for their grandchildren, or that those who do not readily engage with care for grandchildren are 'unnatural', 'selfish' or 'unwomanly'.
- The grandmother effect does not mean that grandfathers won't be equally attached to their grandchildren.
- The grandmother effect does not mean that all daughters will want a mother's input in childcare.
- The grandmother effect does not mean that a grandparent won't have a preferred grandchild, or decide to give more care to one adult child's children than another's.
- The grandmother effect does not mean that a step-grandmother, with whom she does not share genes, will be less attached to step-grandchildren than a biological grandmother.

The grandmother effect *does* mean that there is a universal tendency to engage with – and protect – grandchildren. Indeed, grandparents report that when a grandchild is in their care, they are even more watchful than they remember being with their own children. They worry whether they are still sharp or quick enough to ward off disaster. In a delightful account of her toddler grandson launching himself into the pool, Anna Quindlen remembers wishing she had been wearing a swimsuit and that she had left her lovely watch behind; but, even as these thoughts are running through her mind, she is jumping into the pool after him. She warns all grandparents: 'Be ready… because no matter what happens – coyotes, mean bigger kids, thunderstorms, carnival rides – you are going to do whatever needs to be done to keep this boy safe and happy.'[43] And that, throughout the vast cultural changes across the centuries, is what grandparents do.[44]

Four

Eternal Family Dilemmas: Bonds and Boundaries

'What counts as too close?'

Like any parent who has lived through their child's adolescence, I have been given hard lessons in the importance of parent/child boundaries. 'I'm not you', 'I don't want the same things as you' and 'I need to do it my way' are the markers a teenager lays down and a parent learns to deal with. Yet deep inside our maturing child remains an infant's sensitivity to approval. New grandparents find that a new parent is extremely sensitive to comments about their own parenting. My daughter, as a new mother, saw any suggestion to resolve the baby's crying as an instruction about what she should be doing, and criticism of what she was doing. It was like dealing with a prickly teenager all over again.

My younger daughter was, initially, very different. 'What should I do?' she asked when her new baby cried, her nerves strained from lack of sleep. She looked at me pleadingly, but I had no answer. I could only take my tiny granddaughter, trying this and that with my voice, face and arms, until something seemed to work. For this very different daughter, I was not an annoying judge, but a source of knowledge. It would take some months for her to call out my deficiencies.

When an adult child becomes a parent, they are once again overwhelmed by feelings of what it is to be an infant, and simultaneously begin building up a sense of who they are as a parent. Their own parent's presence provides comfort, but their primary aim is to learn how to be a parent themselves. Borderwork – interaction with others aimed at negotiating comfortable boundaries between them – has to be learned anew.[1] New parents know they are on a steep learning curve. Grandparents, on the other hand, have to relearn something they probably believed they had already mastered.

Grandparents who fail to finesse new borders can become a painful thorn in the heart of the newly configured family. Their intrusion causes stress in one parent or another. New parents who feel unable to manage an intrusive grandparent expend huge amounts of mental energy ruminating on ways to protect their privacy. Borderwork failures result in tension between the two new parents – to the extent that, in some countries, a spouse's failure to prevent their parent from 'invading' the family home is legal grounds for divorce.[2] But how can we, as grandparents, learn to differentiate support and connection on the one hand, from intrusion or invasion on the other?

Myths about Maturity

There is a common myth about human development, which skews expectations and interferes with the ability to manage shifting bonds and boundaries between parents and their adult children. This myth centres on what happens to relationships when children become adults. To understand this myth, we need to go back to the very first bonds forged between child and parent.

In the first days and even hours after birth, infants turn their head towards the person who holds them, prompted by the sound of a parent's voice. They show special interest in a face when the eyes are focused on them, and so it is that parent and infant's eyes lock into a 'love gaze'.[3] Gradually the infant distinguishes within this face a full lexicon of responses and, by the age of about four months, learns that the pupils of the eyes dilute with love and contract with fear, and that a genuine smile comes with distinctive crinkles around the eyes.[4] The movements in a parent's face prompt the infant to exercise her own facial muscles. These early facial exercises are frequently rewarded with a bright smile, a hug and a cascade of warm laughter.

A parent's face is highly responsive to the infant's. It automatically engages in a kind of mimicry that does not simply mirror the infant's face, but shows the infant that her expressions have meaning. The parent transforms the infant's expressions by emphasising and exaggerating certain features. The open mouth of the wailing infant, for example, is mimicked by a parent but also modified with an expression of gentle surprise. Through this process of imitation and inflection, the infant learns that the parent understands her feelings and is also on hand to soothe them.[5]

This is one of the many ways parent and infant engage in what is more commonly called bonding. The connection is intricate and deep, bringing to life an infant's sense of being a self in relationship with others. Through this connection, children learn how to eat and talk, how to manage their bodily functions, whom to trust and whom to fear, what is safe and what is dangerous. Parents scaffold a child's picture of the world – until adolescence.

Teens shake this scaffold until the foundations rattle. They often seem intent on proving their parents wrong on every score. Instead, they turn to friends to arbitrate questions about who is to be trusted and whom to fear. The family's gauge of safety and danger is thrust aside as teens thrill to the risk of forbidden activities. Parents' approval and disapproval, once vitally important, is now constantly contested. Friends and influential peers form their new cultural toolkit. The infant's 'eye love' is replaced by 'that look' of the adolescent.

But children, whether as surly teens or independent adults, remain profoundly sensitive to a parent's approval and disapproval. Parents often forget how easily a child, no matter their age, can be hurt by what they say. They don't realise that their assumptions about what their adult child 'needs to hear' or has yet to learn are badly out of date. They are unaware that, because the adult child retains within them a larger than life-size image of a parent, their small remark, however softly spoken, sounds in the child's mind like an announcement made through a megaphone.

To retain a comfortable connection between this pair, borderwork is required. On the part of the adult child, this involves a signal that, 'You've gone too far,' and, 'This is my private concern,' and, 'This advice feels more intrusive than helpful.' It is a way of reminding their parents – and themselves – where they begin, and where they end. It is confusing and exhausting work, and they do not always do it with patience or charm, any more than they did as teenagers. But as parents of a new parent, their parents have to listen in a new way. As Annette Byford reflects in her book *Once a Mother, Always a Mother,* 'Being a parent of an adult child presents you with more demands for change and more and new and varying challenges than I had ever imagined, and, frankly, at times more than I feel sufficiently prepared for.'[6]

Blurred Boundaries: Connection and Confusion

For many mothers, a daughter's pregnancy opens the floodgates to memories of their own pregnancies. 'It's difficult to stay in the here and now when I see her pregnant waddle. And watching how she sits down – slow and heavy – really takes me back. I feel her pregnancy in my own body. I look at her and I rush off to pee. I feel the pressure on my bladder, and in my legs,' Jill admits. She describes her thirty-one-year-old daughter Becca as 'a cool cookie, nothing woo-woo about pregnancy in her eyes, just a thing she has to get through to get the baby. I thought I was the same. But now that *my* baby is having a baby, part of me is caught in some elemental identity melt. I don't know where her body ends and mine begins'.

Becca's father Paul is also thrown back to earlier stages of attachment. 'She was always independent, so none of the other big steps to adulthood surprised me. Didn't surprise me when she chose a career we never knew existed. Doesn't surprise me that she argues a big case in front of a judge. But this is different. My sister says, "What are you fussing about? She's a grown woman." And I think, "Yeah, it's about time. Yeah, I know she's all grown up." But part of me wants to bring her back home with us and say, "Little girl, you don't have to do this on your own." Hell, I want to say to her, "I'll do it for you." How's that for a messed-up mind?'

Of course, Paul cannot have the baby for his daughter. Of course, Jill isn't the one who's pregnant. But rather than read this as enmeshment – the inability to distinguish between one's own experiences and that of a close family member – or a 'messed-up mind', these grandparents-to-be articulate a common and very normal experience.

The new closeness grandparents feel when 'my baby has a baby' also increases their vulnerability to breaches between them and their adult child. Once it was the child who experienced existential anxiety in the face of conflict with a parent: 'Will an angry parent reject me, cast me out, abandon me?' Now it is the grandparent who fears a breach with their adult child: 'Will my child cut ties with me and freeze me out? Will I lose access to her and my grandchild?' Grandparents' eagerness for an early visit to the newborn infant serves multiple purposes: to see the grandchild, to help the new parents, but also to reassure themselves that they are a key part of this newly configured family.

Becca is glad to have her parents nearby when she gives birth. Her parents will look after her ten-year-old stepson, while her partner Alex stays with her and the new baby. But when she returns home from hospital, she finds what she calls her parents' 'fussing' intrusive. 'I have to work this out myself,' she informs her mother brusquely. Later she barks, 'I need you to stop talking now,' and, 'Just give me a minute!'

'OK, OK,' Jill says, stepping back, halting her approach towards the crying infant. She tries to laugh it off: 'Like when you were two. And you were always shouting, "I can do it myself."' But she is clearly hurt, and somewhat shamed by having her daughter bark at her in my presence. I wonder whether, if I weren't there, she would scold Becca, as she might a child.

Becca's insistence that she 'work this out myself' is not childish, but it does share something with the toddler's heated refusal of help. Just as a toddler's brain is geared to learn quickly, a new mother's inexperienced brain is highly receptive to learning about her baby. Soon she will be able to interpret the meanings of different cries – hunger, pain, fear – and know the repertoire of her baby's movements and breathing. It is often said that this comes naturally and it does, but only through intensive study.

New parents, as we have seen, experience something called 'baby brain', which is often supposed to result in deficits of memory and logic. The brain of new parents does exhibit change, though the remoulded brain involves growth and focus rather than any deficiency. Brain imaging techniques allow neuroscientists to see distinctive neural patterns in response to an infant's cries and an infant's laughter. The brain becomes highly sensitive to cues from the infant, poised to attend to and learn from interactions with the baby.[7] Soon parent and baby engage in nuanced interactions that flow so smoothly and are so finely coordinated that they have been described as a 'dance'.[8] Becca's brain is intent on learning, and at this point her mother's 'help' interferes with her concentration and her learning. She *is* like the two-year-old who is enraged by help and, like the two-year-old, her anger stems from the imperative to learn to do these things herself.

How upset a grandparent is at a new parent's impatience depends on how secure they feel about their relationship. Jill says that the past ten years with Becca 'have been great. To see her blossom like she has. And so smart. Knowing what she wants, that's great.' There is a pause and Jill focuses on something at the far end of the room as she collects her thoughts. 'Those teen years were rough. She was ruthless in the way she took me down. We never came to blows but it felt physical, I was shattered. I didn't know whether we'd survive it. So maybe that's why I've treasured the last, relatively calm, ten years.'

New friction between them activates those old fears about 'whether we'd survive it'. I heard these fears voiced by other grandparents, too, who describe relationships with the new parents as a minefield. They are on tenterhooks about saying 'the wrong thing', just as they were in their child's adolescence. They are exhausted by the need to watch their words and disheartened when they are 'misjudged' – for example, when their 'smallest suggestion is taken as some high-handed order'.

From the adult child's perspective, however, it is they who are being judged. Remember, the adult child does not feel fully separate, psychologically and emotionally, from their parents. They retain within them a special sensitivity to what they believe their parents think of them. The childhood idealisation and dependence remain alive – transformed, of course, and often muted, but easily revived, particularly when the adult child feels uncertain themselves. This then raises a fear in the grandparent: what if the border drawn by the new parent marks an exclusion zone? What if the grandparent is seen to be 'invading the family home' and is therefore 'divorced' from the younger generations?

Grandparents' challenge with borderwork continues long after a new parent's postnatal sensitivities have subsided. Carrie, seventy-one, moved countries to be near her ten-year-old granddaughter. After several years of harmony between her and her adult daughter Sophie, her son-in-law and her grandchildren, Carrie's usually tolerant daughter 'exploded when I suggested she could put less pressure on [my granddaughter] about her school performance. She didn't talk to me for two weeks. This was a real body blow. It reminded me how I hated it when my mother criticised how I was raising my kids. If Sophie sees me like I saw my mother, we might not come back from that. And if she wouldn't talk to me, where would that leave me and my granddaughter?'

Sudden conflict can erupt at any time, revealing fissures in even the most robust family bonds. Such eruptions are difficult to predict or avoid because they arise from childhood dramas that seem forgotten – until they are not. Carrie's daughter Sophie explains that she still 'falls into roles I hate'. Sometimes she 'reverts to old patterns' and believes she is 'programmed to accept what mum says. So I think I am doing fine, that mum living nearby isn't an issue. I'm still the mother in charge of my kids. But sometimes she says something that crashes my confidence. Am I like one of those hothouse parents I hate? Why am I so anxious about how well my daughter does in school? Is mum right, and I'm getting it all wrong?' Carrie's comment – meant as something Sophie might consider – is heard as criticism announced through a megaphone, leaving Sophie spinning with self-doubt.

Fortunately, day-to-day life among people we love presents many opportunities for repairing ruptures. When I return to Carrie and Sophie some months later, grandparent and parent are once again allies, and Sophie is seeking her mother's support in dealing with teenage upheavals. Sophie discovered that her daughter, now fourteen, has been exchanging sexually explicit and what Sophie describes as obscene messages with a boyfriend. Sophie turns to her mother to moderate her dismay and 'nausea'. Like many parents, Sophie has 'shaken-head syndrome, seeing my little kid transformed to a sexual teen in the blink of an eye'.

The grandmother is able to say, 'You're shocked and that feels awful but don't lay that at your daughter's door. You deal with it. Just make sure you have a sensible conversation about those health risks. And social risks, too, because these things end, and the aftermath can be awful.' As so often, the grandparent's broader view – 'I've been here before, with you and your brother' – normalises what seems cataclysmic. The new parent who so recently protested 'I need to do it my way', 'I need to figure it out myself', or 'I can manage on my own' now turns to the grandmother to ask in amazement, 'How did you get through this when I was a teen?'

Borderwork with In-laws

We have seen how the deep bonds between parent and child make a new parent supersensitive to comments about their parenting, sometimes as a throwback to unfinished business in borderwork, sometimes as unresolved complaints about grandparents as parents. 'You were never this patient with me,' a new mother says to her own mother, and the grandparent's positive interaction with a grandchild is transformed into an insult. 'You always have time for him, but you never had time for me,' a mother says to the grandmother who offers over and over again to look after her grandchild. 'I don't need any parenting advice from you,' a parent says to her parent, flooded with memories of the times her mother – in her view – got it wrong. But we have also seen a different, frequently more negative sensitivity to the grandparenting input of in-laws.

Within a family, the primary members generally know how to argue and how to mend breaches while maintaining their dignity and status. As Agneschka explains, 'I have very close family, very, very close family. And I raised my children for eight years as a single parent. So I'm a rock, I'm the anchor in the whole family. I'm the matriarch at some level.' Her daughter, equally self-confident, tells her, 'I've got this. I don't want to rely on your advice.' After a beat, Agneschka declares, 'That's my daughter.' The peace they broker is: 'We are both self-reliant: our similarities make us argue, but they also connect us.'

It is more difficult for in-laws to broker such peace deals because arguments seem dangerous. 'Once you squeeze the toothpaste out of the tube you can't get it back in,' Nisha's partner Seth explains. The message is: 'If we argue, I will say mean things (the mean things I think but keep inside me). Once mean things are said, they cannot be unsaid.' This is the nub of the good behaviour syndrome described in Chapter One, where grandparents try to silence themselves as they interact with a new parent – particularly with their son- or daughter-in-law.

Grandparents' anxiety about how their behaviour might be perceived by a child-in-law is a prominent theme in all discussion platforms for grandparents. On *Gransnet* there is a special section and a special acronym for it: AIBU or 'Am I being unreasonable?' This question occurs and recurs in the minds of many grandparents – especially in relation to a daughter-in-law. 'I told her I found it helpful to have a bedtime schedule. Was I really telling her what to do, as she seems to think? Am I being unreasonable, or is it my daughter-in-law?' Or, 'I talked to her just to keep her mood up, but she told me she needed quiet when she was with the baby. I apologised and then kept quiet, but she's still sullen. So I apologised again and got, "It's OK!" So it clearly wasn't. Am I being unreasonable in showing her I want to do what she wants, or is [my daughter-in-law] being unreasonable?'

Such constant self-questioning is exhausting. It undermines day-to-day confidence. It is humiliating to be under pressure to please someone and comply with their erratic responses. Nonetheless, self-censorship is seen as a basic requirement by many grandparenting gurus. Without it, grandparents are warned, they risk exclusion both from the new parents and their grandchildren. Regardless of your established authority and the proud and loud voice you may have in other areas of your life, setting boundaries to your speech is seen as a prerequisite to bonding with your grandchildren. Such rules sound like common sense, but, as I show at the end of the chapter, there are better paths to maintaining bonds than silencing ourselves.

Differences among In-laws: Norms and Cultures

When two distinct families are blended into one, as happens when our adult child chooses a life partner, we discover new patterns in the configuration of our family. The older generation expects that their status and influence will not change, but it does. The new partner expects they will have first rights to loyalty, support and influence. Adult children then have to balance loyalties to their parents, to their partner's parents *and* set boundaries between themselves as a couple and both sets of parents. Of course, such loyalties should not compete against one another, but they often do.

With a newly combined family come new rules, but it is not always clear precisely what these are. Every family has expectations about how its members should behave. Every family subscribes to a version of normal without seeing how strange those norms seem in another family. Some rules cover behaviour: can each member decide how to spend their own evening or weekend, or is there an imperative to do things together? Are family members expected to converse over the breakfast table, or is silence acceptable? Sometimes rules extend even to what family members should think and feel. How much disagreement is OK? Can strong emotions – either positive or negative – be expressed?

These rules, often unspoken and even unacknowledged, can leave one feeling like an outsider among in-laws. If you don't know the new family rules, then you may discover that your habit of reading the news while buttering toast is 'rude'. You may be declared unfriendly or cold because you decline to join a family hike – something your own family accepts and expects, but which your in-laws take as a rejection.

Also embedded in each family are assumptions about each member's power. Does 'what mother/father says' dictate the behaviour of others? Does 'mother/father know best'? Does family harmony require daily maintenance with constant praise, whereby one member says to the other, 'You're so thoughtful and kind.' In one family these remarks seem supportive; in another, they are cloying. In one family criticism is routinely used to monitor harmony: 'Don't speak like that to your mother/father/brother'/'Don't be so grumpy'/'You have nothing to complain about', but in another these micro judgements feel inappropriate, controlling or demeaning.

Then come wider cultural issues about politics, diversity and fairness. Disagreements about political, social and moral issues can put primary family members at odds, too; but there is a distinctive surprise, threat and outrage when conflict erupts between in-laws. Without knowing how to argue, disagreement poses an unknown risk to family connection. Avoidance then seems the best option – a superficially sensible tactic, but one that constrains and distorts communication. This is regrettable, because diversity within a family is potentially enlightening.

Diversity within a family today is not exceptional, yet often takes people by surprise. When Anna Quindlen held her grandchild in a baby carrier, people asked her, 'Where did you get him?' Fielding the question as neutrally as possible, she relied, 'From my daughter.' A common follow-up query was: 'Oh, is he adopted?'

Anna Quindlen reflects that her grandson shows what 'our country looks like now… The child who has one parent who is black and another who is white. The child who has one parent who is Latino and another who is Swedish and who ricochets among languages.'[9] At the latest count, one in seven babies born in the US, and one in three babies born in the UK are multiracial or multi-ethnic, more than triple the figure at the time grandparents' own children were born.[10,11]

People often say that we look for a partner who reminds us of a parent. Hence the adage, 'He married [a woman just like] his mother.' But in looking for a life partner we are just as likely to be attracted to someone who has qualities, characteristics and abilities we believe our childhood family lacked, making it likely that our parents will see a partner's family as 'not like us'. Combine this attraction of differences with a diverse society, and you get 'an arc of progress [that] bends towards grandchildren that are like us and yet not'.[12]

With this new norm come different cultures, different religions, different ethnicities and vastly different experiences. These large cultural differences do not necessarily affect how well the new family functions more than do the different micro-cultures of each family – unless ignorant stereotypes loom up about race, class or religion. 'My daughter-in-law is really posh, will my grandchild grow up to be a snob?' Or, 'My grandchildren's new step-mother is a born-again Christian, will she draw my grandchild into her church?' Or, 'The other grandparents are Jewish, will they insist that all Fridays and Saturdays are set aside for Shabbat observance?' Or, 'My daughter's parents-in-law are working class, will they value education the way we do?'

Many grandparents, however, approach in-law differences with curiosity rather than suspicion. 'Of course [my grandchild] must learn Portuguese. How else will she be able to communicate with her other grandparents?' Bettany tells her daughter, who is wondering whether the toddler should be exposed to two languages at this time. But later, as her granddaughter approaches puberty, Bettany is no longer so accepting. She worries the family, including her bilingual granddaughter, will move to Brazil and see the other set of grandparents every day. She fears that her granddaughter will see her Brazilian side as her true family, and that she will become a 'shadow of a grandmother'. Her anxiety opens up a very common, but rarely recognised theme: competition between the two sets of grandparents.

Competitive Anxiety Between Grandparents

Competitive anxiety – 'Which grandparent has the most influence?' and, 'How can I modify [what I see as] the bad influence of the other grandparents?' arises from both mountains and molehills. One grandparent feels despair and disconnection as a granddaughter takes First Holy Communion or a grandson is circumcised. 'Why do the other family's customs take priority over mine?' and, 'This is not who I want my grandchild to be.'

We have less power than we would like to protect our grandchildren on the terms we choose, but over time we have more power than we think. Teenage grandchildren frequently spoke of learning about two very different cultures from two sets of grandparents. Sixteen-year-old Noah explains that his mother's father teaches him about Iranian culture, while his father's mother teaches him Hebrew songs 'from her weathered copies of the Haggadah which are signed by those who came to family Seders going back fifty years'. His 'dual background has led [him] to think about how people on opposing sides can find common ground by studying other cultures.' As different cultures fuse within a grandchild, grandparents' clashing cultures give way to Noah's – or any grandchild's – eagerness 'to hear all sides of a debate'.

But the power to balance another grandparent's values with our own rests on our strong bond with grandchildren. Often the competition between grandparents is not about cultures but closeness. 'Do the other grandparents have a closer connection to our grandchildren?' we may worry, and, 'Do they have easier access to my grandchildren?' These concerns from many grandparents echoed anxieties I heard from young girls who constantly worried that another girl was no longer their very best friend.[13] And, as with young girls pondering over social alliances, questions that appeared petty had existential implications.

One grandmother is offended at not receiving an invitation to her three-year-old grandson's birthday party, because the other grandparents were coming and, the parents believed, there was not space for everyone. Another, who travelled to Belgium to visit her son (part of a same-sex couple) and grandchild, is brushed aside by the other grandmother at bath-time because, it was explained, she 'already knew the routine'.[14] Living close by, this other grandmother seemed more keen to display her familiarity than to share grandparenting during the short visit. Another focus of competition was money: gifts that outshone anyone else's, extravagant holidays, homes with endless rooms for hide and seek, gardens with meandering paths, ponds and magical dens.

Stories about rivalries between grandparents are difficult to assess because they are one-sided. I hear them only from grandparents who feel threatened and marginalised. While their stories suggest motives – the other grandparents want to secure a higher status – is this a reality? Are grandparents who enjoy greater influence or easier access to grandchildren impervious to competition? Do only the 'lesser' grandparents suffer? I cannot yet answer these questions, but all grandparents should keep in mind Noah's experience of the two very different, potentially clashing cultures of his grandparents: 'Throughout my life I have juggled these two branches of [my] background. From the outside, they may seem conflicting, yet I consider them complementary.'

The Power of Geography

A key question in discussion about grandparenting and connection is, 'How far away are your grandchildren?' Grandparents who have grandchildren nearby are thought 'lucky', while a sympathetic 'Ahh,' can be heard in response to, 'My grandchildren live thousands of miles away.' But these responses – envy or sympathy – are sometimes reversed when a new parent is asked, 'Where do your parents-in-law live?' Living together, 'on top of each other' or 'next door' can offer enviable possibilities of easy childcare, but may blur the distinction between 'invasion' and comfortable connection. Yet, in spite of the value they place on their own independence, and their genuine concern to respect the space in between generations, many grandparents are urged by the new parents to uproot themselves from their home, their neighbourhood and their friends to move close by.

To someone like me, who hopes to spend the rest of my days in the house I have lived in for nearly fifty years, in a city I never, ever want to leave, seeing others take such a step is nearly beyond my comprehension. When I explored how other grandparents made their decision, I found myself in a landscape resembling Alice's giant chess set in Wonderland, except the pieces were not king, queen, bishop and pawn, but personal, moral and practical principles: what are the practical implications of relocation? What is most important to me now? Going forward, what is the best way of securing the life I value? What responsibilities do I have here, and how can those be managed if I move elsewhere? This momentous decision often involves moving closer to one adult child than another – a choice that can generate envy and resentment between siblings. Since there is no simple rule book for making decisions, I decided the most illuminating approach is to explore how thoughtful, reflective grandparents arrive at such decisions themselves.

His second grandson was four months old when Donal learned his son was moving from the UK to Australia. 'I asked him about the new job and I showed – I hope – the interest I should have in these things, but I was forcing myself to stay on the subject. What was really happening was that my head was spinning. All I could think about was the distance. Those miles between us seemed like a chasm, and I was going to fall in it. What would it be like, seeing my grandchildren only once a year, or at most, twice? Sure, we could do FaceTime, but that's different from sitting on the floor and playing with them and letting them show you what they're doing. One thing that pulls at my heartstrings is having my granddaughter come here, to our home, and see how she thinks it is hers, too. She takes my hand and leads me around. She looks for the cat. Then she wants to "make something with Granddad" and pulls me into my workshop to look for spare pieces of this and that to see what we can make. How's that going to work when she's in Australia?'

Parents and grandchildren are likely to see geographical distance as manageable with phone calls and visits. Grandparents, however, are aware how quickly time passes. They are less confident about opportunities to make up for lost time. 'The distance weighs on me,' Donal concludes. He shakes his head and repeats, 'It really weighs.'

Like many grandparents, Donal and his wife Cat took this blow in their stride. Their daughter lives on the west coast of the US, along with her husband and their children, so they were used to long-distance grandparenting. Every spring, they made the journey to see their daughter's family, exhausting their funds and annual leave from work. As these trips lasted several weeks, they rented a serviced flat near their daughter's home, rather than risk 'being under their feet'. They were both fifty-eight, still relatively young, when their son moved to Australia, and both still working. But with two families so far away, they decided to retire a little early. Once they turned sixty, they began spending six weeks of the year visiting their children and catching up with their grandchildren on the different continents.

Soon after they retired, their daughter-in-law was in a skiing accident. With a badly broken leg, she welcomed the 'extra pair of hands' her parents-in-law offered. They spent three and a half months in Sydney helping to look after their youngest grandson – now a demanding toddler – and the school-age granddaughter. 'Seeing them every day, and doing lots of little inconsequential things with them was very different from those intense visits, where we crammed everything into a couple of weeks. This way, we were really getting to know them… The small interactions are important for being part of their lives.' The opportunity for daily 'inconsequential interactions' set a clear marker for what their relationship with grandchildren could be.

Five years later Donal said they now felt 'much older. We have both had some health scares. We are now fully retired, and not so active – especially me. Not immobile, just much slower. Several long-haul flights a year are not sustainable. It's nice to think that you can just keep going the way you've always kept going, but we've had a few wake-up calls that forced us to sit down and sort of map our future. We can contemplate a real change now only because both our parents – who required a lot of care in their final years – have passed. Since then, I've taken on a lot of admin-type care for my brother who is immobile, and I worry about that, but I'll set up what I can now, and oversee what I can from wherever we move to.'

Grandparents with more than one adult child confront the question, 'Which family should we be close to?' Sometimes the age of the grandchildren is key; there are more opportunities to help out with younger children. Sometimes grandparents view one adult child as more likely or more willing to help in the grandparents' later years. Sometimes more practical matters guide the decision, such as a country's immigration laws and health provision. Donal said, 'This was a hard one for us, since both our children live far from us and far from each other. But once we made the decision to move near one of the families, we sat down, conferred with our children and thought it through.'

Donal and Cat prepared for 'a necessary conversation with both our children and their partners. We gave them time. We asked them to be frank. We braced ourselves to listen. In the end, when we decided to move to Sydney, our daughter in the US seemed put out, like there was some jealousy going on, which was silly, but we were relieved. We could shed the fear that we were going to be unwelcome. But we're aware that it puts responsibility onto our son and daughter-in-law. Whatever they say, that's got to be a factor.'

After Donal and Cat decided that they would move to their son's home in Australia, they asked, 'How close is too close?' The proximity that is attractive to grandparents might arouse unease in the parents. Perhaps their son had seen distance from the grandparents as a perk. Perhaps the visits that seem far too short for the grandparents seemed to drag on endlessly for the parents. If the adult child has been 'biting their tongue' or self-silencing, strong opposition to the grandparents moving closer can remain hidden.

The burden such a move places on parents should not be underestimated. Moving from one city to another means that grandparents' local networks are still just about accessible. But the move Donal and Cat planned, from one continent to another, meant that their son's family would be their primary source of support, at least for a while. What obligations does such relocation put on the new parents and grandchildren? Does the younger generation worry that, with their ageing parents moving nearby, they will be expected to look after them?

A common assumption is that the older generation living nearby places a burden on the younger one when elder care is required. What I heard when I spoke to adult children surprised me. The adult children said that with their parents nearby, the care load was easier. A check-up visit to see whether they are well, to deliver the medication or groceries they need, or to check the boiler is working, takes an hour rather than several days. A grandparent could be invited to a meal rather than a week's stay. A response to any emergency would not be complicated by travel arrangements.

All these considerations only make sense, however, when both grandparents and new parents genuinely want such close bonds. Given the modern-day stereotype of a nuclear family, with parents' enjoying carefree independence once their children are grown, many assume that ties of care and responsibility across generations are unusual and unwelcome. This assumption requires a radical overhaul.

Tighter Bonds in Modern Times

We often imagine that multigenerational gatherings only take place on special occasions – holidays, funerals and significant birthdays. As we have seen, it is supposed that grandparents, in spite of their long intimate histories with a new parent and their delight in the new generation, are tangential to everyday family life. By this metric, the purpose of raising children is to produce independent adults who leave home, stand on their own two feet and live within the boundaries of their own new family.[15] This model of typical family life obscures the reality: most families are extended families, even when they are not living in one household.

The 1950s are viewed as the heyday of the traditional nuclear family, constituted by parents and their two or three children. But when two British sociologists, Michael Young and Peter Willmott, observed kinship networks in London's East End, they found tight-knit *extended* families. The mother/daughter bonds were particularly strong, leading to a grandmother/new mother/grandchild bond so powerful that sons-in-law often struggled to have any say in family matters.[16] This continuing influence is probably a driver behind misogynistic mother-in-law jokes: the older woman is punished with public ridicule for her high status in the home.

In the 1970s, Michael Young set out to explore whether connections between grandparents, parents and grandchildren remained close, and whether families beyond the working-class, urban ones he originally studied also relied on intergenerational bonds. He and his team looked at school records throughout Britain to see who was registered as the emergency contact, the person a school calls in the event of any emergency, if the child's parents cannot be reached. In an overwhelming majority of cases, Young found that the emergency contact for a child was a grandparent. In some schools this applied to 75 per cent of the children.[17] This data suggests that many new parents acknowledge grandparents as a reliable source of care, and view grandparents as a key part of the family.[18]

For all the value supposedly placed on adult children's independence from parents, new parents today are likely to have far more contact with their parents than those of previous generations.[19] This closeness between adult children and their parents (which leads to closeness between grandparent and grandchild) results from many things. Changing work patterns, with both parents in paid employment, the significant number of single-parent families, and the high cost of childcare increase the potential role of grandparents in day-to-day life.[20] The demands of work, greater control over fertility and reduced infant mortality have led to a reduction in the number of children born to women (from 2.07 for women born in 1950 to 1.94 to women born in 1977).[21] With 38 per cent of families having only two children, there are 'more vertical than horizontal linkages in families... [with members spending] a longer time occupying intergenerational family roles than before'.[22,23]

Connections between the new parents and grandparents of today are also shaped and strengthened by the extended dependence of older teenagers and young adults on their families. New parents are likely to have lived with their parents well past the age of eighteen. As young adults spend many years in education and training, after that initial leave-taking for college or travel or a job, they will often return home. In the UK, 70 per cent of young single people in their twenties, and 30 per cent of single people in their thirties share a home with parents; in the US, for the first time since the Great Depression, a *majority* of young adults aged eighteen to twenty-nine are living with their parents.[24,25] Even those who do leave home for a while are likely to return, transforming the empty nest to a revolving door. As Maggie Smith's character in *Downton Abbey* remarks on the nature of parenting: there is an inescapable 'on and on-ness of it'.

We can see the increase in intergenerational bonds, too, reflected in data on housing. In the past decade, the number of multigenerational households has mushroomed by 30 per cent. For the most part, these extended family households consist of young adults living in their parents' home, but 15 per cent of multigenerational households consist of new parents living in their own home, plus a grandparent who has moved in with them.[26] This family configuration – grandparents who are living in the younger generation's home – increased steadily but very slowly from the 1970s until the pandemic of 2020. Then, with the risks of and prohibitions against mixing households, along with the increased burden of childcare caused by school and nursery closures, a whopping 10 per cent of grandparents moved in with the new parents, forming 'bubbles' where members of the same household did not have to isolate from one another.[27]

Measures that were meant to isolate grandparents from young family generations had the opposite effect. Grandparents stepped in to help with childcare, and responded to the financial hit of higher costs of living. They also protected themselves from the emotional difficulty of being separated from their grandchildren.[28] Twenty per cent of all home purchases now involve grandparents on the lookout for homes that will accommodate adult children and their families. Often funds for the new multigenerational home come from grandparents selling their own home, combining generational assets.[29]

Other grandparents find unexpected ways to ensure proximity to their grandchildren. My cousin, the artist Judith Seligson, a grandmother of two young children, now co-rents a flat just down the hall from her daughter's flat. The twist? She shares the flat with her grandchildren's other grandparents. The children move freely from their parents' home to their grandparents' home, while the two sets of grandparents pool their resources to ensure a closeness to their grandchildren that neither could afford on their own.

Grandparents hope that their children will grow up to be self-reliant and financially independent, but they also want to retain close ties to their adult children and to provide help when needed. A recent *Culture of American Families Survey* shows that older parents say they would encourage an adult child to move back to their home if the child had difficulty covering the costs of housing. Looking at the results of this survey, the sociologist Carl Desportes Bowman reflects, 'The quest for long-term connection has taken center stage. Parenting is still about formation [of independence], but its overriding concern has pivoted from formation to connection.'[30]

Boundary Failure

Maintaining connection between three generations requires delicate negotiations. As we have seen, it requires restraint from grandparents, whose parenting views no longer have priority. It requires acceptance and tolerance of other grandparents who may have very different ways of expressing love and engagement. When the necessary negotiations about authority, influence and access fail, then it is not only the bonds between grandparent and parent that suffer. Boundary failure can also fracture bonds between the new parents themselves, as each partner feels betrayed. One partner complains, 'You don't protect me from your interfering parents.' And the other partner wonders, 'Do I have to betray my parents to be loyal to my spouse?'

In the early years of this century, a divorce lawyer in Italy was alarmed by the high number of couples seeking divorce as a result of tensions with in-laws, particularly between mothers- and daughters-in-law. At the same time, the government was concerned to see Italy's divorce rate increase by 45 per cent from 2000 to 2002. Data was gathered to tease out possible causes for the rise in divorce. Many issues were familiar: immaturity, infidelity and problems with money. But 30 per cent of divorces were attributed to complaints about 'an intrusive and overbearing mother-in-law'.[31]

Further examination of data by the Italian National Institute of Statistics revealed that proximity to a husband's mother was highly correlated with divorce. Tracking the matter further, it emerged that the likelihood that a marriage would last increased with every hundred yards' distance between the couple's home and that of the husband's mother. Unable to legislate on where people should live, Italy's highest court of appeal ruled that a woman has grounds to separate from her husband if he fails to prevent his mother from 'invading' their family home.[32]

A family's breakdown is rarely due to one single cause. But the court's ruling against mother-in-law intrusion will resonate with many couples as they wrestle with the need for both bonds and boundaries. Couples need their privacy and domestic spaces, where the rhythms of love and conflict can develop without interruption. Sometimes these needs cannot be met in the presence of grandparents.

Even minor annoyances relating to voice, manner and habits, can eat away at the greater substance of a relationship. 'She drives me up the wall', and 'Sitting through a meal with him is torture', are complaints not easily addressed with reason and fairness. When Mica visits her daughter and grandchildren, her son-in-law will often be holed up in his office, seeing friends or 'taking this opportunity' to exercise. 'I don't think he likes me,' she concludes ruefully. But she accepts this; it does not interfere with her visits, and her daughter is not shy about asking for her help with the children.

My own slip-ups as a grandmother continue. My desire to engage segues to intrusion. When my granddaughter is tying laces on her skates, her father encourages her, 'You can do this,' but before I think about what I'm doing, I am on my knees doing up the laces myself. I come up with some excuse – 'I want to make sure they're tight enough around her ankles,' – but this is just a cover for ignoring my son-in-law's preference that she does it herself. When she is tearful after a parental scolding and I offer her a treat, I am chided, 'This isn't a time to reward her.' Like other grandmothers, I try to bite my tongue, except that I generally bite mine *after* I've spoken. Boundary setting and bond maintenance between generations is, I must acknowledge, a lifelong enterprise.

A Guide to Life-long Borderwork

Reminders for Grandparents

Borderwork is familiar to any grandparent who has lived through their child's adolescence. 'I'm different from you', 'Don't look at me and see yourself', and 'I have to make my own decisions', are identity reminders from teenager to parent. The lessons that were learned when our children were teens, however, can be undone by the elemental, physical and symbolic experiences of pregnancy and birth. This brings grandmother and new parent closer, but within the closeness new tensions can emerge.

A new parent, confused by blurred boundaries, needs to engage in establishing their identity. The teenager's 'You don't really know me,' now becomes 'I am the authority on this child. I am the mother. You may be a welcome participant in this bond, but you are not central to it.'

The first lesson is to listen to the complaint and not take offence at its tone. Grandparents may need to relearn these hard and humbling lessons, keeping in mind that their voice is amplified in their children's hearing, no matter how grown up they are. Rejoinders such as, 'Don't talk like that to me,' or, 'I was only trying to help,' which imply, 'You should be grateful, not critical', should be avoided. New parents need to map out their own space and authority. They won't always do this graciously.

Arguments and tensions do not have to escalate. Grandparents need to step beyond their comfort zone and allow disagreements to be aired. If they encourage the new parents to air their criticisms, they can do better in the future. If they focus on their own motives – 'She's upset with me and I was only trying to help' – they learn nothing about the new parent's needs.

It is difficult to focus on improving interactions when someone is angry or critical. When someone accuses us of something, particularly if that person is close to us, our brain's alarm system is activated. We are poised to run away, fight back or shut down. But this does not help us sustain the relationships we value. When an adult child says something hurtful, do your best to take a beat, set your defensiveness aside and proceed to understand.

When grandparents do not understand why a new parent is bad-tempered, they could encourage them to speak out. One invitation might be, 'Can you help me here? I feel that I am making something difficult for you, and I want to step up or step back – whichever is appropriate – but I need guidance.' A shorter version could be, 'Talk to me. I'll do my best to listen.' This assures a new parent that the conversation is not going to be about their bad temper or your good intentions, but about communication and collaboration.

Grandparents should also remember that the other set of grandparents is equally in love with their grandchildren. It is worth reflecting whether you, as grandparent, assume greater authority or intimacy with your shared grandchildren. A reminder to the parents – 'Shouldn't the other grandparents also be invited?' or 'Isn't it the other grandparents' turn to spend the holidays with you?' – acknowledges the wider family and assures the parents that you are willing to share family connections.

Grandparents who feel constantly sidelined by the other grandparents are likely to benefit from speaking out. In the first instance, they could explain to their adult child how they feel, giving examples to show why they feel marginalised or excluded. It may be that their child, as new parent, is protecting their partner from intrusion. It may be that a new parent is giving in to the other parent's wish to give their family precedence. To keep the peace with a partner, one new parent complies with the other's wishes. Perhaps they hope their own parent won't notice being sidelined as grandparent. It will be difficult, but helpful, to explain to your adult child that you do notice unfair treatment and how you feel. Even more helpful is to be clear and specific about what you do want. 'I would like to be included in a birthday celebration, too,' is more effective than, 'You constantly ignore/slight/insult me.'

If the other grandparent is directly shunting you aside then it is appropriate to speak directly to them. Try a soft opening, such as, 'I need time with him, too,' or, 'It will be a treat for me to do this today.'

Reminders for Parents

Identity and boundary reminders are often expressed under pressure. New parents can work on this – if they have the energy and brain control, both of which are often drained by the demands of parenting. It helps to have a set of phrases to draw on before the bad temper erupts.

- 'It's more helpful if I get the hang of this myself,' can (or should) pause a grandparent in their bid to sort things out.
- 'This is a no-talking time for us,' can remind a chatty grandparent that you (and the baby) need quiet.
- 'This isn't a time for mixed messages,' can alert a grandparent to let you handle a child's tantrum or scolding yourself.

Learning how to ask for the help you want is as important as deflecting the 'help' you don't. Ready-made approaches to suggestions of what grandparents can helpfully do are useful. Being very specific can make your instructions efficient. 'I need some time out. Are you OK to take over?' can set the stage for a twenty-minute break while the grandparent takes charge.

If a grandparent starts to ask a series of questions, you could either be very clear about what you think they should do, or specify that you do not care what they do. For example, if asked 'Shall I take her out?' you could respond, 'He needs to get out. A short walk would be great,' or 'You can do anything you want. I don't mind. I just need a break.'

Polite, indirect, probing requests have their place, but not in intergenerational borderwork and bonding. 'Perhaps you'd like to…?' or, 'Might it be a good idea…?' or, 'Would it be OK if…?' are too tentative. In this context, speaking out and owning your needs are essential to maintain intergenerational bonds.

Suspension of some politeness is essential, particularly between in-laws. The good behaviour syndrome – driven by the fear that once conflict begins, it will never be resolved – makes nuanced intergenerational borderwork impossible and leaves family members feeling very uncomfortable about being together.

It is difficult to accept boundaries when you fear that these are aimed at excluding you. Parents can ease grandparents' fear of exclusion by combining boundary setting with reminders of connection. Some version of, 'I need to be alone now, but I will need your help later,' can be very helpful in assuaging grandparents' anxiety.

Try not to be offended or anxious if a grandparent notes that the other grandparents seem to have more access to your children. If this is how both parents want it to be, then this message can be conveyed, and should be accepted. But if you are trying to keep everyone happy by submitting to your partner's preference over your own, while not saying anything to your own parents, then no one is likely to be happy. A modest proposal of making an occasional special invitation to your parents could go a long way towards easing their sense of being sidelined.

Five

The Challenge of a Changing Love

'It's hard to keep up'

It is difficult for grandparents to keep up with a child's rapid change. I believe I have bagged the perfect set of books for my grandson at a second-hand bookstall, but by the time I present them to him, I discover his interest in them has passed. He thanks me for the gift, but I see his indifference. 'He's read them all,' my daughter explains, and his younger sister adds, 'He says they're dumb.' The Lego I brought her is completed within twenty minutes. She says politely, 'It goes with my other new Lego.' When she shows me her other set, I see that the set I have given her is below her level. Six weeks have passed since my last visit, and their former selves have been left behind.

Nonetheless, my granddaughter, now aged seven, is happy to see me. We find things to do in her room. She wants to make dolls' clothes, and her mother supplies us with scrap material. She wraps it around the doll, then cuts and sews the ends together. I insist on using patterns; I think I am showing her how much better my approach is. She gives a sociable 'Mhmm' in acknowledgement, but continues using her own method. I imagine her disappointment when her completed garment slips around the plastic body, but she seems satisfied. We turn to a Lego hospital that she wants to organise. When I search for the instructions, she tells me she doesn't need them, and asks me to read to her while she gets on with things herself.

I take a breath and search for a rhythm that works, where I am neither instructing her what to do with her own toys, nor imagining her inner disappointment because things do not turn out the way *I* would want. I read to her as she works on her construction. Sometimes she interrupts to ask me what a word means. Sometimes she corrects my pronunciation of a character's name. She is giving me a chance to make up lost ground.

I pick them both up from school and she runs towards me, bumping into me with a hug. But the ten-year-old boy whose inner world I once shared is now a builder of barriers. His face, especially when it breaks into a smile, has an irresistible allure; if I look at it straight on I have to linger, and the emotion showing in my face annoys him. As we walk home, I cast only sideway glances. But when he walks ahead, my eyes can feast, at least from behind. I get to take his hand only when we cross a road. Once safely across, he drops it, giving it a little shake, perhaps ridding it of my touch. Even that small tolerance of hand-holding won't last long. Maybe a few months. Maybe less. Next year he will walk to school on his own. Another milestone. Another challenge. Will I be able to find a new link to him?

In Lesley Stahl's delightful book, *Becoming Grandma*, she muses with her grandmother friends over the magic of grandparent love. 'It's unconditional love,' they conclude, adding, '[Grandchildren] give us unconditional love back.'[1] Perhaps we nod in assent as we locate within ourselves that early uncomplicated and undemanding affection. But grandparenting goes beyond that easy joy of very early childhood. If we are to see what grandparenting is really like, we need to lift it out of the warm box that fits only the good times. Bonds between grandparent and grandchild, like all relationships, have rough edges, require borderwork and need to be re-imagined as the child changes and grows.

Grandchildren in later childhood and early adolescence may reject a grandparent's encompassing and gushing love. They baulk at what they see as being 'babied'. They are irritated by excessive praise. They no longer seek unconditional love; they seek *responsive* love, in sync with their developing interests and personalities. Some grandparents find it more difficult than parents to keep up with their grandchildren's rapidly changing interests. Once they enjoyed their lightning-quick insight into a grandchild's inner world, but now they feel shut out; some speak of 'mourning' the lost attunement they enjoyed with the younger grandchild.

Grandparents, too, might take a small step back as grandchildren reveal personality traits and physical traits that can make them uneasy. The adorable baby grows into a child who is surly, cranky or unkind. A grandparent's attachment allows for variable feelings that are unthinkable to a parent, such as finding one grandchild more interesting or appealing than another. There may be unconditional *attachment* to all grandchildren, but the actual, enacted *love* is shaped and reshaped throughout their lives together. Boiling down this love to something 'unconditional' obscures the challenges to grandparents in retaining its vitality and leads to a relational laziness. 'I love you no matter what you do,' may well be true, but in later childhood and adolescence, when grandchildren search for understanding and resonance in others, unconditional love of this kind is often beside the point. When I spoke to children about what they liked, or did not like, about being with grandparents, the relatively short negative list focused on failure to keep up. 'To them I'm always a baby,' complained seven-year-old Maggie. 'They ask me stupid questions. "How's school?" and, "Do you have a girlfriend?" It's never a real conversation,' explained ten-year-old Jared.

Keeping the relationship current takes patience, curiosity and effort. There will be hits and misses. The relational tropes that worked yesterday may not work today. The next visit might pose bewildering questions: 'What is my grandchild interested in now?' and, 'How do I draw him out?' and, 'How can I show him my interest?' and, 'How do I update my repertoire of interactions?' A child will take your hand and show you the way, but a teenager might not be so accommodating, or trustful.

The Teenage Years

It is said that 'at around age 10 into their teen years, kids start drifting away from their grandparents.'[2] Often grandparents anticipate teen rejection, just as parents do. Joan Bakewell, while enjoying the golden years of grandparenting young children, looked ahead sadly to a ruptured relationship. During the 'tough teenage years,' she wrote, 'grandparents will definitely not be part of the scene. I can expect to see them less often as visits to the dinosaurs at the Natural History Museum give way to discos, shopping and back-packing.'[3] But while some kids do drift away from grandparents, many do not. It is counterproductive to expect to be obsolete, when it is possible to do the good work necessary to maintain this important bond.[4]

This can be hard work, challenged by an older child's belief that they have 'no use' for grown-ups. They are compelled, nonetheless, to engage with their parents. Daily life involves requests for money, food and *things*, ranging from socks to smart phones. They need a parent's signature on school forms, they need parents to chauffeur them around until they can drive – and then they need parents for access to a car. Parents are an inevitable feature of their lives, and provide necessary supports in times of trouble. Grandparents, on the other hand, can be avoided. Why would teenagers bother with yet another grown-up in their life?

I understand why some teenagers might want to avoid grandparents. I remember all too vividly a visit from my grandmother when I had just turned fourteen. She was sitting on our sofa, her face tanned but showing white in the deep folds of her skin. Her hair was dark, as were her eyes that had always brightened on seeing me. This is what I expected as I approached her. But instead of her face lighting up as she clapped her hands to applaud my existence, she fingered her necklace, turned to my mother and remarked, part accusation and part query, 'She's got fat?'

Humiliation drew a line between us. I had been spending many hours staring at my reflection in the mirror, wearing different clothes, taking different positions and always asking myself, 'Do I look OK or am I fat?' All the careful bargains made with my reflection ('If I hold myself this way, it's fine'), fell apart in an instant. My grandmother cast the deciding vote: yes, I was fat. A single comment closed me to her, or her to me.

It was not until I was in my late teens, protected by a new slim physique, that I could enjoy her company again. Even then, it was more performance than genuine pleasure. I entertained her with my new maturity, and enjoyed my arch satisfaction: she could not now repeat her cutting remark.

As a grandparent myself, I am haunted by that unforgiving teenager whose trust in her grandmother was forever changed by a thoughtless remark. What could my grandmother have done to return us to our previous state, wherein her dark eyes provided warmth and her scent – talc, rosemary and cedar – could soothe and comfort me? But perhaps she had little interest in my forgiveness. Perhaps the distance between us was secured not only by my grudge, but also by her lack of interest in this larger grandchild, who was no longer the cute toddler of my early years.

What, I wonder, might I unwittingly say that could breach my bonds with my own grandchildren? Biting my tongue – taking care in what I say before I say it – is not something I do well, nor, as I have said, does it facilitate strong relationships. But self-silencing is not what grandchildren seek. They want a grandparent's excited curiosity and warm understanding. They want a genuine and interesting exchange. They want a grandparent to tap into their new powers of thought and observation, and provide empathy, or at least tolerance, for their proliferating anxieties.

Behind Their Screens

One frequent complaint I hear from grandparents is that they cannot lure a teenage grandchild away from their phone, tablet or computer. Grandparents complain that their digital exchanges with their grandkids are so oddly coded they cannot understand even brief replies. They fear their grandkids will never learn the basic elements of communication. Unable to compete with a young person's fascination with a screen, some grandparents grumble about 'kids today' – complaints that do nothing to close the space between them. What I saw when I observed grandparents and their screen-struck grandchildren, however, is that grandchildren were tuned into a grandparent's presence even as they appeared to be glued to their phone.

Axel, seventy-nine, marked his only grandson's tenth birthday by taking him on safari in Tanzania. 'It was magical,' he explained. 'The boy was a wonderful companion, trusting, engaged, grateful for everything from ice cream to a helicopter ride.' Axel wanted to mark the boy's fifteenth birthday with something equally rewarding for them both, and decided on a sailing trip that would include the stunning port of Istanbul. 'That view from the Bosphorus is heart-stopping. I was ecstatic as we approached it. I thought of its long history, and I felt timeless. I looked at my grandson, thinking we were sharing a terrific experience, but what was he doing? Looking at his phone. Not even taking pictures like a tourist. Just glued onto something else. I was more than disappointed. I was angry. I must have shouted, or something, because he put his phone away and looked, and listened while I enthused, but the magic had gone. From then on, I insisted that he take on more crew duties. Maybe I was too harsh, but I just couldn't deal with him any other way.'

Axel was convinced that the trip had been a waste of time. But teens take in more than they appear to. On the last day of the trip, his grandson embraced him and, sobbing, told him that this was the best trip ever. When he calmed down, the grandfather asked, 'What did you like most about the trip.' The boy thought for a moment and then said, 'Being the crew.' The instructions and insistence that everyone on board was crew, which the grandfather had thought was resented as a punishment, had been a high point. 'I've had many stellar moments in my life, significant public successes. But this took the biscuit.'

When I spoke to teenagers about time they spent with grandparents, I asked them about screen time and visits with grandparents. They explained that they used their phones because 'grown-ups' conversations are boring', because they were 'embarrassed and don't know what to say' and because they 'don't know what else to do'. Being chided for using their phones, being scolded for being unsociable or typical, made them more uncomfortable, and less likely to engage. When I asked them what would ease their discomfort or boredom, they said, 'not making [looking at my phone] a *thing*' or 'constantly reminding me I'm looking at the screen'. As Axel's grandson explained to me, 'Looking at my phone didn't mean I wasn't doing anything else. It was just good to have something I could turn to when Granddad was talking like he does to other people, like it's both of us talking but it's not. When he kind of forgot about it, things were OK, and I could dip in and out, myself.'

It is helpful for grandparents to keep in mind that the new world of screens does not totally transform adolescence. Teenagers have always had a keen focus on their social worlds, with their attention drawn by their peers' views and thoughts and activities even when they are with their family. Grandparents might as well be pragmatic: banning phones will not help them engage with grandchildren, nor do grandchildren 'disappear' from important relationships when they use their phones.[5]

Memory and Empathy

Most grandparents I spoke to expressed empathy with teenage sensitivities. Erin, sixty-nine, recalls how impatient she was as a mother of a teen. 'My daughter was exasperating. Nothing I said was right. Her mood swings frightened me. I felt she was standing on the edge of cliff and always ready to propel herself over the edge. You know, always on the brink of disaster. She refused to study. She stayed out all hours. Her friends were awful. They drank. They smelled. I couldn't see any good in them. I never thought she'd [start acting like] a grown-up. But she did. She survived and thrived. But now *she's* facing the same fears about her fifteen-year-old, my Niamh. There's a wicked part of me that's pleased, and I want to say, "Now you understand what you put me through." But I also sympathise with a mother's worry. I sympathise, but I don't share her worry. Niamh is lovely. We have a lovely time together. When it's just us we can enjoy a peaceful magic, when I feel whatever happens, this relationship will stay with her. I can't worry about all the little things my daughter worries about – whether she's getting the best possible grades, or going with the best crowd. I know she'll be fine, eventually.'

Niamh enjoys the judgement-free zone her grandmother provides, and enjoys the special time they spend together, apart from the rest of the family. When Erin visits, grandmother and granddaughter go on outings to escape what Niamh calls 'the weird vibes at home'.

Teenagers are hyper-alert to a parent's every gesture, sound and word. They read negative meanings into a parent's sigh, or suspect the worst when a parent hesitates before speaking. Teenagers' brains process social information in distinct ways, different from the ways a child's or an adult's brain works. One effect is that they see threats where there are none, and interpret a neutral expression as one of anger.[6] 'What are you laughing at?' and 'What's wrong?' a teen demands, when a parent had not meant to signal any criticism.

By the time their grandchildren undergo teenage conflict with parents, grandparents know that 'butting in' will elicit no thanks from either parent or grandchild. What surprised me in talking to grandparents, however, was how their sympathies bent more towards their grandchild than towards the parent.

'I see what it is that annoys Niamh. Her mother always watches her in the way mothers do. They can be having a nice conversation, but there's something about my daughter's responses that clearly irritate a teen. It's a kind of running commentary. Niamh will be telling her about some tiff with a friend, and my daughter's saying stuff like, "Good for you. You were trying to defend her," or, "Next time take a breath and think what it's like for her." And then the dear girl explodes and tells her, "Get off my case. Give me a break!" Her mother's advice is good advice, but this constant summing up of what she did right and what she did wrong… It's claustrophobic. So I understand why Niamh explodes, and I see that her mother doesn't get it, but I concentrate on my phone or my book or whatever. I know from bitter experience that intervening will make both of them angry.'

Niamh and Erin lunch in restaurants, or look around art galleries and clothes shops. Or they hang out at Erin's house and watch television, with Niamh explaining who's who on *Love Island*. Niamh, on occasion, looks through the collection of make-up Erin has amassed over the years, much of it barely used, and harvests it for her own use.

Erin and Niamh are fortunate in forging such a good grandparent/teenager match, but they are not exceptional. Donna M. Butts, executive director of *Generations United*, observed that when grandparents and their teenage grandchildren get beyond the stereotypes of an old person who is past it, on the one hand, and adolescent rebel, on the other, then a special closeness develops. Caught between their peers who offer new, exciting experiences, and their parents who pressure them about schoolwork and warn them against unsuitable friends, teenagers often find a haven with grandparents, who are genuinely interested in their activities and more relaxed about their possible futures.

Instead of seeing her as a difficult, rebellious teen, Erin is amazed at 'how well Niamh keeps it all together' given 'all the mess that comes with being a teen'. Erin remembers the acute self-consciousness that plagued her own teenage years and her conviction that her face and physique were not what they should be. 'Everyone says social media makes things worse for teen girls. Maybe it does, but I think when people say that they forget how bad it was anyway, even in my day. We had magazines. We had movie stars. We had mothers who were always dieting and who pressured us to diet as soon as we gained a few pounds. We had that battle with the mirror. You know, posing and positioning ourselves to see if we could find the right angle, when we looked OK?'

I do remember. Erin and I are roughly the same age, and in my day, too, body dissatisfaction went with being a teenage girl. Adolescence gave rise to a 'looking-glass self' long before the era of selfies and social media.[7] The teenage self is fragile, constantly shaken by the question, 'What do people see when they see me?' Teenagers are convinced, too, that they are constantly being watched and judged. The closest grown-ups are likely to get to a teenager's self-consciousness is in so-called 'nakedness dreams', in which we find ourselves at a formal occasion and suddenly realise we are undressed. Our dream then turns into a struggle to cover up or put on clothes, but the shirt we grab slips from our grasp, and our legs won't fit into the trousers. While we are struggling some dignitary approaches us. We scan the distinguished face for some sign of disgust and wake with a jolt, enjoying the sudden relief that this was only a dream. But for teenagers, this nightmare is very close to their day-to-day lives, when they feel both totally exposed and totally unprepared.

The vividness and immediacy with which grandparents of teenagers recall their own teen experiences initially surprised me. In exploring further, I understood why the passage of time sharpened rather than dulled their memories. Parents of teenagers are generally too focused on the here and now dynamics – the rapid, bewildering changes in their teenager's responses to them, their search for ways to secure reasonable boundaries, their anxieties over the teenager's new vulnerabilities to influence from friends and from the fathomless shapes of social media – to take an it-will-pass approach. When they note similarities between their own experiences as teens and those of their teen children, it is usually to shudder over either their own reckless teen behaviour or the sound of their own parents' voices speaking through them. 'I'm turning into my mother,' parents of teens often observe, wincing with recollections of how they saw their 'awful parents'. But the grandparents remember how those tough times passed, how conflicts were resolved, how their tearaway teenagers became responsible grown-ups.

It is not that grandparents do not worry about the well-being and safety of their teenage grandchildren. But the perspective of age gives them both resignation and optimism. They are more resigned to their lack of control; as Lucia, whom we met in Chapter Two, reflects, 'Whatever happens in life, happens.' They are also more optimistic that any poor behaviour or mistakes are part of a phase, rather than a sign of ingrained bad character. After all, in most cases, their adult child offers proof that a stormy adolescence does not presage a ruined life.

When a grandchild gets a less good grade, or has unsavoury friends, or pressures parents into letting them travel during a summer holiday and refuses to get a job, parents fret anxiously over a child's blighted future. Grandparents are more likely to see such setbacks as a mere blip in a flexible and zigzag route to personal success.

Gender Bias and Changing Generational Sensitivities

A common complaint I hear from parents is that grandparents express old-fashioned views about gender; their ideas about what it is to be a girl or a boy shape interactions with grandchildren. A grandparent, for example, tells their grandson that 'boys don't cry', but I also hear parents complain about a grandparent who 'coddles' their son and encourages him 'to act like a baby'. There is no definitive position on gender norms that can be described as typical for the parent or typical for the grandparent; but disagreements commonly arise about how to adhere to – or to challenge – gender norms.

'When [my mother-in-law] Celia comments on [my eleven-year-old daughter's] appearance, I cringe,' Saskia explains.

'It's nice to be told you're gorgeous, but when that's the first and last thing she says, and when it's so heavily laid on, and when it's accompanied by primping and grooming, I want to pull [my daughter] away and shake her and tell her to go outside and play rough and be real sassy.'

When Saskia asks her mother-in-law to 'dial down the beauty stuff,' Celia scoffs. 'Don't be ridiculous. It's just harmless fun.'

Dismissing a parent's concern is not a smart grandparenting move, so I'm not surprised that Saskia reminds her mother-in-law of the pecking order. 'I'm her mother and am trying to protect her from a whole lot of junk out there. I know you don't mean any harm, but you're bringing all that stupid beauty stuff too close to home. Can't you find other ways of having fun with her?'

Celia's perspective as grandparent is very different. 'I think she's gorgeous,' she tells me, stunned by what she sees as an 'outburst' from her daughter-in-law. 'I think she's gorgeous because I love her and I say so because I love her. When I tell her, "You're the most gorgeous girl in the world," I'm not really comparing her to anyone else. I'm just looking at her and I can't imagine anything more gorgeous. How can that make her vain? Or encourage her to think looks are the only important thing? I should have a grandparent's prerogative to say that to my granddaughter. And the stuff with make-up? My granddaughter's choice. I take the lead from her. I let her mess up my stuff and then I show her how to do it properly. That's not something her mother will do – and that's fine, but she's really distorting things by seeing this as a clash of values.'

As so often in grandparent/parent conflict, a point about a wider principle, such as gender-linked messages, turns into a personal dispute over who has a 'prerogative' to speak as they see fit. Since, in the heat of such personal conflicts, we easily lose sight of the other's intent and meaning, it can be helpful to look at Saskia and Celia's from our comfortable distance. Tracking the very different perspective of grandmother and parent provides a road map for resolution when we ourselves are in the hot seat.

Saskia's position is likely to have resonance with many parents and grandparents. She does not want her daughter inducted into the cult of beauty. She does not want her daughter to believe she must be beautiful to be lovable. She wants the important people in her daughter's life to encourage her to be outspoken, courageous and confident – not pretty and pleasing.

While many of us can applaud Saskia's aims, we can also see why Celia is amazed and offended to be told her admiration of her granddaughter puts any of that at risk. Before I became a grandparent, the gushing adjectives grandparents used to describe their grandchildren would transport me into a very bored place that I had to wait out politely. I would offer a minimal smile and avoid saying anything that would prolong the tedium of the grandparent's enthusiasm. Now I hear descriptions of grandchildren as 'the most beautiful child' and 'out-of-this-world gorgeous' in a very different way. What sounds like boasting is a grandparent's renewed appreciation of the promise that shines in young humans – who are indeed beautiful and wonderful (as well as smart, curious and adventurous).

The grandparent who offends a parent by telling his grandson to 'man up' is trying to encourage traits that the grandparent believes will be needed in later life. When chided by a parent, the grandparent is likely to think (though perhaps not say), 'You think I'm a bad influence on my grandchild,' or, 'You want to undermine my connection to my grandchild,' or, 'You want to put me in my place.'

Whether or not a grandparent actually voices these defensive allegations, it is useful for parents to have to hand a formula for upholding their values, vis-à-vis those implied in a grandparent's behaviour, while moderating any perceived insult to the grandparent.

Saskia could assure Celia, 'Your influence is valuable, but I am sensitive about gender stereotypes. I hope you can support our resistance – as parents – to the pressure to be beautiful that she faces every day.'

Stating your aim in such personal terms, and soliciting understanding and support from a grandmother often helps, but it is important to admit that no guidance, however wise, always has the desired effect. As Celia continues to brood over Saskia's 'high-handedness', I ask Saskia whether she is using the formula I suggested: clear statement of aim, grounded as a personal preference rather than a high moral principle, and warm request for support. She admits she finds it hard to follow the formula, because her resentment of Celia's gender biases has many layers. She resents her own treatment as a child, when she was told to 'act like a lady' and 'dress nice' – while recognising that her mother-in-law had nothing to do with how she was raised. However, she does blame Celia for the biases she believes are embedded in her husband, who was raised by her mother-in-law. '[My husband] is on the side of the angels, but his gut reaction is for men to do stuff and women to help them do it. I see it coming round again with [Celia's] emphasis on being pretty, so you can please the men.'

Grandparenting exposes you to what you feel is unfair criticism and censure. Out of the blue, you hear complaints you never heard before. One child-in-law blames you for her dissatisfaction with the spouse she married, and your own adult child, watching you interacting with your grandchild, spots new flaws in how you parented them. Some families are torn apart by these accusations and the defensiveness they generate. A much better outcome is through acceptance that a degree of resentment and conflict go hand in hand with love and intimacy.

Parents may complain about a grandparent's failure to toe an enlightened line, but some grandparents, particularly when they consider the impact of racism, believe that parents unnecessarily prime children to look out for danger, while they see clear water ahead for their grandchildren: 'I can count on the fingers of one hand the times someone made me notice that they were noticing me as "other" or "lesser",' Letisha, sixty-five, said. 'My grandkids need to know how to handle that when it happens, but it'll be a small thing in their lives, even smaller than in mine.' Other grandparents, with different experiences, see biases of their youth persist today. Downhearted by continued injustices, they complain that the parents are oblivious to the dangers their grandchildren face. 'It's the same as when I was a kid – things haven't got any better,' Carl, sixty-two, reflected. 'I coached my sons how to behave if they were ever stopped by the police. I never believed I would have to give my grandsons the same lessons.' He wants, as a grandparent, to slay old prejudices, yet there are times when he sees them loom over future lives, as strong as if his youthful battles had never been fought.

If parenting is associated with inevitable guilt, then grandparenting is associated with inevitable regret that the world is not a better place. We hope for a bright and fair future, but we see a minefield of biases, both internal and external. There are times when I am struck, as I look through my granddaughter's eyes, by the stagnation of gender stereotypes, even when I know that so much has changed. I take my granddaughter ice-skating. The rink is crowded. The music reverberates harshly against the ice, glass and metal. This is not something her brother would enjoy. But he is with his father, and I have her on my own. I hold one skate blade upwards before I put it on. I show her the edges and remind her to feel them – inner versus outer – as she skates. It is hard to get her attention. She is too interested in the people around her. There are the glamour skaters, in sleek leggings, skirts decorated with sparkles, hair like Taylor Swift. The beauty of these young women is too far removed from me to envy or emulate. But her fixed attention on them reminds me of what youthful glamour once meant to me; I have mixed feelings about her blatant stare. 'Enjoy their loveliness by all means,' I want to say, 'but don't let that be your inspiration. And don't be intimidated by it.'

I know these are not things I can say. Even when I think she will understand the words, I know such mental furniture is not rearranged so easily. I give up on my lesson about the anatomy of skates. When we join the skaters on the ice, I coach her to improve her forward stroking, but she stops to watch a lesson taking place in the centre of the rink. The boy is probably a year younger than she is. He is doing a routine – two backward crossovers, backward outer edge on one foot, quickening to a one-foot spin. He does not nail it but he moves with elegance. I ask my granddaughter if she would like a lesson. She hunches her shoulders in a gesture I read as, 'I don't, but I'm not sure I can say, "No."' Or perhaps she does not know how to say, 'Yes.'

'You could learn to do that,' I tell her.

'I think it's too hard,' she says, and my heart contracts.

'In time you could do it,' I insist. I assure her the coach will work with her as she is now, and take her forward.

I see that I have not convinced her. My heartbeat quickens with the urge to grab hold of her diffidence and rip it out. Where did it come from? This self-doubt?

We find a quietish patch of ice, and I show her what I am working on. I am trying to do a sit-spin. Her eyes widen with concern as my spin ends with an ungainly plop on the ice. Then she laughs as I make a thumbs-up sign. 'My coach says if you don't fall when you practise this, you're not doing it right. I will get better at this,' I tell her. 'We're both improvers.' She nods, but what else can a polite girl do? I can't let go of my fixation on bequeathing to her my love for the sport. But she shows no interest in my next lesson on a backward glide. Today she wants to play a game of racing away from Granny.

When she tires of the chasing game, she lets me catch up with her. I take her hand – careful not to squeeze it as, I have been reminded, is my annoying custom. It feels strange just holding it, without carrying on a conversation in pressure. Her hand moves, perhaps to get a better grip or find a more comfortable position. Unlike her brother she is too polite to pull away.

'I'm tired,' she declares. I swallow my disappointment, let go of her hand and we step off the ice.

In the hubbub of the changing room, I muse over just how far I can slay her eagerness to please on the one hand and her resistance to challenge herself on the other. I begin to compose feminist sound bites, ready to dole them out at the first opportunity: 'Your needs are important, too,' and 'You need to see how capable you are.' But as I watch her return her skates, I see in her walk that special saunter and spring of a child enjoying her independence. I keep the sound bites in my mental file, but realise that she will have to find her own way through her own social minefields.

If grandparents are no longer the leaders when it comes to parenting, but become followers of the parent, we can be 'searchers'. We are curious, and take joy in our discoveries of who our grandchildren are. We may still have our ideas of what counts as a 'bad influence' or 'wrong direction', but we have to negotiate these alongside our knowledge that we don't have a full grasp of their generation's cultural environment. This doesn't mean I won't try to influence where I can. But I have to find indirect routes, and I have to be patient. I want to get inside her head and challenge her diffidence. I want to find out how much of herself is preserved alongside this wish to please. And I also have to deal with my shocked recognition of persistent gender norms. Didn't I work to protect her from this? If not, what use am I?

It is often said that grandparents think the world moves too fast for them to keep up. What strikes me is the slow pace of change. The struggles we had as teenagers and young adults and our determination to make things better for our children continue as we grandparent.

Gender Transitions and Grandparents

The so-called culture wars of gender transitioning are highly personal to many grandparents in my study. It is often assumed that grandparents will be too confused by the issues to engage positively. After all, it was not until 1980 that something called 'gender identity disorder' appeared as a diagnosis, a term that was retired in 2013. When today's grandparents were parents, what is now known as gender dysphoria was considered too rare to ponder. Today, too, it is rare, but even with a prevalence of 0.5 per cent to 1.3 per cent of children and adults, the concept of gender change is salient, and six (or 8.3 per cent) of the grandparents in the group on which my cases histories are based, had a grandchild who was transitioning, or seriously contemplating transitioning to another or non-binary gender.[8,9]

Accepting radical, unexpected change in a child they have known and loved since birth is a challenge to any grandparent or parent, but within my participants, grandparents accepted transition with greater equanimity than parents.

When Greg heard that his son Stevie, aged seventeen, was planning to transition to live as a girl, he was devastated by his child's 'willingness to trash the father/son history we had together, to want to change everything I thought he was.' Stevie's grandmother, Tessa, seventy-three, felt, as a grandparent, 'at one remove. I didn't have to face the institutional aspects of the change. I didn't have to consider questions about medical interventions. I knew I had no say in this, so that's very different from a parent's position. I could just be there and listen to them gripe, and work out the new pronouns. If I slip up they're more forgiving because I'm old and I'm used to being told by any of my teen grandkids or my adult children that I'm getting things wrong.' Greg was amazed by his mother's acceptance of her grandchild's decision, but they did not quarrel over the support she offered.

Adam, sixty-eight, said he didn't see what the fuss was about, and couldn't understand his daughter's anxiety about her child Leslie's transition. 'It might be a phase. It might be forever. But he's still our kid, and still with us. He hasn't been drawn into a dark cult. He's still working towards making a life. I've spent many days with dark thoughts about what might happen to my children and then to my grandchildren and I just accept they'll do what they do, and mostly, as long as you don't lose sight of them, they're OK.'

Some teens are disappointed if their parents are *not* upset by a decision that to them seems momentous. Part of the pleasure of drastically changing an identity, for teens, is shaking parents out of their complacency and getting across the message 'I'm not the little kid you think you know. I'm different from who I used to be and you need to keep up.' Grandparents, who usually know they do not know their teenage grandchild through and through, find it easier to admit they constantly need to be updated as to who the teen is. What surprised me most was that while grandmothers were described by transitioning grandchildren as 'accepting' and 'tolerant', grandchildren were more likely to single out a grandfather as 'taking it in, like whole'.[10]

Boundaries and Loyalties

A common quandary for grandparents is how to support a teenager without showing disloyalty to a parent. Even subversive grandparents – those who induct grandchildren with unofficial lessons of how life works and the skills they'll need to work it – are wary of outright criticism of a parent. Erin listens to Niamh complain about her mother, but avoids taking her side against her mother. 'I don't want to form an alliance of disrespect,' she explains.

Erin reminisces about her own experiences as a mother of a teenager and, with some misgiving, tells Niamh tales of what her mother was like as a teenager herself. But when Niamh, encouraged that an adult is listening to her parent-bashing discourse, concludes with, 'She doesn't understand anything,' or, 'She's worse than any of my friends' mothers,' or, 'She's a hypocrite,' Erin shuts it down with a neutral, unengaged response. 'I change the subject. I order dessert. I say it's time to go. I know how frustrating this is for Niamh, but I can't pretend to be on her side while she trashes her mum.'

Taking the grown-up position of neutrality vis-à-vis parents is harder for Wahida, who has 'a whole bunch of trouble getting on with [her] daughter-in-law'. Exchanges between Wahida and her daughter-in-law, Carol, are kept to a minimum. Carol brings her daughter to the door when Wahida comes to see her. There is no polite chitchat, no hospitable ritual, no pretence that the relationship is anything but strained. At the age of twelve, Mariam relays back to her grandmother 'all the things Carol is saying about [her]'. When Wahida worries, 'Maybe I shouldn't hear this,' Mariam retorts, 'I thought that's what people did. Mum always asks what you say about her.'

Wahida is stunned. 'My heart goes out to this sweet kid who's trying to give people what they want, and getting mixed up because she's with people who are so mixed up.' She acknowledges that 'it's hard not to be haunted by the things Carol says to my granddaughter, especially about me. I try not to bad-mouth her mother, but it's hard. I want to set the record straight when people are so unfair.'

It is challenging to maintain a show of grandparent/parent solidarity when a parent seems bitterly unfair. It is also difficult when a grandparent heartily disagrees with parents' teachings and practices. Another grandmother, Nicky, dislikes many aspects of the religion in which her granddaughter is being raised, but tries to show, neutrally, an alternative way of living, of being good and respectable outside the rules of the father's religion. 'It isn't easy,' she admits. 'It's one thing holding my fire in company, but when it's just [me and my granddaughter] talking, it's tempting to make my pitch.' While Erin declines her granddaughter Niamh's invitation to join a discourse of parental disrespect, and Wahida does her best to mute her criticism of her daughter-in-law, Nicky remains on the lookout for an opportunity to draw her granddaughter away from the hard lines of the father's religion. 'If she comes to me as a rebel, I'm not going to tone her down. I'm not sure how I'll play it, though. You'd be amazed how much time I spend practising things I might say. Or planning what steps I would take if I thought she needed my protection. At some point I'd be willing to say she can stay with me, and I'd do my best to keep them away from her. It would be the end of my relationship with my daughter, but I'd take that on to protect my granddaughter.'

Three different approaches, three different contexts, map out three different ways to manage cross-generational tensions. None presents a perfect model, but each is a genuine effort to balance protection of a grandchild with respect for the parents.

Safe(r) Havens

Engaging with and protecting a grandchild are particularly challenging when we have a grandchild with a disability. Layla admits that she isn't proud of [her] initial response to her grandson's birth. 'There weren't many times of the day when I wasn't thinking about this, and feeling sad and angry. I kept wondering, "Why didn't [my-daughter-in-law] get her baby tested?" Or, "Why did [she] have to wait until thirty-eight to have a child?" I blamed my daughter-in-law and I blamed fate and my attitude really boiled down to, "Why did this happen to *me*?" It was a while – oh gosh, over a year – before I absorbed it and could connect to him. Now – well I hope you're going to anonymise this, because I love him to bits, and I don't want a different grandchild and it would be awful if Berat ever learned how I felt when he was first born.'

We talk about how I 'will change things around' so that neither her son nor her grandson, should they ever read this, will identify her as the grandparent with these feelings. Yet she insists, 'I want to describe what I felt because I don't think it's something I would ever talk about otherwise. I don't think it's something anyone else would admit either, but I'd be very surprised if I was completely alone in how I felt. Anyway, [admitting to] that low, really low starting point, could be useful to other grandparents, because I've gradually found ways out of it.'

Layla found that letting the parents take the lead was essential 'for me to step back and let them figure it out themselves. Because I wasn't the one sorting everything, I could let go of all that worry over what we needed to do.' She notes that her grandson's condition 'totally changes a family. It's changed me, but it's changed my son and daughter-in-law more. I'm not proud of this, but I don't feel easy – I don't feel warm about [my daughter-in-law]. But she's thrown herself into raising him to be as much as he can be. She's on top of all the learning techniques and the social support available. I look into these things too, but when I tell her about some programme somewhere she switches off and tells me she's got this. And she does.'

Berat's grandfather, Emir, found acceptance of his grandson's Down's syndrome much easier. 'He is what he is,' he remarks, shrugging away my questions. 'He doesn't seem so different from any child. Maybe he's not so quick, but many kids are not so quick. He has a few health issues, but they seem in hand. I don't understand [Layla's] fussing.' Their son, Ayaz, describes Berat's relationship with his grandfather as 'the best in the world. Granddad treats him like anyone else, just wants to get to know what he likes to do and what makes him laugh. They spend hours together, looking at books or going places – anywhere with animals is a big hit. And the disability label disappears. I don't think it ever will with his grandmother. It's a misplaced pride, in my view. And that edge between her and [my wife] doesn't help.'

Among my relatively small number of participant families, grandfathers were singled out as achieving the warmest and most relaxed relationship with a grandchild diagnosed with a disability. I observed one seventy-three-year-old grandfather whose grandson, Tom, has been diagnosed with dyslexia – affecting the fluency of reading and spelling – and dyspraxia – affecting his physical coordination. At the age of four, the grandson was a good match for his grandfather, who was sometimes unsteady and slow on his legs. As they walked, holding hands, at intervals each of them would comment on their own or the other's missed step with an exclaimed 'Ooops'; this interaction ensured that any physical unsteadiness was accepted as a normal part of life.

Some grandchildren, like Berat, have a diagnosis from birth, but even then, the diagnosis did not dictate what his life might be like at four or fourteen. The grandfather, Emir, objects to the word 'disability' and 'diagnosis'. His engagement with his grandson transforms his view of diversity. The child himself becomes the norm. 'Down's isn't a disease, and it doesn't stop the little guy from doing what he wants. It doesn't stop him making friends, and it won't stop him falling in love either happily or unhappily as we all do.'

Some diagnoses come later. Mental health issues, attention deficit disorder and autism are generally assessed in later childhood or adolescence. Here grandparents sometimes regret the loss of the 'bright spark' they once saw in their grandchild. Some grandparents scoff at a condition with such a broad diagnosis as autism spectrum disorder; in their view, it 'doesn't change anything about how I see or understand him'. Their dismissiveness sometimes reassures the parents, and sometimes irritates them: 'We have to deal with this and it doesn't help when you deny it's there.' In each very different case, grandparents fared better if they moved away from asking, 'How can I fix this?' to asking, 'How can I support the parents as they find their way around a condition's many meanings?'

Searching to Connect

Teenage boys have been found to say that a grandfather is the family member they trust most and whose support is particularly effective in periods of family stress.[11] How does this fit the stereotype of the inarticulate, sulky teen boy, quick to grunt and slow to speak?

Among the grandfather/grandson pairs participating in collected case studies for this book, interactions were often low-key. Their conversations meandered. They did not talk much, but watched television, mended bikes or prepared meals. As Leslie thought about why he said he trusted his granddad most, he said, 'He doesn't badger me, or try to pin me down. Dad always says, "If you want to make a decision, you make it logically." He sets out pros and cons of one route and the other. "You take your exams again and you might do much better, but you spend the whole summer studying. You accept the grade you have, and you can spend the summer doing an internship. You decide." But then it's no longer my decision because that's not how I make decisions. With Granddad, talk about this stuff is chill. He doesn't get cross if I opt for one thing and then change my mind. He's not always judging me.'

Teenagers put 'being judged' at the top of the list of things they hate about grown-ups. Parents may say, 'We're not judging you. We love you unconditionally.' But teenagers are smart and know that when a parent is making suggestions, they are directing them and implicitly criticising the teen's deviation from their advice. Teens also know that 'being judgemental' includes praise as well as criticism. Parents' positive comments – 'You're doing this so well,' and, 'Keep working at this, you're nearly there' – exert a kind of control. So teenage grandchildren delight in a grandfather who lets them take an equal, or lead position in whatever they are doing.

I only made sense of this research on teenage grandchildren and their grandfathers as I struggled to reconnect with my grandson after the pandemic. My initial approach to him involved overt displays of affection. I wanted to revive the playfulness and physicality we once enjoyed. But hugs and cuddles were no longer welcome. He drew away, and my discomfort increased his confusion and anxiety. His grandfather, on the other hand, was more pragmatic in his engagement and was somehow able to show genuine interest at our grandson's level. By the sailing pond in Harrogate's Valley Gardens, they are both engrossed with a remote-controlled model sailing boat – our daughter's birthday present to her father, knowing her son would also like it. The grandfather is as focused on mastering control as the child, demanding to have 'his turn' as adamantly as any kid. Each sulks, with relative good humour but no irony, when the other's turn is 'too long'. They exchange views on how to hone their technique and crow at their rapidly improving skills. I sit on the park bench, with a sense of how it might be in heaven, looking at the people you love engrossed in the playfulness and curiosity of living, oblivious of you but somehow buoyed by your wonder at each movement, inflection and gesture.

I continue to watch for opportunities to re-engage, trying both to respect his new sensitivity to personal boundaries and to show him I am there for him, ready to open my arms at any time. I look at our bond as a Sleeping Beauty that will spring to life at his touch.

'Want to help?' I ask as he peers at my tablet, which shows a game of Wordle that I am trying to solve. It is a rare sign from my grandson that he is interested in what I am doing. We then move on to another game, Spelling Bee. We each say the words we find in the jumble of letters. He wants to achieve genius status; when we are stuck, I suggest looking up a website that will unscramble the letters. He is horrified. 'That's cheating!' He returns to the task. He is competitive, but when I find a word he hasn't spotted, he is delighted; when our eyes meet, his smile ignites our old connection. Then we both dry up, still shy of his target. As soon as he wakes the next day he is eager to see the list of possible words. 'How did we not get that?' and 'We tried that but it didn't work!'; we are together again in a world of our joint making.

Next year, possibly even next month, I will have to find another hook for connection. But having found this new one, the first since I have secured since our lockdown separation, I feel a new lightness, and trust in the nimbleness of the relationship.

Grandparents Change Too

Grandchildren also face the challenge of adapting to changes in grandparents. My younger grandson tries to tell me a secret. His face is flushed with excitement. He puts his moist lips to my ear, and I feel his warm breath and a spray from his toddler's lisp. He draws away from my ear and looks at me, expecting an emphatic response – a gasp of delight or horror, perhaps. But we are at a party, and the background noise dulls my hearing. He repeats himself, raising the volume but maintaining a whisper. Still, I do not hear enough to make sense of his message, so his sister, standing nearby, repeats his words aloud in her crystal-clear diction. He steps back, his brow furrowed and lips turned down. His pout is so cute that I am half inclined to laugh. But I know how much pain lies behind the frown. He wanted to be the one to relay this 'secret'. I have let him down.

It is the decreased hearing associated with age that grandparents tell me has the greatest impact on intimacy. Grandchildren accept the slower pace of their grandparents and, once they are beyond the toddler stage, are usually careful not to run too far ahead, to wait at the kerb, to accept that it will take longer to get to the park or bus stop. The inability to lift a child into a car seat or buggy sometimes puzzles a young child, but this weakening of age does not diminish closeness. Failure to hear the joke that they so proudly tell, however, embarrasses them at having to repeat a remark that has lost its punch. Asking them to speak more loudly, when they are confiding in you, discourages them from doing so again.

A grandparent's urge to protect and teach comes up against limitations imposed by age. My older daughter was abroad when she heard her grandfather was dying. She rushed home, wracked by grief that surprised her as much as it did me. For some years he had withdrawn into illness and worry about the wife he would leave behind, and lacked the energy to engage with a teenager, whose cohort unsettled him with their open sexuality. Arriving home after a summer in Peru, she was excited to relay her adventures, but he cut her off mid-sentence, and spoke of other things. I now realise that he had probably simply not heard her talking.

As my husband and sister-in-law conferred with the medics about his end-of-life care, my younger daughter was told to 'talk to her grandfather'. When she worried he would not hear her, they told her he would. But she, knowing better, held his hand, pressed it at intervals and spoke loudly but gently into his ear: 'I'm here. I'm Julia.'

Our grandchildren adapt in their own ways to grandparents' infirmities. We cannot protect them from the slights of mortality, but we can model responsiveness to change – and use our hearing aids.

A Guide to Maintaining Connection

An effective way to extend the repertoire of interaction is with one-to-one time. Most grandchildren respond to a grandparent's interest and engagement with *their* interests. Steps that can take you forward include:

- Asking them what they would like to do with you, but also contributing ideas of what you would like to do with this special time. Go to their – or your – favourite store, restaurant or park. Some grandparents establish a custom of taking a grandchild away for a particular birthday. Other grandparents enjoy taking a grandchild to a tennis match or football game. One grandparent, seeing 'what a good barrister my granddaughter would make', introduced her to some lawyers and took her to observe court hearings.

- Focus on your grandchild, but don't sideline your own experiences and interests. Show them photos of you with their parent, or of you as a child. Tell them stories about 'when I was your age'. The time of your youth will seem very far away to them, and it will be difficult for them to imagine their parents at their age. But it is also fun.

Address a parent's concern that you, as a grandparent, are not a good influence, by explaining your aims, in the hope of finding common ground. Either grandparent or parent can admit how difficult it is to rid our culture of biases. Instead of accusing the grandmother of imposing gender stereotypes on her granddaughter, Saskia could say, 'I find this difficult too.' The grandmother, hearing the parent's complaint, could admit, 'I do this without thinking. I don't want to limit her. I don't see her as limited. What can I do differently?' And Saskia could explain, 'I try to draw her away from the mirror and I feel you are pushing her towards it. That's OK sometimes, but more drawing, or going for a walk or gardening would add something, and make me less anxious.'

You can listen to a grandchild's complaints about parents without encouraging or endorsing them. Forging an alliance of disrespect will not strengthen a relationship. Over time, a grandchild is likely to be uneasy about their own disloyalty. The best message a grandparent can offer is, 'I'm willing to talk about anything. I won't be shocked by anything. And I will do my best to stand beside you if you want to step away from what I see as a constraining culture, but which you may well see as a source of connection, support and faith.'

After exploring your grandchild's interests, try involving them in something that interests you. This could be sport, travel, film, art, hiking, running or fishing. There is, in my experience, a special delight in introducing a grandchild to something they would not otherwise discover.

Think about something your grandchild can teach you. This could be something helpful, such as finding ways to use your phone more effectively, or to post things on new social media sites. It could also be something that may not actually interest you but enlightens you about their interests. My grandson, for example, introduced me to all the *Warhammer* characters, explaining the specific powers and limitations of each. Other grandparents listen to a running commentary on the people who feature in their grandchild's favourite programmes or books or films. Some grandparents find that looking at a grandchild's school curriculum extends the range of possible conversations.

Grandparents who don't see their grandchildren regularly can keep up with their grandchildren's age group by volunteering at schools or in their community. Nothing can compensate for absence but this can help them make the best use of the time when they do meet. And even when you are at a distance, try to make it to special events such as graduations or significant birthdays.

Your grandchildren will change. Their bodies will change and you may feel you have lost something as they leave the physical appeal of childhood behind. They may dress and decorate themselves in ways that make them look too 'different'. You may have to work a little harder to refresh your love.

When Your Grandchild Needs to Learn Your Rules

Many grandparents express concern about a teenage grandchild's lack of respect. A rude grandchild stirs up resentment towards the parents ('Why haven't they taught him how to behave?') and diminishes their pleasure with grandchildren. However, I was surprised how effective grandparents were in teaching their grandchildren to be respectful and cooperative.

Building a strong bond with grandchildren doesn't guarantee their good behaviour, but they have more invested in your goodwill if the bond is strong.

- Focus on them. If grandchildren think your mind is elsewhere, they see this as disrespectful. Just as you would expect them to put their phones away when they are with you, ensure that when you are with them, you are not looking at your digital screen or talking to friends.
- Make your rules clear. You may not be able to set day-to-day rules, but you can say, 'On my watch you don't use your phone at the table or eat in front of the television.'
- Communicate with parents. It makes sense to tell parents which rules apply on your turf. Grandparents can set their own rules, but we don't want our grandchildren feeling their parents are disrespected or discounted. Even subversive grandparents, who want to support a child's exploration into alternative views, are likely to form a more comfortable bond with a grandchild who knows their parents are aware of the grandparent's mission.

Six

Intergenerational Heartbreak

Part 1: Parent/Child Estrangement

'We're no longer family'

The bonds holding a family together are strong, but not unbreakable. Ruptures occur, a bloodline version of divorce that reverberates throughout generations. Such a break is never clean or final. Ghostly echoes remain of those who have been cast out. 'I no longer speak to my mum,' thirty-four-year-old Joe tells me, 'I don't take her calls, either. But every day I hear her voice inside my head, and every day I ask myself whether I'm doing the right thing, for me and my children. Over and over again I play out scenes in my head. I picture us coming back together, and her embracing her grandchildren, but as that reel plays on, I hit the wall of her anger and criticism. I never make peace with the separation.'

Many people assume that parents are more likely to cut the bond. Horrified by an unsuitable lover or a teenage pregnancy or some treason against ingrained beliefs, a parent declares, 'You are no longer a child of mine.' In fact, most estrangements are not instigated by a disapproving parent but by a son or daughter, and not in the heat of adolescent battles but in early adulthood, between the ages of twenty-four and thirty-five.

Parents are then stripped not only of their own children but also their grandchildren. Estranged grandparents describe the loss of contact with grandchildren as even more painful than the loss of their adult children. Barbara Graham likens separation from grandchildren as being struck 'by a rogue tornado' causing 'grief unlike any I have ever known.'[1] Professionals working with estranged grandparents describe the love for a grandchild as 'more raw and pure, its disappearance more disorienting and bewildering, the need to connect with the grandchild more desperate and vital.'[2]

It is difficult to get reliable data on the number of grandparents forced to separate from their grandchildren. Often they do not know how to explain their situation to others, because they do not understand it themselves. In conversation with anyone other than the closest, most trusted friend, they brush aside questions about their grandchildren, silenced by shame and heartache. But 14 per cent of the people who use the website *Gransnet* reveal that they have difficulty having contact with their grandchildren for reasons other than distance and, of these, 37 per cent have not had any contact with their grandchildren for the past five years. Other data shows that at least one million grandparents in the UK are currently denied contact with their grandchildren, though with 11 per cent of mothers – more than one in ten – saying they are estranged from at least one of their adult children, the number may be much higher.[3,4]

Are those who put up barriers between grandparent and grandchild ungrateful and cold? The stories of heartache told by bereft grandparents might lead to this conclusion. But adult children who instigate estrangement do not do so lightly. They are not holding a grudge over some slight offence. They believe that a functional relationship with a parent will never be possible. They cannot envisage contact that does not involve pain and humiliation. Distancing themselves from parents is their survival strategy. Yet *every* member of the fractured family longs for things to be better. This chapter explains why it is so difficult to reconnect with an estranged child, but also offers guidance towards repairing even years'-long breaches between parent and child, thereby uniting grandparent with grandchild.

Untangling Stories of Estrangement

Stories of family estrangement are frequently messy and incoherent. They have long, knotty histories and many different versions. It takes a lot of patient listening to understand why the normally life-sustaining parent/child bond is severed.

Breaches between generations often result from mismatched expectations or values. Grievances are deeply felt, but can be difficult to articulate in ways an outsider can understand. Minor complaints accumulate until everything is viewed through the lens of resentment. Grandparents, looking through a very different lens, are flabbergasted at being deemed unfit associates of their grandchildren.

Estrangement sometimes results from physical or sexual abuse. As a child, Gavin accepted his beatings as normal. It was what he thought he deserved for being 'bad'. After leaving home at nineteen, he looked back on his childhood and thought, 'How could my father have done that to me?' Seeing his father age and mellow, he asked why things had been so difficult for him between the ages of six and fourteen, at which age the beatings stopped. Gavin was amazed when his father denied 'ever giving [him] more than a little cuff.' His mother backed up this story. 'You were a difficult child. We had a duty to raise you right. I don't know what's in that head of yours, but we spared the rod, more than most parents. All parents shout. All parents punish their children. That's what they do to raise them right.'

Gavin puzzled over the discrepancies in memories, but accepted his parents' assurance – until, that is, he saw his father playing with his three-year-old son. 'There was something in his rough play that brought it all back. I felt sick. I couldn't get us out of there quick enough.' Gavin hasn't seen his parents for three years. He declines their repeated requests to 'see that great grandkid of ours'. He feels 'sorry for [his] parents but is committed to protecting [his] son'. The grandparents, holding different memories, see themselves as innocent, and their son's behaviour as incomprehensible. In their view, Gavin's 'sense of reality' is 'distorted' or 'deluded'.

Abuse comes in many forms. Joe's mother is similarly stunned by her son's refusal to let her see her young grandson. For Joe, however, the reason is clear: 'She makes me feel worthless, and turns everything I've done into a mistake. She calls or texts me, every day, with lists of what I "have to do" and "what I did wrong". I never feel whole in her presence. She shreds my self-esteem.' Joe tries to explain to his mother that her approach was hurtful and unhelpful, but his mother Val insists, 'You know I'm just trying to help you out. It's up to you whether you listen or not. You can ignore my advice, like you always do.'

Val, sixty-five, has 'no idea what [she] did wrong'. She believes 'there is something wrong with Joe. I gave him everything I could, and this is how he repays me.' Because of Joe's rejection, she feels, 'My whole life as a parent has been taken away. Everything I thought we had – the wonderful times, the love – he's taken from me. All the memories I have of me and my son are poisoned, because he tells me I'm not fit to be a grandmother.'

Eddie, thirty-two, hopes the volatility of her relationship with her parents is something her own daughter will never experience. 'I felt like things were always about to break apart. Like I was one heartbeat away from being cast out,' Eddie tells me. 'Every place outside that house felt safer than anything in it. I lived with a constant dread of her scolding. She'd harp on one of my sins and keep digging, finding more and more sins.' Now an independent woman with a young child, she asks, 'Why would I put my little one in her path? I don't want my daughter's life to be infected by their chaos.'

Sometimes, as we saw in Chapter Four, borderwork fails and it is only by severing the bond that a boundary can be secured: 'I can't have her calling me four times a day and asking me how the baby's doing and then telling me what I should be doing,' Helen says. 'I can't deal with [my mother's] control. She tells me what to do and then throws out these dire predictions: "If you do that, you'll smother her." Or, "If you don't get her on a schedule you'll never have a moment's rest." I try to fend her off by telling her I'll do what she advises, and then just ignore her, but I end up worrying over what she's told me, looking up arguments for and against. I try telling her I [am] too busy to talk, but she says I can phone her later. When I don't, she rings me and then tells me the reason I am so busy with the children is that I am not managing them right. I end up losing my temper and shouting or crying, and she says, "See what happens when you don't take my advice."

Eventually my husband encouraged me to draw a line between us. He told her I needed time apart from her for a while. I hate that I hurt her, but not dealing with her is a relief.'

Some adult children distance themselves from their parents, and block contact to grandchildren, not because of what their parents have done but because of their own disappointment and shame. Niall does not want to have any contact with his parents because he feels he is the black sheep in the family. His siblings have jobs and partners and live with their children. He lost his job, his marriage fell apart, and he himself has limited access to his nine-year-old daughter.

His parents protest, 'We don't blame him. He's had a tough time, and we are sympathetic. We want to support him. We'd love to be able to comfort him. We miss him and we miss our granddaughter, and we just want to connect.' Niall scoffs when I convey this message. He is convinced that what he sees as his low status in the family is at the forefront of everyone's mind. Unable to overcome his self-disappointment, he cuts himself off from the people in whose presence he feels it most.

At the end of the chapter, guidance is offered for mending even entrenched family breaches, thereby allowing grandparents to engage with grandchildren; but breaches brought about by an adult child's personal shame are particularly difficult to address – and particularly tragic, since the parents themselves are often blameless.

Bad Influences?

Sometimes parents restrict grandparents' access to grandchildren because they perceive powerful and malign influences:

'The children pick up bad language,' or they 'are impossible to handle after the time she spends spoiling them,' or they 'start believing all sort of nonsense.' Or, like Joe, they fear that a grandparent will 'smash the kid's self esteem'.

When I talk to the opposing teams – the parents and the grandparents – I hear radically different accounts of the same situation. Like divided views everywhere, issues are rarely confined to the articulated complaints. Unspoken fears and fantasies inform the adult child's accusations.

Sometimes the adult child imagines a less flawed self, and believes that is who they would be now, if only their parents had been different. They want to protect their own children from being damaged by the chaos or humiliation they themselves felt.

'I can't for the life of me see what crime I've committed,' Barb tells me. At sixty-six, she is recently retired. She expected that her son and daughter-in-law would welcome her greater availability, and that she would spend more time with her seven-year-old grandson and four-year-old granddaughter. 'They're struggling with childcare. There is so little give in their schedules. They used to call on me, and sounded so relieved when I stepped in. Really grateful. Of course we have different views about raising kids. Times change. So what? Why does it matter? I mean, why does it matter *so much*? So much that they say, "We don't want you near our children." I don't get it. I really don't get it.'

Barb, like so many grandparents who are excluded from their grandchildren's lives, speaks of pain 'like an unhealed wound', of anger and of humiliation: 'What did I do that was so terrible? Don't they understand I would do anything for those children? Do they really think I would ever harm them? Do they really see me as a bad influence?'

She also worries what her grandchildren will think: 'Do they think I don't want to see them? Do they think I'm too busy for them?' She worries, too, about what the parents say about her to her grandchildren. 'Are they being told I'm an awful person? Are they making me into a monster?' She notes, regretfully, the speed at which they grow up. 'Even if this stupid thing goes away in a few months, they'll be different. I'm missing out on seeing them grow.'

When grandparents are confronted with accusations of what they said or what they did, they are frequently amazed: 'We're fighting over *that*?' The issues seem so small, and the effect so large. But there are many different measurements of harm. Klaus, Barb's son, explains: 'She says things that I now see are meant as a joke, but I remember how much these remarks hurt me when I was a kid. To this day I worry about my "funny feet" and my "squishy nose". She loves the kids but there's a mean streak in her. I don't think she's aware of this, but it's there.'

A grandparent can have very good reasons for believing that they provided their own child with good, even excellent parenting, and that their grandchildren would benefit from their input. A parent can, at the same time, have very good reasons for thinking that the grandparent is capable of disturbing or misleading or shaming a child. There are arguments about 'what really happened' in every family. Normally everyone rides out the bumps, accepting different memories and different views. But for some parents, suffering from past insults and put-downs is magnified by a child's vulnerability. 'I don't want my children to go through what I went through,' Klaus says. Barb focuses only on her own love and tenderness, and Klaus focuses only on his childhood pain.

Barb is not wrong when she says her remarks are meant as jokes and delivered with affection. Nor is Klaus wrong when he says her remarks hurt him and made him self-conscious. On the basis of the many family exchanges I have recorded in my research, I can imagine a conversation between the grandmother and new father as going something like this:

'For heaven's sake, it was a *joke.* I was being affectionate. It was meant to be playful. And, you know, it was a joke from about thirty years ago, which you're still going on about. You know I love your feet and your nose. You're too sensitive. Do you really think my grandkids won't know I love them and think they're nothing other than adorable?' Barb might well say if she were faced directly with Klaus's complaints.

And Klaus would say something like, 'You're insensitive. Listen to yourself. You are telling me I'm wrong to feel what I feel. You're undermining me again. You can't help yourself.'

At this point the interaction could spiral downwards as each persists in defending themselves rather than listening to the other's complaint; or it could be a bridge between them as the complaint of each is acknowledged: 'I'm amazed that I hurt you. I will take more care from now on,' and, 'I know you didn't mean to hurt me.'

From the Perspective of Pain

Grandparents denied access to grandchildren have their own stories of heartache. They report feeling bewildered and powerless. They feel 'erased' from their grandchildren's lives. They describe anger 'at how little [their adult child] cares about the pain she's causing me.' The pain, they say, is 'always with

[them]'. A toy in a charity shop reminds them of the playtime they are missing. A birthday reminds them of developmental milestones they cannot witness. Quintessential occasions of family gatherings, such as special holidays and religious days, become hollow-eyed reminders of emotional loss. Petra, whose daughter shut off contact after she had a period of abusing alcohol, admitted that she would lurk near a grandchild's school in the hope of getting a glimpse of her grandchild. 'I know this is a dangerous game,' Petra admitted. 'If her mother found out she'd go ballistic, maybe even try to get an injunction against me. But the sight of [my granddaughter] – even a glimpse – gives me so much pleasure and reassurance.'

When Petra gets home, she opens the pages of a special diary she keeps, hoping one day to show it to her granddaughter. It contains descriptions of things she has done, such as visiting a garden centre or going to the theatre, and how she would like to do these things with her granddaughter. 'I want her to look back and realise that I was always her gran. I don't know what her parents tell her, but if they say I'm a worthless alcoholic, or I don't want to see her—' Petra pauses as her voice breaks. 'Well, with this diary I can show her I always thought of her, always held her close in here,' and she points to her head, and then to her chest.

To grandparents, the parents' rejection appears reckless as well as cruel. After all, they argue, they have so much love to give a grandchild. They would agree with the psychologist Joshua Coleman when he says, 'For a generation obsessed with closely hewing to theories on attachment between themselves and their children, it is remarkable how many seem to disregard the profound attachment that their children have to their grandparents.'[5]

Estrangement and In-laws

Some grandparents describe a close and comfortable relationship with their adult child deteriorating after their child married. Marriage brings a new person into the heart of the family, and this newcomer comes with their own set of desires, needs and expectations. Most families accommodate and benefit from the adjustments, but sometimes they foment shockwaves throughout the family.

Estrangement is painful no matter who instigates it, but if an in-law is responsible, grandparents at least avoid the difficult question about what they did wrong as a parent. And because it is easier – generating less self-blame and soul-searching – many excluded grandparents conclude it must be their child-in-law, rather than their own child, who is responsible for the breach.

'In-law manipulation' – when an in-law repeatedly denigrates or criticises a partner's parents – is an insidious bid for undue power over a partner and their children. Overwhelmingly, victims of coercive control are women and perpetrators are men, and a common tactic of such abusers is to isolate a partner from her family.[6,7] When a son-in-law engages in in-law manipulation, it is reasonable to consider whether the motive is to clear the way for his own spousal abuse. He may want to isolate his partner, to deprive her of emotional support and to hide his abuse from others. On the other hand, in my experience, when a daughter-in-law tries to put distance between her partner and his parents, she is more commonly focused on her partner's well-being.[8] Mel, for example, believes that she has to set boundaries because her husband cannot. 'He never stands up to her. If she wants to visit, he won't tell her it's not a good time. If she pries into the kids' health or schooling, he won't tell her to butt out. If I want my privacy or space or sanity, *I* have to be the bad guy and tell her to butt out.'

But in some cases where a daughter-in-law manoeuvres her own children away from grandparents, protectiveness disguises bids for status and control. 'My daughter-in-law keeps changing her rules, so it's hard not to break them. "I told you I didn't want you to get her a *big* present," she says. "I don't want you to take her to *that* restaurant." And when I've gone to considerable trouble planning something I know my granddaughter wants to do, she says, "It won't work. She has too much schoolwork." She doesn't come right out with, "You can't see her," but she makes it very difficult. It's so humiliating—' and here Aggie struggles to control her voice. 'It's humiliating but I put up with it because I need some hope that I can still see my granddaughter.'

Rudrashki, sixty-eight, believes her daughter-in-law 'convinces my son that I always insult her. It's nonsense. She twists my words. She tells him I undermine her, and that she shouldn't have to put up with this. My poor boy has to tell me I'm not invited to a family dinner. He has to make excuses why she won't come to visit me.'

Fortunately, Rudrashki's son Rakesh is happy to meet with her separately, and he brings the grandchildren to her. It takes courage for a new father to forge a separate relationship with his parent when his partner wants to reject her. Rakesh accepts his wife's view of his mother without sharing it. Confusing and hurtful though the daughter-in-law's breach with Rudrashki is, her son ensures it is not a barrier to good relations with her grandchildren.

For some grandparents, however, no pragmatic compromise is offered. 'I started getting emails from my son dragging up complaints that clearly came from her mouth not his,' Jenni, sixty-seven, explained. 'He said he worried about my reliability – but it wasn't about things like being a good driver or being sober, or being attentive when I took my grandson to the playground. Everything was pretty vague and general, about how I could be emotionally unavailable. Then he said they – that's him and my daughter-in-law – could tell that [my grandson] was confused or anxious after he spent time with me. What can I say to that? The boy jumps up and down with excitement when I see him. He runs into my arms. He comes into my house and takes off his shoes, and goes to find his toys and asks where the dog is and opens the cupboard to get the food he likes. He's at home with me. He knows his way around the house and he knows his way around my heart and we're equally joyful, just being together. These things – me being emotionally unsafe, him being confused by our time together – are nonsense, but my saying so doesn't mean anything. He's just mouthing *her* views, and it's like she's a cult leader so he has to stand by them.' Her daughter-in-law also returned every present she sends to her grandchildren. 'It's like anything to do with me is tainted.'

Jenni pauses, and then adds, 'But the eldest, my darling girl, my first grandchild, isn't so sure. She holds back, looks kind of embarrassed when she smiles, and her eyes sort of wander away from me. She knows there's a situation here. Maybe she's not sure it's still OK to like me. And who know what they say about me now. It's enough to drive me crazy.'

'If anything can drive a parent to madness,' Joshua Coleman observes, 'it can be watching their own [adult] child slowly disappearing from their grasp and influence, replaced by a child who suddenly parrots the accusations and feelings of the other parent.'[9]

A parent can protect grandparents from their partner's animosity, as Rakesh does, by taking his children to visit their grandmother without involving his wife. More often, however, a man stands by, feeling helpless, as their wife sidelines his parents.[10] To explain this compliance, we have to explore a little-known feature in marital moral dynamics.

Many psychologists have observed that within a couple, men have a tendency to comply with their partner's judgements about other family members. For many men, the close friendships of childhood fall away in late adolescence, as need for others becomes associated with weakness, resulting in what the psychologist Niobe Way calls a 'crisis of confidence'.[11] Over time, among their small sphere of three or four male friends, they seem to lose the skills for intimate discussion.[12] For heterosexual men, their partner is the best available close friend, on whom they rely so heavily that they are sometimes accused of 'emotional gold-digging'.[13] As with all close friends, their partner's views of what's right and what's not, and what's acceptable or not, are highly influential. While a wife might discuss any issues regarding her parents-in-law with a close friendship group – 'Am I right to be angry?', 'Should I say anything?' or 'Do I have to put up with this?' – men are less likely to test and fine-tune their views outside of conversations with a wife; her opinions then have a privileged position. Moreover, siding with a wife's views offers her support and comfort – something many men want to do, feel they should do, but are not always clear how to do.

Less common, but more insidious, are cases where a wife relies on her personal influence to isolate her husband from other family members. 'My better half' is a familiar way of referring to a wife. It may be merely a stock phrase, but it defines a type of romantic partnership in which a man hands over his moral compass to his female partner. In this moral handover, one partner (usually the man) has a higher social status than his wife. This might come from his financial position, or he may have a distinguished career. His wife looks up to him and showers him with compliments, but at the same time has far stronger ideas about the character and value and motives of people in their lives. Her views may be motivated by her desire to take full possession of the man she greatly admires, the man who she thinks she is lucky to have. She may frame her criticisms and resentments in terms of protecting him from others' failure to acknowledge his status. Underlying these acknowledged motives may be others, such as the wish to demonstrate primary ownership of him. At the same time, she may form a powerful alliance with her own parents in securing greater family influence, to compensate for her partner's greater social influence.[14]

In many such partnerships, a man feels so gratified by his wife's admiration, and so safe in her judgement of others, that he sees no reason to challenge her view – even when her view is that one or both of his parents is too toxic to enact the role of grandparent. He may, also, be less adept at naming his feelings, or catching the underlying meanings in daily interactions, and therefore give way to his wife's *narrative power*: she controls his interpretation of who did or said what, and what was meant. An additional element is the man's deep well of empathy for his wife, an empathy so tightly focused on her that it shuts down empathy towards his own parents.

Difficult and Necessary Steps Towards Reconciliation

Family break-ups in which parents block grandparents' access to grandchildren usually involve deep, distorted and disguised dynamics. These are difficult to correct, but the guidelines below suggest possible routes to reconciliation.

To repair family breaches, a grandparent must take on the very difficult task of seeing themselves from the adult child's perspective. Whoever instigates estrangement – adult child or child-in-law – grandparents must start the process with their own adult child. They need to acknowledge some truth in the negative view their child has of them. The adult child does not treat the estrangement lightly. They see estrangement as necessary, either to their own well-being or to the well-being of their children. Whether or not someone, such as a spouse, is touting a toxic story of who you are and what you have done, you have to be willing to listen to your adult child.

Many parents reasonably believe that they have been good parents, perhaps even great parents. The estranged child, however, believes that their parent did not give them what they needed. Estrangement is rarely based on one incident or even one series of actions. It is usually so complex that even the adult child who has spent months and probably years thinking about this, cannot easily articulate their reasons. Estrangement is also varied, so no single set of guidelines will fit every case. But in most cases, an estranged adult child harbours a deep sadness at the breach and longs to find a way to reconnect. Below are steps that have been found most likely to lead to reconciliation by those who have worked closely with family estrangement.

Steps to Reconciliation

The first, very big step is bridging opposing experiences of the same family. This involves what Joshua Coleman describes as 'an attitude unlike any you've ever experienced before [with] a willingness and certain bravery to see yourself as your child sees you, and actively look for evidence that what they're saying may have a kernel of truth'.[15] This difficult step involves accepting your child's perspective and setting aside your personal pain and sense of unfairness. This is the only way to reduce a child's defensiveness and create the opportunity to look at the problems together.

Many grandparents assure me that they are willing to do this. But keeping an open mind when someone believes their well-being depends on breaking ties with you, while hearing their accusations and complaints, is extremely difficult.

Therapists working with estranged parents often suggest starting with a letter that invites the adult child to talk things over. In the letter, you should admit that you know you haven't been the parent they need and that you want to understand their complaints. You must show willingness to explore whether there is some way you can make amends. This does not mean you have to endorse your adult child's view. You do, however, have to acknowledge their experience, and engage with it generously.

If they agree to meet or if they agree to write, then you will need the courage to set aside your natural defensiveness and hear their accusations. You'll need empathy for their suffering, both past and present. This is hard for many reasons. It's hard because the accusations probably seem unfair. 'That isn't what I meant,' or even, 'That isn't what I did,' many grandparents insist. But fairness isn't the aim of these meetings. The goal is reconciliation, and this is not based on fairness but on compassionate understanding.

Listening is also difficult, because we value our child's view of us. Their early belief that whatever a parent is doing is right, and their trust in what a parent teaches, is foundational to their – and our – early attachment. Learning that their experience of our parenting conflicts with our experience of being a parent, is confusing and hurtful. Not only are we deeply sorry that we did not give them what they believe they needed, we also feel the blow to our self-esteem. How can we think well of ourselves if we have not been a good enough parent? Yet the route to reconciliation demands that we say, 'OK, I'm willing to listen to your side and see things from your perspective.'

This does not mean you have to *believe* everything they say. Sometimes what they say is deeply distorted. Unfortunately, if the adult child is in therapy, a less scrupulous therapist may make matters worse by diagnosing their parent as a narcissist, a sociopath or a depressive, or suffering from alcoholism or a personality disorder. It bears repeating that no diagnosis on the basis of one person's description should have clinical standing. If you find yourself in this situation, the gentlest way to address your child's belief in their therapist's diagnosis to say calmly that because their therapist has never met you, their diagnosis *might* be wrong. At the same time, you can again assure them that you want to know what they think, and to hear how they feel you let them down.

Having listened, you need to demonstrate that you understand their feelings. This might involve admitting, 'I can see how you must have been disappointed/hurt/scared/angry. I didn't see that at the time. That must be awful for you. I'm so sorry.'

In many cases parents know they made mistakes. Perhaps they were overwhelmed with anxiety about their own relationships, or about money, their job, or about their own health and stability. They tried to protect their children, but now they realise their efforts fell short of their aims. In these cases, it is time to say, 'I was hurtful/unfair/neglectful on many occasions. I am deeply sorry and nothing that happens now will take away my regret. But now I really want to make amends.'

Getting to this stage is a huge advance. It takes you to the crucial point at which you pivot from looking back to looking forward. You can then ask your adult child, 'What can I do to make amends?' Or, 'What do you need from me for you to let me back in your life and back in your children's lives?'

Accept that any form of communication may take some time. Your adult child may not be ready at the same time you are. The habit of ruminating over 'the terrible things you did', may be so ingrained that they may need more time to reset their thoughts.

What Happens Next?

Even if you do reconcile – and there is a good chance you will – estrangement can be repaired but not forgotten. Your adult child might be hyper-alert in case you 'do the same things again'. You, also, are likely to be sensitive to the possibility of causing offence when you don't mean to. Each of you probably fears another conflict and another breach. It will take time to gain confidence and feel comfortable with the newly repaired bond. This will be easier if you ask your child to tell you what they want you to do. So instead of defending yourself when they are critical, ask, 'What do you think would be a better thing to do?'

When, after a period of separation, grandparent and grandchild are reunited, there is as much caution as celebration. Before the reunion, acknowledge the parents as the power-holders, and ask, 'What would a good visit look like to you?' and, 'What are you worried I might do?'

One way of reconnecting with your grandchild is telling them what you've been doing during the period of separation. Some kind of record, maybe a photo album or a diary such as the one Petra is keeping, can show a grandchild that you have been keeping in touch with them in your mind and in your heart.

When Barriers Remain

'Invisible grandparent' is the term Pat Hanson, a health educator and grandmother who has not seen her granddaughter for thirteen years, uses to describe a grandparent who is unable to participate in their grandchild's life.[16] The grandchild is a huge feature of the grandparent's life, but cannot be seen.

Pat's daughter cut ties with her when the youngest granddaughter was four. She writes about ways she went about healing 'the hole in her heart'. She staved off depression by writing letters – hundreds of them – and saving them 'for the hypothetical day [her] granddaughter Annie might look [her] up'. In these letters she builds a picture of herself that counter her daughter's negative view. She writes other letters, too, that express her anger and bitterness towards those enforcing the alienation, but these letters, written for her own benefit, she burns. She also writes her grandchildren birthday messages, documents her family history and shows how she is thinking of them (on their first day of school, for example) and includes pictures of scenes she has enjoyed day to day. In these different ways, she hopes to pass on her legacy of love.

Seven

Intergenerational Heartbreak, Part 2: Divorce

'I'm going through this, too'

Divorce is a brutal force that disrupts every relationship in the family. In the process, nice and reasonable people make unreasonable demands and bizarre accusations. They seem bent on destroying those they once loved. There may be good divorces but I have not seen one. There are many ramifications of divorce, but here I look at the divorce between the generations. A key challenge confronts grandparents: to recalibrate their connection with their child's ex-partner, who may have the power to divorce them from their grandchildren.

Grandparents describe constant, health-breaking anxiety in the wake of their children's divorce. They worry about their child's well-being, about housing, money and social status, but even if these can be managed, one worry that transcends all others is the impact on their grandchildren. Some plead with the parents to avoid divorce. 'It's bad for the children,' they say. Or they suggest, and offer to pay for, marriage counselling. But the parents know that divorce is not good for the children. They have probably already tried some version of marriage counselling. It is likely that the marriage has been a source of profound unhappiness long before the grandparents learn of it. Most adult children hide their marital struggles and their criticism of a partner in case the marriage eventually works out. 'I didn't want you to think badly of [my partner] in case we did stay together,' my daughter explained to me.

As I know from my own experience, a child's marital break-up stretches grandparents' sympathy in three ways – towards their own child, their grandchildren and in many cases their child-in-law. As soon as their adult child embarks on the relentless, costly route to divorce, many grandparents describe a rapid reversal of the good feelings they once had towards the spouse. The person they hoped would love, champion, support and respect their child has – from their understandably biased viewpoint – let them down. The visceral disappointment in their child's partner colours memories of what they felt in the past. Grandparents who never before criticised their child's partner now conclude that they 'never really liked [their in-law]' or always felt uneasy about the union. This might not be true, but current feelings reshape memories until no good ones remain.

As they seek new ways of being there for their own child, they witness the cascading effects on their grandchildren. A grandchild's bad behaviour may be simply part of childhood's routine, but is now seen as a signal of special distress. How, grandparents reflect, can they protect grandchildren from the parental storms? They speak of having all the worry of a parent, but none of the power – though as I will show, grandparents have more power than they think to rescue grandchildren.

In the UK, one out of every three children will live through their parents' separation.[1] Parental rupture is known to impact children's well-being, but the *average* effects are small and the individual experiences of each child are different. And grandparents' closeness to a grandchild cushions the blows.[2] This closeness is emotional rather than geographical: even when grandchildren live far away from their grandparents, they often say they *feel* close and are able to confide in them.[3,4] The sooner grandparents step in to reassure grandchildren of their continuing connection, the better.[5]

Grandparents' need to learn new routes to connection acquires a special urgency. What might be a normal phase can be seen by a worried grandparent as a distress signal. The open and easy bond I so greatly enjoyed with my oldest grandson was disrupted, first, by the school closures linked to the pandemic and then by his parents' divorce. The boyish shyness that led him to press his body against mine in times of social doubt, gave way to episodes of acute anxiety during which visits from grandparents were no longer a pleasure but a disruption of his space. 'Too many people in the house' disrupted his day and prevented him from 'doing [his] own things'. He tolerated my presence, but clung to his mother. I stood back, helpless, grieving for my grandson's loss of his once easy childhood.

His younger sister is keen to finesse her closeness to everyone in this fractured family. I feel I have more chances with her, a more sustained future, during which we will keep coming together, but in new ways. When she gets a phone, she woos me with texts. 'Hi Granny. How are you?' and 'How many weeks or days do I have before I see you?' she asks. I melt at these gestures of affection, but also regret that she takes on the burden of maintaining links between people so at odds with one another. At times the burden is too great. She huddles beneath a large hoodie. Nothing is right, not the feel of her socks nor the fit of her shoes, nor the texture of her trousers. When discomfiture descends, she doesn't want to go anywhere or do anything. I search for the shrewd, observant nine-year-old who is now submerged, at times by cheerful compliance, at times in passive defiance. I sit quietly by her, hoping that my empathy and interest in the real thoughts behind the mood swings are somehow conveyed to her.

It is reassuring to step back and take a cool look at what research shows us. Teenagers who have a grandparent involved in their lives – particularly after their parents' separation or divorce – report fewer emotional symptoms and more pro-social behaviours than those with less grandparent involvement. So I remain alert, ready and available, even when my message, 'I am here for you,' seems useless to them.

Grandparents Caught in the Aftershocks of Divorce

If divorce is like an earthquake at the heart of a family, then any new alignment takes a long time to navigate. Maddie, whose daughter divorced two years ago, believes that grandparents should expect different stages in the aftermath. The first is when your adult child needs emotional support. A grandparent is there to 'keep the pieces from falling', and to offer some semblance of cheeriness and good family stuff to grandchildren. The second phase involves practical help. More childcare may be needed as established schedules change and your adult child functions as a single parent. Grandparents might assist with the grunt work of moving home. Or, where possible, they might provide financial aid to cushion the blows. Third, there is a time when your adult child is once again steady and taking charge of their future. A new normality gradually takes over, new routines are set, and there may be new rules to learn and new kinds of borderwork required.

Many grandparents say that their relationship with an adult child is much easier in this third stage. Such a life-changing event often brings an adult child closer to their parent. In some difficult cases, however, the rupture and realignment lead to estrangement. Seeking a clean break from a bad marriage, an adult child may sever all ties from their former life. They might believe their parent sided with their former partner, and feel misunderstood and betrayed.

In most cases, however, grandparents offer key support to both their adult children and grandchildren in the whirlwind of divorce. Most parents act in the best interests of their child and seek to maintain grandparent/grandchild connections; but divorce is one of several things that can skew a parent's measure of a child's best interests. Angry, hurt and resentful, an ex-partner might be convinced that their ex-partner's parents are not good for the children. The absence of any evidence for their lack of fitness as grandparent does nothing to weaken their determination to banish a grandparent.

This destructive dynamic is common enough to be given a name: 'grandparent alienation syndrome' – a crueller version of the in-law manipulation described in the previous chapter. Of the seventy-two grandparents from the thirty-two families that participated in my research, twelve described themselves as estranged from at least one grandchild. Both grandmothers and grandfathers were included where possible, so the twelve individual grandparents represent eight different families, a full 25 per cent of the participating families. In hearing about their experiences, I found myself in a dark world, where empathy and good intent had drained away. Family interactions can be painful and messy, even without divorce, but the hopes and intentions of family members, even as they quarrel and complain, usually aim towards resolution and a better connection. Grandparent alienation, however, is gratuitously mean, and everyone loses. Children become confused and anxious ('It's weird being suspicious of Granny, but…') and miss out on a potentially beneficial relationship, and the grandparents suffer daily, bitter grief. Setting out the most common tactics of the alienating parent makes difficult reading (and difficult writing) but will, I hope, help grandparents make sense of what is happening. Only then will they have a chance of managing it.

Tactics Used in Grandparent Alienation Syndrome

Grandparent alienation syndrome consists of a three-pronged approach. The first and most obvious is that the parent – the former child-in-law – sabotages time that the grandchild spends with the grandparent. Because the aim is hidden, the grandparents, confused and still hopeful, do not protest. Fahad tells Halima, 'You are welcome to see the children any time.' He assures her, 'We will always be family, whatever happens between [me and your daughter].' However, Halima finds that when she makes arrangements to see her grandchildren, 'something comes up and he has to take them to some activity or a doctor'. This means that she can see them only when they are with their mother – her daughter – but even then he will step in. She undertakes the four-hour drive to her daughter's home to stay with her grandchildren while her daughter is on a deadline at work, but Fahad arrives fifteen minutes after Halima's daughter leaves the house. He declares, 'My children need their parents, not their grandparents. If their mother is too busy to do her share, I'll take them to mine.'

Someone who engages in grandparent alienation almost always wants to control others. Fahad's cold confidence, and Halima's wish to avoid open conflict, give him the upper hand. He drives the children away unhindered. On leaving he tells Halima, '[Your daughter] is too wrapped up in herself to see what the children need. I know she's your daughter and you're going to defend her, but I'm the one with parental responsibilities.' The parental responsibilities Halima's daughter shares are ignored.

Another guise of grandparent alienation syndrome is threat, often disguised as 'protection'. When Maria's former son-in-law blocks her visits with grandchildren, he explains, 'It isn't safe for you to drive in the dark. You're old, and your vision isn't good enough. I want you to be safe, so this visit isn't going to work.' When Maria insists she can see well enough, he says, 'I'm going to arrange to have that assessed. Probably you shouldn't be driving at all. Come to think of it, I'm not going to allow my children in your car. If I find out you've been driving them, I'll have to take out an order to protect them from you.'

Maria is an adult; she can decide for herself whether she wants to drive at night. Maria's daughter, Soulla, has equal say in whether or not she wants Maria to drive her grandchildren, but the alienating partner threatens them: first with disaster scenarios ('You'll kill the children'); and second by denying access ('If you don't respect my wishes I'll have to cut you off completely').

A third alienating tactic involves taking charge of narratives about what the grandchildren need, or the competence of the other parent to see what is 'really going on'. The ex-partner assumes the authority of decision maker. Often these are dressed up as regret. 'I do this with a heavy heart,' Colin says when I ask why he cancelled his children's holiday with his ex-wife's parents. 'But I don't want the children to be more confused than they already are. And they need to be with me.' Colin's former wife, Amy, retorts, 'That's ridiculous. He won't be spending time with them. The [idea that] they are "with him", when they're at his home, is ridiculous. He's always out. He's always busy. The children just sit around and play on their computers.'

Amy knows Colin has no real grounds for denying access to her parents, but people who engage in grandparent alienation are not open to argument or negotiation. Amy is angry and upset on both her children's and her parents' account, but Amy has learned, 'Once he makes up his mind he doesn't change it.'

Controlling and coercive people have a dark intelligence that allows them to quash resistance. Soon after I interviewed Halima, she received a letter from Fahad's lawyer instructing her not to try to contact the grandchildren again. He warned that if she failed to comply, he would challenge her daughter's access to her own children. In all probability, the father would have had no success in the family court, but the threat was enough to ensure that Halima complied. In one of the very few academic studies of grandparents alienated from grandchildren, grandparents said they felt like 'puppets and [the alienating parent] pull[s] the strings'.[6]

An alienating parent may also groom the grandchild to sabotage the relationship. Sometimes this is through denigration: 'Your grandparents are mean/selfish/bigoted people.' A more common method involves sowing small seeds of suspicion: 'Was your visit with your grandmother OK? Did you feel safe? Did your grandfather fall asleep when he was looking after you?' Or with a tone or look, a pall is cast over a visit: 'Are you going to be able to survive three whole days with them?' The questions alone cast a shadow over the grandparents, ensuring that the grandchild feels uneasy and suspicious in their presence.

Dilemmas Faced by Alienated Grandparents

Grandparents describe a profound sympathy for their grandchildren in the wake of divorce. Maria sees her grandchildren's confused and anxious loyalty to each parent. She does not want to burden them with her own longing, nor does she want to defy their father's wishes. In fact their father warns her that 'his children keep no secrets from him' and if she contacts them without his permission, he will know. Maria wants her grandchildren to understand that her lack of contact is not her choice, but neither she nor her daughter is comfortable in admitting that their father has banned her from them.

Young children, caught in the middle of family wars, depend on parents to interpret their world, to show them who is friend or foe, who can be trusted and who should be feared. They are inclined to believe what a parent tells them about others but they are also shrewd observers. They believe the father who declares, 'Granny can't be trusted not to drink,' and yet they see that their other parent sees Granny as reliable, sensible and trustworthy. 'You can smell it on her breath,' their father says, and they wonder whether he means the minty or garlicky or coffee scent that they notice as the grandparent hugs them. The scent that was once comforting now generates suspicion. As one alienated grandparent reflected, 'I don't think they know what's real any more because they're told so many stories.'[7]

Grandparents sometimes have to choose between supporting an adult child who is unable to have contact with the children, and supporting the other parent who has full custody.

'[My son's] only conduit to his children is through us,' Stan explained. His son had been estranged from his former wife and their children for two years. His former wife won't let him see the children, and she tells Stan, 'You can see your grandchildren on condition you don't tell [Stan's son] where they are.' Like most grandparents, Stan complies with the mother's conditions, however unfair they seem to him. He decides he can tell his son *how* they are and what they are doing, and in that small way form a connection, however fragile, between estranged parent and children.

Aggie's son Olly separated from his wife Tiffany soon after his second son was born. Olly is a lawyer capable of aggressive argument in court, but is no match for Tiffany who is able, in Aggie's words, to 'dictate all terms and conditions.' Olly is desperate to see his sons, but Tiffany keeps him at bay. She insists that they 'need to get used to you being away.' She claims that, after spending time with their father, they 'are very upset and impossible to settle.' She says she keeps a mood diary for the children that 'proves visits with [their father] are bad for them.' A mood diary is a potentially useful record of a child's ups and downs. It can help locate the context in which a child is subject to violent or very dark moods. But Aggie believes that Tiffany is weaponising this, and using it for her own purposes.

After a long month during which neither Olly nor Aggie had any contact with the children, Tiffany agreed to mediation. They were delighted with the outcome: Olly was able to spend Saturday mornings and Wednesday evenings with both children. Aggie planned to be with him and her grandchildren as often as possible within his window of time. But within a week, Tiffany decided against this arrangement.

In the UK, the outcome of mediation is advisory, not legally binding, unless the agreement is made into a court order and approved by a judge. Reneging on agreements is common among those engaging in grandparent alienation. After all, the ultimate aim of the alienating parent is to gain control over a former partner and their parents, and any fixed agreement limits that control.

After several weeks, much argument and pleading, Tiffany agreed that the children could meet with both their father and grandmother, but not in one of their homes. 'I don't want them getting confused about where their real home is.' So Olly and Aggie took them out, sat them in a cafe, and they took turns entertaining the active toddler and crooning over the infant. 'I sat there in public with tears running down my face and staring at that baby,' Aggie explained. 'I saw the sorry looks on people's faces, and was horribly embarrassed I couldn't stop crying. We're trapped in a situation with someone who wants to torture us, and we'll be shackled to her for a very long time. Down the road there might be some reprieve from a court decision, but this takes such a long time and she can be so convincing because she has total belief in her position.' Aggie saw the only route to contact with her grandchildren was to forge a bond with their mother. 'My son feels betrayed. He thinks I am siding with her. He barely speaks to me now. But I feel there's more time to make things up with him. If I don't see my grandson now, I'll never really get a chance to be his gran.'

A surprising version of grandparent alienation can also occur following the death of an adult child. This by-product of traumatic grief came to light in the wake of the attacks on the Twin Towers, as a significant minority of grandparents, who lost their own child, were then struck with a double tragedy. Instead of clinging to grandparents as a precious connection to the dead partner, some surviving spouses cut grandparents off. There is no official count of such tragedies, but of the 3,000 children who lost a parent on 11 September 2001, the families' advocates heard more than a hundred reports of 'conflicts in which parents of a World Trade Center victim, desperate to remain connected to the children of their lost offspring, had found themselves in bitter struggles with a surviving spouse who would rather they did not'.[8]

Grief, like the trauma of divorce, transforms intergenerational relationships. Usually the death of a partner brings the surviving parent closer to the grieving grandparents, but a mediator who works with bereaved families estimates that in as many as one in ten families experiencing death, bitter conflict arises over views about the burial or about money.[9] Sometimes past tensions harden into lasting grudges. Sometimes the surviving parent remarries and hopes the new family will wipe out all the grief associated with the dead parent. To their horror, grandparents Barbara and Victor were denied access to their grandchildren when their daughter-in-law complained they upset the children by showing them pictures of their father.[10] Based on the registry he has kept of surviving relatives, Bob Doyle, whose own son died in the World Trade Center, admitted, 'It can get so ugly, it's beyond belief.'[11]

Splitting – the Ability to Live with Bad Faith

Surely people who inflict this cruelty on both grandparent and grandchild must know they are behaving badly. 'How can he live with himself?' grandparents ask as they tell their stories. The implied answer – 'No good or reasonable or decent person could possibly see such behaviour as acceptable' – does not help us either understand or manage these difficult situations.

Parents who put up barriers to grandparents insist, with apparent sincerity, that they are 'forced' to take action. Grandparents are told, 'It's your own fault. Your actions led to this.' In short, those who instigate grandparent alienation syndrome claim the moral high ground. They blame either the grandparent or the grandparent's adult child for making their prohibition necessary. They are likely, too, to dismiss the grandparent's grief: 'Stop feeling sorry for yourself. What matters is the well-being of the children.'

In trying to answer grandparents' tormented questions – 'How can they say/do/think that?' – we have to look at a psychological process called *splitting*, which, as the name suggests, results from compartmentalisation of good from bad.

Most of us accept a mixed bag of traits, good and some bad, within ourselves and in others. Generally, people have fairly innocuous ways of managing our need to see ourselves as someone who is basically good, reliable and reasonable, capable of love and loyalty, even as we acknowledge our mistakes. We shore up our self-worth when we fluff our lines ('It could happen to anyone'), break a glass ('The stupid glass was too slippery'), get someone's name wrong ('It doesn't matter'), quarrel with a colleague ('They can be so annoying') or fall out with a friend ('We'll get over it'). But when someone has no tolerance for the mix of good and bad traits, they split people into 'good' and 'bad'. Denying the bad in themselves – the petty motives, the urge for revenge, the personal failure – they project this onto others.

Divorce, whatever its cause, is an emotional trauma that can overwhelm healthy defence mechanisms. The terrible sense of failure and loss shakes self-worth to its roots. When splitting occurs, the feeling, 'I have failed', and 'I have betrayed this relationship', and, 'I am hurting someone important to me', morphs into, 'You are the failure', 'You are the betrayer' and 'You're responsible for both your pain and mine.' Their ex-partner and anyone associated with them, such as the ex-partner's parents, are also painted with all the negativity associated with the divorce. In this way, a person feels cleansed of blame and shame, since all faults lie elsewhere. Any shift in perspective, any plea for forgiveness threatens them with the realisation that they, too, harbour some 'bad' within.

It is no coincidence that 75 per cent of parents who alienate children from their grandparents do so in the wake of divorce when they are struggling with guilt and a sense of failure.[12]

Grandparents Also Divorce

Grandparents' lives, too, have dramatic ups and downs. They, too, divorce and have to find new ways of living. Grandfathers who are separated from the grandmother seem to have a particularly hard time. They are less confident about maintaining bonds to grandchildren without the grandmother, who is usually more proactive at arranging contact. They are at greater risk of depression, especially when they describe themselves as 'having no friends', either because friendships have faded or because they have moved away.[13]

Many grandchildren are deeply upset when their grandparents divorce.[14] They see this as an affront to the stability they expect from their elders. Older grandchildren worry that a grandparent is sad or lonely. This can be an opportunity for grandparents to speak about their own challenges, while modelling a 'good divorce' that demonstrates how family bonds can be maintained, even as they are altered.

What Legal Recourse Is There Against Grandparent Alienation?

In 2018, the Solicitor General for England and Wales noted, 'Grandparents play a significant role in family life. There is something special about the bond between a grandparent and grandchild. Grandparents provide stability when it is needed. They can give a sense of history and show how important it is to belong to a family. They can give family support when it is needed, such as when it is difficult for more immediate family members to be called on.'[15]

This powerful statement, however, has not yet been incorporated into social policy or law in the UK where, as is also the case in all fifty US states, grandparents' automatic rights are limited to applying to a court for visitation rights. The Madras high court in India, however, recently upheld the visiting rights of grandparents when a mother sought to exclude the parents of her deceased husband, citing evidence that an affectionate relationship with grandparents is beneficial to grandchildren.[16]

When the terrible possibility hits me that one of my daughters might predecease me, I shut down. I know people who have survived such loss, but all I can imagine is darkness. Now another terror is conjoined to this one: the possibility that, as a result of losing my daughters, I could also lose access to my grandchildren. I talk to my daughters about making wills and appointing me legal guardian. They rebuff what they see as an inappropriate suggestion with good humour. They want younger guardians for their children, perhaps without the indulgent passion they see in me, and, of course, with greater likelihood of a longer future. They assure me they will nonetheless stipulate their wish that grandparents continue to have a place in their lives. I have to rest my case and comfort myself with the low probability of this situation arising. My hope, however, is that this book, in showcasing grandparents' central family roles and capabilities, alongside their social and legal marginalisation, will join the forces for change, so that grandparents will, at last, have legal security to enact their love.[17]

A Guide to Mapping Routes Through the Maze of Estrangement

A book about grandparents should leave us with a warm glow, shouldn't it? Why then have I included two very difficult chapters on estrangement and alienation?

I cannot do grandparents justice if I ignore their challenges and heartache. Vulnerability is an inevitable accompaniment to strong attachments and the limits of our ability to protect those we love. The tragedy of grandparent alienation is double-edged. Not only does it cause enormous sadness for grandparents, it also deprives grandchildren of support that minimises adverse childhood experiences.[18] The guidelines below are possible steps for engaging with grandchildren in times of family rupture.

- **Control your own feelings**

This is no small task. There is a common saying, 'You're only as happy as your least happy child.' When your child and grandchildren are unhappy, you will be, too. Overcoming this unhappiness will take time. In the meantime, it can be managed.

Most people already have techniques for managing negative emotions. Hobbies, puzzles, work, exercise, films and time with friends potentially reduce anxiety. Any activity, physical or mental, that absorbs your attention, even for an hour a week, is highly effective in emotion management. Examples from grandparents themselves include reading (anything from technical manuals to poetry to commercial fiction), watching a film, listening to music, talking to friends, writing a journal or hiking.

- **Expect change**

You will need to find new ways to engage with your grandchild. Higher levels of patience and attention are required. A watch-and-wait approach might be necessary as the family structure is rearranged.

- **Provide continuity when you can**

Special occasions – Christmas, birthdays and summer holidays – are all likely to be different post-divorce, but grandparents can accept these changes while providing a familiar environment.

- **Try to appear neutral with grandchildren**

Your view of your child's ex-partner may nosedive, but your grandchildren still love both their parents. They may be very angry with one or both parents, but don't be tempted to endorse this anger. Your apparent neutrality will help grandchildren manage their conflicting loyalties.

- **Be canny and pragmatic about your relationship with your former child-in-law**

This may require listening to their explanations of why your own child was at fault for the marriage's break-up. This can be very difficult, as Soulla discovers. She feels 'a visceral repulsion' when she talks to her daughter's former spouse. 'He tells me how cold she is, and how she'll always be unhappy because she can't make friends. He goes on and on and I get the worst headache just listening to his voice. But I listen because I want him to think I am not set against him. And I want to talk to him about arrangements for the kids. So I guess that means sitting still when he complains about my daughter's character.'

- **Be alert to signs of grandparental alienation syndrome**

One telltale sign of grandparent alienation syndrome is a grandchild's display of disrespect. Even with the best intentions, divorcing parents might disparage their ex-partner's family in front of their children. In grandparent alienation syndrome, however, disparagement is persistent and sends the child the message that, 'Your grandparent deserves contempt.' A grandchild may then express the parent's view through disrespect.

When Carla's nine-year-old grandson started mocking her, 'You're such a worrier. You always think the worst is happening and no one can enjoy themselves with you,' she heard in his words her former son-in-law's language. 'I turned on him and I said, "Don't mock me, Charlie, don't you ever mock me." I'd never talked to him like that before. He was so surprised he couldn't speak. There was silence. And I said, "I won't be mocked by you," and he heard me, and then I gave him a big hug, and he gave me a hug, and it was fine.'

Carla delivers a sharp reminder to her grandson that she is worthy of respect, and then seals her message with a hug – a reminder of their strong connection.

Another approach is to open conversations with your grandchild on how people's views and experiences differ. People within one family can have very different takes on others' strengths and weaknesses. The goal is to shift the assumption that there is only one possible perspective, or that to be loyal to a father (for example) the grandchild has to be disrespectful to you.

- **Expect but resist low-status signals from your former child-in-law**

Many grandparents feel that their former child-in-law is downgrading them from a primary relative to one of lesser status. Greta explains, 'Any time I get with my grandchildren she sees as some special gift from her. "I'll let you see the children at Christmas." Like I owe her so much because I can see my grandchildren. It's like I'm downgraded from a grandmother who has a right to see them, to some distant figure who has to petition for access.' Greta lets these slights wash over her. She decides, 'I'll allow her the pleasure of insulting me, and have these little "wins", but if she pushes me away from the children, I'll fight back.'

Grandparents often experience further marginalisation when a former child-in-law remarries. The parent wants to incorporate the new step-parent's family into the central family unit, and cast their former partner's parents to the periphery. It is important not to instigate open competition over this. The aim is not to complain about an insult to you or your status, but to persist calmly in your efforts to secure time with your grandchildren, too.

- **Learn to talk – or not – to grandchildren about divorce**

There are good reasons to encourage children to reflect on and talk about their feelings. But this cannot be forced. Nothing closes a child down as firmly as a grown-up saying, 'Let's talk about this.' Talking – deep, meaningful talking when you take in and respond to what the child is saying – is often opportunistic. Don't be surprised or alarmed if your grandchild does not want to talk about their feelings or their parents' divorce. It is OK for a child to focus on childish things, and leave their parents to the messy stuff. After all, children are witnesses in this drama. They often have little control over which parent they will be with and when. They have no control over whether they will be moving from their familiar home. Their loyalties are divided, and they are unsure how to allocate them.

Eight

Modern Families: Navigating Diverse Relationships

'Don't define us by your idea of family'

The definition of grandparent as the biological parent of a biological parent holds only for a minority of grandparents. Families come in many different shapes. Sometimes two grandparents are female or male or other. Sometimes a new relationship – our own or a child's – creates intergenerational bonds as loving and enduring as those linked by genes. The different forms and features of family have no bearing on its significance or success. What marks a well-functioning family are love and responsiveness.

In her decades' work on atypical families, Professor Susan Golombok found that it is the quality of relationships, rather than structure or form, that determines the well-being of a family and its members.[1] Grandchildren initially take the family they are given as normal. They may encounter surprise or contempt or fascination about their family's structure in the wider world, but it is their own experiences of whatever they call 'family' that interest me here.

One third of women over the age of sixty-five are *step*-grandparents. In fact, step-grandparents are more numerous today than genetically related grandparents and form one of the fastest growing demographics in the Western world. The character and quality of these intergenerational relationships, and the associated joys and tensions, are equally diverse.[2]

The emotional pull between step-grandparent and grandchild can be as strong as that across bloodlines. Step-grandparents often experience the same 'grandmother swoon' to a new baby as a grandmother who shares the baby's genes. The love and support that step-grandparents offer have the same benefits to grandchildren as that provided by their biological grandparents. The impulse to care for and protect our relations serves evolution; it programmes us to love the people with whom we interact most, and those we think of as family. Our profound attachment to our kin, whether or not we actually share their genes, is also a legacy of our so-called selfish genes that programme us to invest in the wellbeing of people close to us.[3]

A step-grandparent's love can arise with the birth of a child, just as it does for a biological grandparent. For Bina, now sixty-nine, love for her grandchild is grounded in her attachment to her stepdaughter, the grandchild's mother. 'I came into Ally's life when she was nine years old,' Bina explains. 'I don't know whether meeting her was what made me want to marry her father, but I knew pretty soon after I met Ally that I wanted to be in her life forever. When her son was born I couldn't stop weeping. It was a gut-punching joy having this little bundle in our lives. But for me, well, it hit me how amazing it is that I now have a baby – and dear Ally's baby – to love from birth. I used to look in Ally's eyes and wonder what she was like in all those stages she'd already passed through. Now I have this little boy from day one.'

Sometimes a step-grandparent's bond has little to do with an attachment to the stepchild. JoAnn said she had 'no special feelings, just a decent goodwill' towards her husband's children. She was twenty-nine when her first marriage ended, and assumed she would remain single and child-free, until she met Tom, whom she married in her mid-forties. 'I never had the maternal urge so many of my friends had. When I went through an early menopause, the doctor pulled a sad face, but I just laughed. I was delighted that this was no longer on the cards. I enjoyed having control over my daily life. And the freedom! When my friends swapped stories about their kids, all I heard about was worry and drudgery. When Tom proposed, he looked at me soulfully and said – as though this was a downside – that he didn't want to have more children. I grabbed his hand and said, "Yes." And I was never sorry. Never.' But when she was fifty-two, and Tom's daughter had her first grandchild, 'everything I thought I knew about having kids changed'. JoAnn is now 'besotted' with her two grandchildren and 'takes them off their parents' hands at every opportunity'. She concludes, 'I love them to bits. Like they're mine.' She then corrects herself, 'They are mine.'

Sometimes, however, a grandparent feels that step-grandchildren compete with their own children or grandchildren. Monica, now fifty-one, also thought she would remain single and child-free, until, as she explains, she married at thirty-eight and had two kids within two and a half years. 'As soon as my first was born, I turned into a kind of earth mother,' she says. Her husband was twenty years older than Monica, and already had adult children, but was 'delighted by his second shot at being a father. He says it keeps him young, and he feels he has learned from past mistakes – mostly mistakes of omission. Older and settled in his ways as he is, he is the ideal new father.' Now he has grandchildren the same age as his children with Monica. 'We laugh about it and I put on a bright face, but it's weird. And it irks me how much he adores his grandkids. Because I don't. They annoy the hell out of me. And they don't get on with our kids. The oldest grandchild and my oldest squabble over just about everything – toys, food, place at the table or the car, whatever. I want to hug my little boy when he cries. God help me, but I want to tear my hair out when [my step-grandson] cries.'

Monica's tolerance for her own child, and her unease with her step-grandchildren, led me to reflect on how common it is for a grandparent to have 'a favourite' grandchild. Favouritism is taboo among one's own children. 'I love you all the same,' parents tell their children. They get around the very different feelings they do have by saying the *nature* of their love may differs, but the *amount* is the same for all. Grandparents, at one remove from the heavily policed norms of parental love, often admit to favourites. The ease with which they relate to one grandchild, the frequency of their meetings, how close they feel, or how much they understand and admire a child all play a part. They see no shame in saying, 'This one I am closest to,' or, 'This is my special one.'

But *disliking* a grandchild is different. Grandparents admit to losing patience with or finding a particular grandchild difficult, but none of the biological grandparents participating in my work admitted to disliking a grandchild. It was, however, an issue that came up a few times among step-grandparents.

Step-grandparents and Relational Justice

What struck me most in talking to step-grandparents was their commitment to relational justice – treating all grandchildren alike, whether step or biological. Maddie's daughter, Eva, married an older man who already had a nine-year-old child. She explains, 'This was a kid who'd been through divorce. That's how it is with a step-grandchild. You take on a child who is already dealing with problems. I warned my daughter about that before she married, but she said she knew what she was doing. So I had to follow. She got married, and suddenly I had a grandson. But he wasn't a new baby I could hold and protect. He wasn't my daughter's baby you have a ready-made love for. But my daughter was working to get on with this little boy, and I had a duty too. It was a duty through a triangle – me to the child because of my daughter.'

It wasn't easy for either of them. Maddie describes a phase 'like an emotional desert because you couldn't get through'. Initially the boy ignored Maddie, while he vacillated between adoration and hostility to his new stepmother. When Eva's own child was born he withdrew from them both. Maddie said, 'He thought of me as the baby's grandparent, not his. He wouldn't even say hello when I came to visit. He wouldn't eat with us. Like he was saying, "I know you're not here to see me." So I marched into his room. He ignored me, kept his eyes glued to his laptop. I sat on the bed beside him and he scrunched his shoulders, you know, kind of warning me not to get to close. I had things for him, books he liked and chocolate. He loved chocolate, and he kind of grunted when I put them on the bed. I sat there and eventually said, "This isn't good enough. You've got to give me something." That really surprised him. He put out his hand for a high five but

I asked for a hug. He was embarrassed but said, "OK, I'll give you a hug."'

Soon Maddie was spending more time with him. She helped him with his schoolwork. She read to him. She took him shopping for clothes. Seven years later, when Eva and the boy's father divorced, she kept the relationship alive. Maddie wanted to support him through this second divorce that, she believed, was even more traumatic for him than the first. He was angry that the 'supposed grown-ups couldn't sort things out.' He rang Maddie to ask, 'Do you know what's going on?'

'I told him that I'd been through divorce myself. I said he should give them a year. All anyone could see now was a mess, but gradually the dust would settle. It would take a year or so for his parents to calm down. And I told him he didn't have to worry about it because it wasn't his responsibility. For him, I was kind of an outsider he could go to for some objectivity, but also an insider he could talk to. And we still talk. And I still help him with things, because you can't just drop a kid like that.'

Maddie adheres to the principle that, whether you are the biological grandparent or a step-grandparent, 'you will treat all your grandchildren equally. It's unacceptable to deny a step-grandchild just because the marriage that made you a step-grandparent ends. I know people do it, but it isn't right. When I married my husband, and I had two young children, my late mother-in-law didn't treat my children like her blood grandchildren. Even at the funeral someone got up and said she had two children and two grandchildren. But she had four, because she had mine, but mine weren't acknowledged. It's decent just to treat all your grandchildren alike.'

Family Loyalty and the Sleeper Effect

Often a child embraces both step-parent and step-grandparent. Harmony reigns in the newly combined family and all seems well. Later, however, resentments emerge, apparently from nowhere. The child whose affection for a new stepmother seemed generous and easy, becomes a teenager hostile to her very existence, issuing the stunning blow, 'You're not my real mother.' The step-grandparent is then also dislodged. Or, the teen idealises the more distant parent, the one whose parental role was marginalised by the divorce. Then, suddenly, a step-grandparent hears, 'You aren't my gran. You have nothing to do with me.'

Unresolved issues over divided loyalties sometimes remain dormant for years, even decades. Harry's parents divorced twenty-two years ago. He was already married himself when his father remarried. Harry 'got on fine' with his stepmother – until one day he heard his two-year-old son calling his step-mother 'Gramma'.

'I went wild,' Harry explains. 'I was furious with [my stepmother]. I wanted to know how long she was going to ignore my mother. I accused her of getting ready to dance on her grave. Everyone was stunned. My father told me my behaviour was shameful, but I'm not ashamed, because I was pointing out something real and important.'

Loyal to his gravely ill mother, Harry marks out a hierarchy of bonds – 'blood' versus 'step' – and protests when others ignore this. His father and stepmother seem to him unperturbed by his mother's current suffering and vulnerability. Her illness refreshes memories of the confusion and outrage he felt when his father left his mother, when he was about the age his son is now. It is difficult to tease out the precise trigger, but latent resentments towards step-parents and step-grandparents are widely recognised and known as the *sleeper effect*.

Biological Grandparents and Their Grandchildren's Step-parents

A new step-parent may be welcomed as a source and support for their adult child, but grandparents are also anxious about their 'suitability' or 'trustworthiness' as the guardian of their grandchildren. Perhaps the new partner will be as unsatisfactory as the previous one. Perhaps he or she will be unable to meet the grandchild's needs? Does the new step-parent realise what they'll be taking on? Will the new step-parent have their own children? Will this new marriage support their grandchild, or will it expose them to further disruption and disappointment?

Perhaps a grandparent doubts an adult child's judgement in a partner, particularly if it is a second or third marriage. Sonia explains that she 'worked hard to get on with her [first] son-in-law. My initial response was, "My God, she could do so much better." But when it was clear she would marry him, I was careful to focus on what was good in him. I told myself, "Well, he isn't the smartest or most appealing guy, but he is good for her, and will be a good father and life partner." I couldn't have been more wrong. All those qualities that seemed good soon disappeared. So, now I don't trust myself – and I don't trust her – to see who this person will be when the going gets rough.'

It is even harder for grandparents to accept the new partner of a former child-in-law. The new spouse can be seen as a replacement or usurper of their own child. When Maddie's former son-in-law remarries, she fears this newcomer – now her grandchildren's stepmother – is an unsuitable mother figure. 'I never thought about this before, how terrified I would be as a grandmother about who my ex son-in-law marries. But suddenly it hits you. You have no link to this person who is going to be your grandchildren's stepmother. I wake up at four in the morning worrying about this new woman in my grandkids' life. She doesn't have children herself. She didn't want children. She has no knowledge of children. I worry about them being with her. So, I gave the kids phones and I said, "Ring me or your mum if you don't feel comfortable there."'

We are back to the conundrum common among in-laws as well as step-relations: will this outsider come between me and those I love? What is this 'interloper' really like? How far can they be trusted? How will this new attachment affect my influence? How will I be able to monitor this new parent figure, with whom I have no connection? Will the new step-parent acknowledge me as grandparent?

Grandparent as Parent

We have seen how many grandparents – 63 per cent of them – help raise their grandchildren in a variety of ways, with one third of all working mothers relying on a grandparent for childcare.[4] They provide adult supervision, help with homework and provide support, continuity and reassurance in stressful times. Grandparents run errands, taking grandchildren to after-school activities and lessons, buying toys or clothes or school equipment, and sometimes giving money either to the parents or grandchildren. Nonetheless, they stand in the wings. The main stage on which big life decisions are made – about discipline, religion, education, dating, diet and safety – is the parents' special domain. But some grandparents are forced to step onto that stage and act as primary carer to their grandchild.

In the United States, 6.7 million grandparents (3.3 per cent of adults between the ages of thirty and sixty-four) live with their grandchildren.[5] Sometimes the parents are also on hand, but 10 per cent of these children live only with their grandparents.[6] In England and Wales, of the 121,000 children cared for by a family member who is not a parent, nearly 60 per cent are living with a grandparent.[7] When parental care is affected by illness, addiction, a prison sentence or neglect, the most common and most effective back-up parent is a grandparent. In a grandparent's care, children have the best buffer against the worst effects of their difficult childhood.[8]

Normally we think of parental failure as individual failure, but individual tragedies take place in a social environment. As this environment worsens, the number of grandparents called upon to parent or co-parent increases. In the 1990s, with the spread of AIDS and the widespread use of crack, the number of grandparents in the US having primary or significant co-care of their grandchildren rose. The rate then increased very slowly until 2007 and 2008, when a combination of recession and the opioid crisis triggered a second spike in the number of grandparents taking on parenting roles, rising from 3 per cent of children in 1980 to 7 per cent in 2010.[9]

Grandparents who take on the role of official guardian face many practical and legal hurdles. They are often in straitened financial circumstances themselves, live in very modest accommodation and engage in demanding, tiring employment. It is not surprising that given these circumstances, and perhaps deeply worried about their adult children, many guardian grandparents report to their GP that they feel burnt out after a period of three or four years, and struggle with fatigue and depression.[10] But, while grandparents in the US and UK usually take on full parenting responsibilities only when things go badly wrong in the parents' lives, things are very different elsewhere in the world.

Across the world, grandparents take on the role of primary parent as a hugely positive step. Individual family wealth rose sharply in rural China, for example, as grandparents stepped in for parents who took well-paying city jobs.[11] In the Philippines, grandparents frequently look after grandchildren while parents work or study abroad. Sandara, fifty-two and living in Manila, is parenting her grandchildren because the parents are in the UK studying for a degree. Her grandchildren, eighteen months and three years old, chat and wave happily to their parents on weekly video calls, but look to their grandmother for their daily necessities, direction and care. She is a traditional version of the feminist grandmother – taking on childcare to support her daughter's (and, in this case, also her son-in-law's) education. When she was a young child herself, her mother spent five years in the US working as a nanny to other people's children, leaving her with her grandmother. She loved her grandmother, and weeps as she tells me she passed away last year. She also loves her mother who is now 'very old and needs watching'.

What is normal in one culture can be mind-boggling to someone from a different culture. Sandara laughed as I puzzled over this arrangement. I asked, 'Who will the children listen to when their parents return? Who will have the final say over how they are raised? Will the grandparent have to step back in their role once the parents come home?' Sandara shrugs off these questions. 'We will argue it out,' she assures me. And I think, 'Yes, that happens in all families.' Arguing – in the broad sense of dealing with different views and priorities and needs – is a way of negotiating boundaries and duties. Her breezy confidence comes, I believe, from not having the fear held by so many grandparents – of falling out with parents and losing access to their grandchildren. Being primary carer gives this grandparent an unquestioned status.

As we have seen with so many working mothers, grandparent care is essential to some careers. In research for her book, *Becoming Grandma*, Lesley Stahl interviewed Whoopi Goldberg, who left her daughter in the care of her mother when she was given the opportunity to have her own one-person Broadway show. Both women agreed that such a once-in-a-lifetime chance should not be passed by. When Goldberg called her mother and asked her to move from Harlem to Berkeley where Goldberg was living with her daughter, the grandmother responded with a simple question, 'When do you need me?'[12] This was not a guilt-free decision for Goldberg. It was not an easy experience for the child, either. But Goldberg said her mother 'wouldn't let me feel bad about this'.

Waiting for a Parent to Grow Up

Teenage pregnancies have decreased over the past decades. In the early 1990s, one quarter of all fifteen-year-olds in the US had given birth by the time they reached the age of twenty, and this has declined to 6 per cent in the US and to below 2.5 per cent in the UK for teenagers aged eighteen or younger.[13] Still, every year about a million teenagers in the US become parents and over 43,000 teenagers in the UK become pregnant. And as the average age of becoming a parent rises to over twenty-seven in the US and to over thirty in the UK, the idea of what it means to be 'too young to be a parent' has also risen. Preparing for adulthood takes longer today, and requires more years of training, education and experience before young people are ready to take their place in the adult world.[14] Grandparents may then step into a parent's role to enable a teenage mother or a young adult mother time to acquire the skills she needs for her own future.

When Ellis had a child at seventeen, neither she nor her mother, Gemma, wanted her future plans to change. Ellis had a place at a university ninety miles away. Gemma was still working in a local bank, but knew 'it must be possible to do this. I won't be the only employee there looking after a young child.' Gemma's granddaughter was born in June. The timing meant that Ellis could spend a few months with the baby before leaving home. The baby's father visited, but Gemma said she 'sees right through him. He always brings some stupid toy, something big and pointless. After holding her for two minutes he hands her back. He doesn't have a clue. He's edgy and embarrassed and always looks for an excuse to leave. I wasn't surprised when he stopped coming. I might have been a little sorry for Ellis, but she shrugged it off, called him "useless" – and I couldn't argue with that. My real worry was that she wasn't much better. She could take [the baby] for a while, but then she got bored and just put her down and didn't seem to mind the crying. She could even sleep through it. But I thought, "OK, let's give her time and when the baby's a little older it will be better."'

When Ellis went to university, according to Gemma, she 'became a good-time girl. As though she had to prove she didn't have any ties. I see her disappearing before my eyes. Sometimes she's up, sometimes she's really down. If she manages to stay in school, I'll thank my lucky stars for that. In the meantime, I do the work, but I tell her I'm the gran. I'm holding the mother position warm until my daughter grows up.'

The ambiguous status of a grandmother who acts as parent calls to mind the grandmother, Catherine, played by Sarah Lancashire in the multi-award winning BBC series *Happy Valley*, who is primary guardian to her grandson; but neither grandson nor grandmother can admit to being a parent/child unit, until the final third series. For Catherine, thinking of herself as the actual parent would be disloyal to the daughter whose death she is still mourning, while her grandson hopes that his father will become his true parent. The grandmother has to relinquish her fantasy that her daughter will return, and the grandson has to relinquish his fantasy that his biological father, a psychopath, will become a loving parent. Only then can grandmother and grandchild accept the reality that the grandmother is the parent.

Orla has no desire for her adopted son, Jed, to take up a role as father to his six-year-old son. She proudly – but not easily – presents herself as her grandson's parent and is taking steps to adopt him formally. Jed was diagnosed with foetal alcohol spectrum disorder, aged fifteen. 'He can't organise himself, or plan ahead, and his girlfriend – my grandson's birth mother – is even worse. They were so clueless they thought they were doing a good enough job with the baby, but when I went round and saw that they were leaving him alone in the flat for hours each day, and sometimes overnight, I applied for custody. His girlfriend doesn't seem to care. My son comes to visit from time to time, usually when he needs money or a bed for a few nights. He is affectionate, but there's no commitment there.'

This is not the life Orla expected to be living in her fifties. 'Never, ever did I think I'd be doing this again. I knew I would have my son in my life, with demands from him you don't usually have with your adult child, but this is a step way beyond that.' For Orla's husband, the unexpected responsibilities are a significant setback. 'I feel my age. To be honest, I feel helpless and sorry for the little chap. I know it's Orla who takes the brunt of this, so I shouldn't complain, but it's hard and the future looks hard too. Partly it's money, that's tight and getting tighter. It's isolating. We can't get together with couples like we used to. It's a little rough,' he concludes, and stands up, making it clear that he has no more to say on this matter.

Grandparents Who Co-parent

About half of children raised by a grandparent have a parent – usually a single parent – living with them and providing at least some care.[15] As co-parent, a grandparent shifts between being the parent in charge to being the parent's helper, according to how well the parent – usually their adult child rather than child-in-law – is functioning. This might vary day to day.

Just before her twentieth birthday, Casey's daughter Poppy was diagnosed with schizophrenia. It was triggered, Casey believes, by the girl's use of tainted cannabis; she was advised that although the condition was manageable, she would have to live with it for the rest of her life. When Poppy was being treated in a secure hospital ward, she was approached by members of a strict religious sect who offered her comfort and companionship along with a strict set of beliefs and codes of conduct. Casey gradually came to accept this as Poppy's choice and one that had advantages in stabilising her mental health. A husband was chosen for her, and she quickly fell pregnant; within four years she had three young children.

When Poppy's husband left her, she fell ill again. 'But what was so difficult was that she didn't think she was ill. She thought she was doing fine. She thought the children were doing fine. I was terrified for her, but even more for my grandkids. I didn't realise this before, but now my grandkids came first. I didn't think, "How can I get Poppy the absolute best treatment?" I didn't think, "How can I protect her role as parent?" I thought, "I need to take those kids." Maybe it was mean, and this haunts me. But I arranged to have her sectioned [under the Mental Health Act] and applied for formal custody of my grandkids. She got better. But I won't give up custody. Poppy's furious with me. She hates me for what I've done. You know, how I'd "gone behind [her] back" and such. This still comes up to bite me, especially when she's down.'

Casey now lives with Poppy and her three children. At first she thought that handing back parental control would be a stepped process, each good day building on the other. Now she sees 'there will always be swings and roundabouts. She's good for a while, and then she's not. I have to do what I can for her, but there's only so much [I can do]. I try to keep things simple for her, let her do what she can with the kids. But I'm the watchman. Always.'

The harmony of this three-generation family is constantly challenged. Poppy thinks her mother is 'a control freak. She's always suspicious and sniffing about my private stuff.' When tensions run high, Poppy tells Casey to leave. 'And that's ridiculous,' Casey explains, 'because legally it's my house. There's no way she could afford to live here without my support. And I can't imagine how she'd manage those kids without me.'

Her husband often chides her: 'You give them too much of your time,' and, 'You stretch yourself too thin,' and, 'What about me? Where am I on your list?' Casey laughs when she reports this last question. 'I don't have a list, but I have a gut. And the gut goes with my grandchildren.'

And these grandchildren are very likely to benefit from Casey's 'gut'. In spite of the parents' significant problems, and their often limited income and resources, children raised by a grandparent have far more positive outcomes than those raised in care, in terms of mental and physical health, education, employment – and in their ability to care for their own children. They are also are more likely to retain bonds with siblings and other family members, to have a sense of connection with a parent and a continuation of cultural and community identity, thereby providing them with significant support throughout their lives.[16]

Child-free Grandparents

Earlier I drew on Erik Erikson's concept of generativity, observing that psychological health in later life depends on continued development of our interests and capabilities. As we age, however, we are likely to dial down our focus on our personal goals and direct our attention to younger generations, even if we are not directly related to them. When, in 2023, I invited grandparents to participate in a research project entitled *Generations of Love*, I had responses from many people who said that they were not officially grandparents; however, their experiences were so much like that of a grandparent that they wanted their voices represented.

Ken, seventy-two, suffered a deeply unhappy childhood and was reluctant to become a parent himself. He is fond of his nephew and niece and takes pride in being an active uncle, but is relieved to have a 'connection without commitment', as he called it. He listens while his brother ruminates over 'all the scary and stupid things' the children did in their teenage years and, subsequently, worries whether they will thrive as adults. He helped his nephew get an apprenticeship, and asked clients for advice when his niece wanted to go to university, something no one in his extended family had ever done. But he did not feel a deeply rooted connection to a child until his niece's daughter was born. 'I went to visit, you know, a routine thing, great-uncle seeing the little one. When I got there what I wanted to do was grab her from her mum's arms. I kind of hugged the doorway because I was afraid otherwise I might just take her and run off with her.'

He visits regularly. He offers to babysit, but usually gets a quizzical look from his niece. 'She's like, "You don't have a clue how to look after a kid." So, I have to be satisfied with visits. I can imagine what they said. "Poor Uncle Ken, he's old and lonely, that's why he comes round so much." But I come round because I can't stand to stay away from her.' When his great-niece was about two years old, he was playing a guitar he'd brought to show his niece's partner. 'This little mite crawled over my legs and underneath the guitar and fit right into my lap. All she wanted was to see the playing movement up close. The point wasn't to cuddle me. It was to get close to the action. But the fact that she was willing to do that, because she trusted me and didn't mind being physically close – that was enough to melt my heart. I was hers forever after.'

Guideposts in Modern Families

In embarking on the role of step-grandparent an important question is:

- **What does it mean to *you* to be a step-grandparent?** Only if you deal with this question can you be upfront with your partner and your step-grandchildren's parents. Perhaps you believe that relational justice requires that you treat step-grandchildren just like biological grandchildren. Perhaps you want to step back so precedence is given to a bond already formed with biological grandparents.

  Being clear yourself, and inviting others to be clear about how they feel, can avoid common quarrels over hierarchies of loyalty.

We have seen how some grandparents want to keep a grandchild particularly close when a step-parent enters the family. They believe the new step-parent is untested, and they want to protect and monitor their grandchildren's well-being. This closeness also provides an important buffer against the worst effects of family tension. But using grandchildren as a source of information about step-parents is upsetting and confusing.

One eight-year-old girl became weepy as she told me about the questions her grandfather asked about her stepfather. 'His questions are weird. I don't know what to say. I don't know what I'm supposed to say.' Her grandfather routinely pressed her to say whether her stepfather made her uncomfortable. What, she wondered, did that mean? Was it that he made her go to school? Was it that she worried over who was going to pick her up? She wanted to please her grandfather by giving him information he wanted, but she also wanted to be loyal to her mother and new stepfather. Her grandfather's questioning raised her suspicions, though she did not know what to be suspicious of.

Here the grandfather's desire to protect his granddaughter from a new step-parent is counterproductive. Confiding in grandparents helps support grandchildren, but confidence cannot be forced. We have to step back, especially with very young children, and be there for them without insisting they talk.

Inexperienced step-grandparents who have trouble relaxing with their new grandchildren can take simple steps towards attachment. Beginning steps include:

- Reading the step-grandchild a story and being silly – using different voices for different characters. You are showing them that you are playful, but not insisting that they play with you.
- Arranging to do something low-key at regular intervals, such as taking them to school or picking them up, visiting the school if you can, attending special events when they are participating.

New step-grandparents sometimes have to try out various things to discover what engages them. One route is to sit beside them and ask them questions about what they are doing. Or, you can focus on something that might interest the grandchild. Work on a jigsaw or word puzzle. Arrange dolls, or dress them. Set up a mock cafe or shop.

Maddie spent some time playing by herself with Lego, until her step-grandson was comfortable enough to join her. She then let him build part of the castle, and helped him when he had trouble following the instructions. 'Eventually I was able to teach him how to follow instructions in the booklet.

I taught him Lego and for the next ten years he did Lego, so it was a great breakthrough because he could learn [and he could] have a hobby. And I was quite proud of that moment that I thought I was really engaging him.' Though he wouldn't ordinarily cuddle her she learned that she could rub his back or his feet when she read to him.

Grandparents who take on the role of parent face many hurdles.

- **They may be dealing with grief over the loss of their adult child**. This could be the loss through death, through absence, or the loss of who they hoped their child would be. Some grandparents express grief through anger: 'I never want to hear her name in this house,' and obliterate reminders such as photos. This move, intended to protect a grandchild, is more likely to heighten anxiety. 'Am I wrong/bad to remember my parent?' the grandchild wonders. 'Should I pretend I don't think about/miss/love my absent parent?'
- **Some grandparents worry that talking about the lost parent will reignite grief unnecessarily**. Grief at the loss of a parent is inevitable. It is better to acknowledge your own and your grandchild's sense of loss, and accept their – and your own – fear and anger. Euphemisms such as 'Your father has gone to sleep' are unhelpful and confusing, raising questions such as, 'Will that happen to me when I go to sleep?' and, 'Where will he wake up?' Normal routines and activities can be reassuring; the aim is for the grandchild's day-to-day life to take up an increasingly large portion of their attention, though the sorrow will never disappear.

- **Some essential grandparents have lost confidence in their own parenting skills.** In cases where a parent is incapable of taking on parenting responsibilities, grandparents may question their own parenting skills. 'My own child messed up. It must have been my fault. How can I avoid harming my grandchild?' Remember the data: children cared for by grandparents are more likely to retain bonds with siblings and other family members, to have a sense of connection with a parent and a continuation of cultural and community identity.[17]
- **Grandparents often find it helpful to think of 'keeping the parent position warm' for the return or recovery of the actual parent, if this is a possibility**. A parent finds it easier to step back in as parent when grandparents update them, via journals and photos, on the grandchild's development. The absent parent is less likely to feel excluded, and more likely to feel confident on their return.

Nine

Memories and Legacies

'What do I mean to them?'

Grandparents lucky enough to witness their grandchildren grow into young adults will have weathered many changes, from an infant's trust to a teenager's search for their own identity, from participation in a child's imaginative world to telling stories that act as an inheritance and a connection to the family's past. But, whatever the longevity of links to our grandchildren, we look to a future and ask, 'How much of me will they retain once I leave them?'

Will my eight-year-old granddaughter have any memory of the hand I place on her shoulder when she is in a funk with her parents, and I want to signal more than sympathy? I want to convey what I cannot say: 'You're in the right. Don't doubt yourself.' In my view she is simply being boisterous, quick to defend herself, or resentful at a scolding she finds humiliating. Her parents want to teach her that she must show respect and patience, but I want her stand up for herself. My husband reminds me that I might look forward to the strong woman she will become, but her parents have to live with her as she is now – and discipline her accordingly. Will she carry my silent applause for her defiance with her, when, in the future, it will be of more use to her?

Does my twelve-year-old grandson consciously remember that early closeness we shared, of his trusting absorption of my phrases and explanations, of the stories we 'wrote' together as he dictated and I recorded? Will any memory remain of those Christmases when I followed him into the chilly kitchen, made his breakfast and shared his delight in his stocking presents, the only adult tolerant of his excited, too-early wakefulness? As he now works on complex patterns in construction and coding, does he see his grandparents' intimate contributions to his capabilities? Do grandparents leave, Anna Quindlen wondered, 'a *trace memory* of being coddled, kissed, attended to, and loved'?[1]

A trace memory, or engram, is a memory stored and secured even when not accessed. Information and experiences are encoded within brain cells, even when the events themselves are forgotten.[2] These memories emerge, not as specific recollections, but through networks of assumptions about self, relationships and the world.

Memory traces are hypothetical, not proven. But they offer an intriguing model of impact and legacy. I am comforted by the notion that the empathy I pour into my grandchildren, the warmth and curiosity I have for who they are and who they will become, and the urge I have to protect them will spring to life when needed, even though my queries, 'Do you remember when we…?' are met with a blank gaze.

Seeking more than a theoretical possibility of memory traces, I set out to hear what grandchildren themselves say about their grandparents. In my explorations of grandchildren's voices, I went into five schools across the UK and spoke to different age groups and distributed questionnaires. Some children lived thousands of miles from their grandparents and saw them only once every few years, while some saw them several times a week.

Some children had four living grandparents, and some had none. All children who knew their grandparents spoke of them with warmth. Some had stories about a grandparent's trials in life: forced migration, poverty, war, prejudice or loss. Some told stories they had been told of minor, common dramas: the time a grandparent, as a child, got lost or encountered a snake on a walk, took the wrong train or lost a wallet. Some had stories about a grandparent's courage in rescuing other family members. Some stories referenced material objects – a doll's house built by a grandparent, jewellery once worn and treasured by a grandparent, clothing from the grandparent's past, or a photo of the house where the grandparents once lived.

Six general themes underpinned the stories in young children. These can be categorised as: grandparents' day-to-day interactions with grandchildren; actions they have done that supported the family, such as rescue stories; amazement at grandparents' courage and resilience; gratitude, often expressed in hindsight; family belonging and identity; and pride in having supported a grandparent.

Regular Grandparenting Activities

The youngest children focused on specific things a grandparent did. Usually these were very different from what their parents usually did:

- 'We play lots of games and I always get to make up the rules.' – Annie, six
- 'They let me leave things I don't like on my plate.' – Stanley, seven
- 'Gran tells me stories about how naughty my mother was when she was a little girl.' – Rishi, eight

- 'I like to go on walks with Granddad because he knows the names of flowers. When I see bluebells, I know Granddad would like them. And the yellow bells, too.' – Finn, six

These seemingly minor interactions lead to deep engagement. The grandchild feels in control of play, released from the usual constraints and boundaries. They register a special indulgence and empathy. They see grandparents as a source of knowledge about the family and about the world.

Rescue Stories

Grandparents were often seen in their stalwart role of stepping up in a crisis. Some grandchildren described a real emergency, while some described what was probably an imagined danger, but the appreciation of a grandparent as protector was a common theme:

- 'My mother had to go to hospital and the teacher got a call and there was no one to pick me up, so I just stood there when other children's parents were at the school gate. And there was no after-school club that day and it was awful thinking about no one coming, and then suddenly there was my gran, and I started crying and she took my hand and took me home. She even had our keys. She made me dinner and stayed with me.' – Sovann, eight
- 'There was all this rain, and it kept coming, and you couldn't see the road because there was just water, and Mum was screaming because it was coming into the house. You couldn't do anything about it, and everything was getting wet. It was so dirty, we didn't want to stay there. Mum thought we'd have to go to the community centre,

and I didn't know what this was like, but she was in one of her states. But Granddad came, even though he lives miles and miles away, and he took my sister and me, and he helped Mum clear out, and everything seemed so much better when he came.' – Ashley, nine

- 'We had to feed the neighbour's cat, and it was about to bite me, but Granny lifted me up and saved me.' – Naomi, five

Courage and Resilience

Children are brutal observers of the signs of ageing. They look upon old age as something that afflicts a different species. Nevertheless, they expressed pride and appreciation of a grandparent's fortitude in the face of frailty and illness:

- 'My grandma had cancer but whenever we saw her, she gave us a bright smile and wanted to hear what we were doing. My mother asked me whether I noticed that Gran's eyes "sparkled" when she looked at me. I just thought those were her eyes but, once Mum said it, I kept seeing it. And I kept thinking about her pain. When my little brother hurts himself, he howls. He doesn't look at anyone or think about anyone else. Gran isn't like that.' – Fran, ten
- 'Granddad can't walk any more, but he plays lots of games with me. He knows lots about history and when we watch things on TV he says, "That's not the way it really happened." I do stuff in his garden because he can't, but he tells me what to do and watches me, and it's just us. He's more patient than anyone I know. I planted a row of marrows and I look after the raspberries.' –Yolanda, eleven

Gratitude in Hindsight

Grandchildren are quicker to regret their insensitivity and ingratitude towards grandparents than towards parents. While it isn't until the end of their third decade that children look back to the hard time they gave their parents, teenagers readily reflect on past insensitivities to grandparents:

- 'I gave Gran an awful time... I hated her because she wasn't Mum. What's even worse is that I could see I hurt her and that made me want to hurt her more. I now see how hard it was for her, because she had to raise a family twice, first with Mum and then with me. I shudder when I think what would've happened to me if she didn't take me on. Mum was gone, and she took me on.' – Juliet, sixteen
- 'I couldn't see why Granddad wanted to give up his nice house and move in with us. I was complaining about it to my mum, and she pulled herself up and said, "He did it so we could have this house." I felt so bad. He loved his house and his hobby room and his garden. I never complained to him after that.' – Jake, fourteen

Belonging and Attachment

Older children and teenagers emphasise the potency of their connection to grandparents:

- 'My grandparents live way far away so I don't see them very often. But they are a huge part of my life. They will always be a part of me. I can't imagine myself not being a granddaughter.' – Saira, seventeen
- 'I think about her face when she sees me. She met me when I got off the train and I saw her first and her face was kind

of blank. Then she saw me, and she just lit up. I'm that special to her.' – Aika, seventeen

- 'My grandfather died last year. I miss him every day. I was surprised how it got to me. Before, I didn't know he was that important to me.' – Greg, seventeen
- 'I thought she'd always be here. I thought I still had time to hear her stories about our family. It was like my window back in time. She made me so proud of being part of this family.' – Lydia, nineteen

Grandchildren's Stories of Providing Care

The average age of someone offering care to an elderly relative is forty-nine years old, but 24 per cent of family members providing care to an elderly relative are aged between eighteen and thirty-four, while some are as young as nine; of these, 17 per cent of these are looking after their own grandparents or the grandparents of a partner.[3] The youngest grandchildren provide care in tandem with a parent, and their experiences are the most positive and straightforward:

- 'I go shopping with Mum, and we bring everything to Gran. And I can put everything away because I know where things go, and I can fold laundry. And now Mum says I can give her pills because I know which ones she needs, and Gran says they work much better when she takes them from me.' – Sahna, eleven
- When a grandchild offers care on her own, the experience is more mixed: 'Mum is away and I need to care for Nan. My friends just hang out after school and I can't join in. Dad tells me Gran won't be with us much longer, and I know that, but I won't be young forever either.' – Annika, thirteen

- I speak to Annika again three years later, just after her grandmother died: 'I'm sort of getting used to things now, how I can just do stuff. It's kind of nice, but also odd. Towards the end Gran got gentler, and said how sorry she was I had to do these things for her. She made me promise I wouldn't do this for my Dad. "Don't let him expect this kind of thing from you." Gran left all her money to me, not Dad, and he pesters me about that, so that's hard. But I keep thinking about what she said. I need to be careful about being roped into caring for someone. I'm glad I did it. But I'm also glad it's over.' – Annika, sixteen

Elder care is not easy, either for those who care or those who need care. Grandparents, itching to exercise generativity – that is, to promote the well-being of younger generations – are reluctant to rely on their children, and even more reluctant to rely on a grandchild. But the grandchildren participating in my work remind me that providing care comes with special compensations and pleasures.[4]

Later Memories

Seventeen-year-old Saira's reflection, 'I can't imagine myself not being a granddaughter,' suggests that our identity as a grandchild is something we carry with us, always. So, it isn't surprising that grandchildren think about a grandparent long after their death, and that the parents and grandparents who contributed to this book also have lasting memories of their grandparents:

- 'I hear her voice every day. The words she used, and her sayings. It's a comforting voice. I mean, sometimes I hear my mother's voice too, but that's critical, kind of telling me off. But Gran's voice sort of softens all the blows, especially when someone isn't nice to me. "People should treat you right. You deserve to be treated right." She gave me real self-respect, you know?' – Ruth, twenty-seven

- 'I remember napping on his stomach – he was lying on his back, and I could feel the rise and fall of his chest as he breathed, and his hand was like a blanket across my back.' – Lisa, sixty-two

Some memories are of being bored with one grandparent, but enjoying a very different relationship with another grandparent. Maya, sixty-five, remembers being 'bored sick' during visits to her mother's parents. 'After the first greetings, which were always exciting, there was nothing to say or do. We had to sit and try to talk. They asked questions and we gave one-word answers. "What'cha been doing?", "Nothing", "Nothing? Still swimming?", "Sometimes." Then we just sat around while the grown-ups talked about the traffic on the journey and then we had lunch.' Yet her attachment to her other grandmother was very different:

> 'So, I didn't feel anything special about my mother's parents, but I was very attached to my paternal grandfather even though he died when I was nine. And I have extreme, I had extreme love for him. I mean, it was almost weird that I could sort of, I sort of talked to him when I was a child after he died. I wrote him notes. I've never told anybody that. But, anyway, I had a very, very close attachment to him. He would come and see me when we lived in Manhattan. He would come after

work and see me, I think once a week, maybe a few times a week. And every time, there was this joy… He gave me a sense that I was cherished, and that's still so important to me now.'

The Ancient History of Grandparents' Legacy

In grandparenting, we engage with lives that will extend beyond our own. We look to our grandchildren's uncertain and possibly difficult futures, hoping that the heft of our love and the quality of our engagement will provide some protection. We also hope for some abiding connection linking us to an elusive eternity. And so we shower our grandchildren with love, and with whatever time and resources we can, but of equal importance are what we teach them about ourselves, our family, our values and our beliefs. Sometimes we lecture. Sometimes we scold. But our most effective method of inducting them into our social and personal knowledge is through the ordinary stories we convey in day-to-day conversation.

For families that have experienced disruption and trauma, stories play a crucial role. Children need to hear about ancestors who had been enslaved or survived genocide to make sense of their grandparents and parents, and few recount family history with as much warmth and immediacy as grandparents. Benny, seventeen, learned more from his grandparents than his parents about his mother's traumatic evacuation from a war zone. His mother, a surgeon, always worked hard 'to ensure a better life' for him and his siblings. His grandparents stepped in to help with homework, drive him to sports practices, all the while telling stories: 'My grandfather loves to talk, and I love to listen… I sat gripped for hours as he recounted adventures in the country he could never return to, and the country he had fled to with his family, arriving with no money and little English.'

Grandchildren also delight in mundane stories about 'when [their parent] was a child' and what life was like in the 'olden days' when their grandparent was young. Stories of family ups and down, dangers and rescues, heroes and victims among relatives become staples of a grandchild's personal social history. Through stories, grandparents help grandchildren understand their personal histories and family identity.[5]

Grandparents' role as storytellers is crucial to our success as a species. Human society advances because of its ability to acquire knowledge, skill and understanding from others, and to share knowledge across generations.[6] Before writing and recording, the conveyors of knowledge, the transmitters of culture were very likely the grandparents. According to evolutionary anthropologists, these elder family members occupied key roles in teaching, monitoring and enforcing social norms.[7] Through songs, stories, rumours, recipes and remedies, grandchildren found links to a still-potent cultural history.[8]

We do not have a time capsule that takes us back to explore precisely how grandparents, in early human communities, transmitted culture. There is no evidence from fossils or artefacts to show grandparents' role in passing on crucial cultural knowledge. But anthropologists studying societies today that are most similar to those of our ancestors, have ingeniously teased out evidence of grandparents' contributions to young children's social learning.

The anthropologist Polly Wiessner stayed with the Ju/'hoansi in Botswana and Namibia who, until recently, lived as they had lived for many thousands of years – one of the very few groups of people who continued to live in forager communities well into the twentieth century. Over a period of years, Wiessner recorded all conversations within these communities that involved five or more people.[9] She found that during the day, conversation was dominated by the seasoned parents, aged thirty to forty years, who talked about things that age group talks about all over the world: what they had to do, who was doing what and whether they were doing it well or badly. They shared jokes – often rude ones – grumbled about others' quirks, disclosed negative feelings about others, and mulled over actual or anticipated conflicts. About one third of the young adults' conversation fell into what Wiessner classified as 'CCC': complaint, criticism and conflict. In short, as Alison Gopnik notes, they engaged in 'the familiar grumbling and grousing … that is apparently the eternal currency of workplace politics.'[10] Children came and went, sometimes listening, sometimes watching for a break in the conversation to get an adult's attention. Conversation between children and grandparents was minimal.

When it grew dark, however, adults, young and old, male and female, gathered around fires. Here, talk was dominated not by the parents' age group, but by the older people in the community. The topics no longer focused on day-to-day chores or difficult people or petty conflicts. Instead, talking consisted of storytelling. Eighty-one per cent of the conversation centred on people from the past, or relatives from far-off communities, on spirits and the strange doings of Westerners. Children were captive listeners of the elders' stories. They cried and laughed and sang as they heard about the lives of others, many of whom were no longer living but still important in their history. Stories of strange people, foreign rituals and puzzling mindsets were brought to life by older, experienced storytellers.

It is easy to see similarities across all societies today, as grandparents grab any opportunity to transmit their ideas. Many would share Alison Gopnik's idea of heaven: 'to sit on the sofa by the fire with a three-year-old, a mug of cocoa, and a stack of picture books.'[11] As they read with a grandchild, they talk about things that are real – such as dogs and cats and children and parents – and things that are imaginary – like dragons and superheroes – and things that are real but act in imaginary ways, such as talking rabbits and wolves and owls. They sometimes weave in family histories about 'what I used to believe' or 'when I read to your mother when she was a child'. They sometimes encourage reality testing – 'Do you think that's what really happened?' – and basic human psychology – 'What do you think he did next?' or 'How do you think she felt?' In so doing, grandparents today are enacting their ancient roles as transmitters of culture.

But we are not the sole influence, and we cannot – and should not – refute the influence of others. We enact our love and protectiveness in a careful dance with the parents, who may or may not share our beliefs and values, and who may or may not meet our standards for the care we think our grandchildren deserve. Moreover, culture constantly changes in ways that limit the usefulness of past knowledge. We pour our hopes into a future beyond our ken. Though many grandparents live to see their great-grandchildren, most of us look to a more limited time horizon, and do not expect to shepherd our grandchildren throughout their adulthood.

Many grandparents say they feel less invested in precisely *what* a grandchild will do with their lives than they were about their own children. When they see the parents fussing over a grandchild's test scores, college choices, career or friends, they realise that, this time around, they do not need to monitor such details. Instead, grandparents, more trusting or perhaps more resigned to their lack of control, describe themselves as 'curious' or 'interested' in who their grandchild *will* become, rather than, as some parents are, fixed in their notion of who a child *should* become. We have seen our own children become adults, shaped in part by our hopes and efforts, but also by forces within and without that we could neither control nor predict. Generally, our concerns for our grandchild are moderated by the unknown scope and menacing shapelessness of their future.

As we age, the future – our end story – seems close to us, but just as unknown as it did when it seemed far away. This leaves us with uncertainty as to how we can give them what they will need in their futures. We ourselves have contributed to the mess we fear we are leaving them. In that regard, grandparents are not wise folk. My grandson took the measure of grown-ups' wisdom during the lockdowns of 2020 and 2021. Why were older people protected while children were denied education and friendship? The blindness and hubris of government, combined with his awareness of climate change and pollution, leaves him with a dim view of grown-ups' wisdom. Who am I to tell him what he needs to be, or learn, or do? When I see him creating Minecraft worlds in which survival depends on excavations from deep within the earth, I am not so sure this is just boys' stuff, or time-wasting screen time. Perhaps he is practising for something I cannot, or do not wish to fathom. I will not live to see his future, and I am less confident than I would like to be that the closeness we had when he was a very young child will remain inside him, living the life it still lives in me. Nonetheless, as I engage with each of my grandchildren, I share with all grandparents the hope 'that I am building a memory out of spare parts' knowing that 'someday, that memory will be all there is left of me'.[12]

Common Myths and Unrecognised Truths About Grandparenting

Myth one: Grandparent love is the least complicated kind of love.
Truth: Grandparents' love exacts careful thought and navigation. They feel love and responsibility, but usually have no direct control or rights over their grandchildren's care. Grandparents' access is at the discretion of the parents. Grandparent love appears easy only when family dynamics are easy.

Myth two: Children give grandparents unconditional love.
Truth: Grandparents have to work hard to keep their love in sync with a grandchild's changing interests and needs. Their grandchild's love is conditional on the success of those efforts.

Myth three: Grandparents have no favourites.
Truth: Grandparents are far more likely than parents to admit to having a favourite grandchild. Favouritism arises from finding opportunities to bond, and the closeness that is established, or a good match of temperaments.

Myth four: Grandparents can enjoy the good bits of children and then hand them back to parents.
Truth: Humans have evolved to be active, engaged grandparents, and that requires hard work. Today grandparents are likely to make significant sacrifices to help care for and support grandchildren.

Myth five: Grandparents have to accept that they do not play a significant role in their grandchildren's lives.
Truth: Listening to the voices of grandchildren, we learn that a grandparent can be as much a part of them as their arms and legs. Research also shows that being close to a grandparent protects a child from the negative impacts of adverse experiences, such as their parents' divorce.

Myth six: Grandparents are so sedentary that children in their care are at risk of illness through inactivity.
Truth: Even when grandparents have mobility limitations themselves, they facilitate grandchildren's activities. They take them swimming, to football practice, to gymnastics, and cheer them on from the sidelines. They also contribute financially to grandchildren's sports and other activities.

Myth seven: Caring for grandchildren depletes grandparents' energy and is not good for their health.
Truth: Grandparents who regularly see and care for their grandchildren have a lower risk of ill health and dementia, and they are likely to live longer than people of the same age who do not.

Myth eight: Grandparents who struggled as parents to combine work and childcare are freed of such burdens when their children are grown.
Truth: Feminist grandparents are keen to protect their own children from the difficult choices they made and are likely to provide childcare for grandchildren.

Myth nine: Grandchildren lose interest in grandparents when they become teenagers.
Truth: Teenagers often find reprieve in grandparents from their adolescent ambivalence towards parents. In fact, teenage boys list a grandparent as the family member they trust most.

Myth ten: Grandparents are so out of touch with their grandchildren's world that they have nothing to teach them.
Truth: Grandchildren love hearing stories about their grandparents' lives and cultures; these help them navigate the diverse backgrounds common in families today.

Notes

Introduction

1 Livingston, G., 'Children Living with or Being Cared for by a Grandparent', Pew Research Center (4 September 2013).

2 Wellard, Sarah, 'Doing it all? Grandparents, childcare and employment: An analysis of British Social Attitudes Survey Data from 1998 to 2009' (GrandparentsPlus: 2011, December). Recent updates indicate stability in data since these publications: Zanasi, F., Arpino, B., Bordone, V. and Hank, K. 'The prevalence of grandparent childcare in Europe: A research update', *European Journal of Ageing* (December 2023), vol. 20(1): 37.

3 Graham, Barbara, 'Preface', *Eye of My Heart* (New York & London: Harper, 2009), p. xiv.

4 Smith, P. and Drew, L., 'Grandparenthood', in Bornstein, Marc (ed.), *Handbook of Parenting* (Mahwah, NJ: Lawrence Erlbaum Associates, 2002), 3(1), pp. 141–72.

5 Of the seventy-two grandparents, fifty were grandmothers and twenty-two were grandfathers, and thirty-five were also step grandparents.

6 For example, the US *Longitudinal Study of Generations* (LSOG) and *Ageing and Retirement* (SHARE) in Europe, the *Three Generation Study* from Oregon Social Learning Center and the *Growing Up in Scotland* study.

Chapter One

1 As Anna Quindlen observed, 'I can't imagine anyone ever thinks to herself, at twenty-five, "someday I will get to be a grandmother".' Quindlen, Anna, *Nanaville: Adventures in Grandparenting* (New York: Random House, 2002), p. 114.

2 Wu, Katherine, 'Love Actually: The Science Behind Lust, Attraction and Companionship' (14 February 2017), Graduate School of Arts and Sciences. Harvard University; NIH (National Institute of Neurological Disorders and Stroke) Brain Basics.

3 Quindlen, p. 64.

4 Attias-Donfut, Claudine, 'The New Grandmother' in *Grandmothers* (*Ageing International*: 2001), 26: 3–4, pp. 64–73.

5 Gopnik, Alison, *The Philosophical Baby* (London: Bodley Head, 2009), p. 15.

6 Ibid., p. 204.

7 Gopnik, Alison, *The Gardener and the Carpenter* (London: Vintage, 2016), p. 192.

8 Quindlen, p. 53.

9 Burn, K.F., Henderson, V.W., Ames, D., Donnerstein, L. and Szoeke, C., 'Role of Grandparenting in Postmenopausal Women's Cognitive Health: Results from the Women's Healthy Aging Project', *Menopause*, (October 2014), 21(10), pp. 1069–74.

10 Attias-Donfut, Claudine, 'The New Grandmother' in *Grandmothers* (*Ageing International*: 2001), 26: 3–4, pp. 64–73.

11 Sadruddin, Aalyia F.A. et al., 'How do Grandparents Influence Child Health and Development? A Systematic Review', *Social Science and Medicine* (2019), 239: 112476.

12 Parsons, Christine, 'New Research Challenges Established Ideas about Infant Crying' (28 April 2022), Department of Clinical Medicine, Aarhus University.

13 Quindlen, p. 31.

14 Diana Lary explained to me that the formal words for grandmother are *zumu* (paternal) and *waitzumu* (maternal, or 'outside grandmother, since traditionally the maternal grandmother did not live with the parents). In north China the maternal grandmother is *laoloa*, and the paternal grandmother is *nainai*; in south China, the paternal grandmother is *ama*, and the maternal grandmother is *popo*. See also Lary, Diana, *China's Grandmothers: Gender, Family, and Ageing from Late Qing to Twenty-First Century* (Cambridge: Cambridge University Press, 2022), p. 8.

15 Fingerman, K., 'The Role of Offspring and In-Laws in Grandparents' Ties to Their Grandchildren', *Journal of Family Issues* (2004), 25(8), pp. 1026–49;

Jamieson, L., Ribe, E. and Warner, P., 'Outdated Assumptions about Maternal Grandmothers? Gender and Lineage in Grandparent–Grandchild Relationships', *Contemporary Social Science* (2018), 13(2), pp. 1–14.

16 Forgatch, M., and Patterson, G., *Parents and Adolescents: Living Together Part 2* (Eugene Oregon: Castalia, 1989), p. 10.

17 Apter, Terri, *What Do You Want from Me? Learning to Get Along with In-Laws* (New York: Norton, 2009), pp. 124–8.

18 Roiphe, Anne, 'Grandmothers Should Be Seen and Not Heard' in Graham, Barbara (ed.), *Eye of My Heart*, pp. 241–50.

19 Eaker, E.D. et al., 'Marital status, marital strain and the risk of coronary heart disease or total mortality: the Framlingham Offspring Study', *Psychosomatic Medicine* (2007) 69, pp. 509–13.

20 Gottman, John, *The Mathematics of Marriage* (Cambridge, MA: MIT Press. (2005), p. 151 ff; Gottman, John, *Why Marriages Succeed or Fail* (New York: Simon and Schuster, 1995), pp. 93 ff.

21 Goodwin, Marjorie, *He-Said-She-Said: Talk as Social Organisation Among Black Children* (Bloomington: Indiana University Press, 1991); Sheldon, Amy, 'Conflict Talk: Sociolinguistic Challenges to Self-Assertion and How Young Girls Meet Them', *Merrill Palmer Quarterly* 38 (1992), pp. 95–117; Tannen, Deborah, *You Just Don't Understand* (New York: Morrow, 1990), pp. 45–55.

22 Eaker, E.D. et al., 'Marital status, marital strain and the risk of coronary heart disease or total mortality: the Framlingham Offspring Study', *Psychosomatic Medicine,* (2007) 69, pp. 509–13.

23 Forgatch, M., and Patterson, G., p. 10; Apter, Terri, *You Don't Really Know Me: Why Mothers and Daughters Fight and How Both Can Win* (New York: W.W. Norton, 2004) pp. 19–21.

24 Gottman, John, *Why Marriages Succeed or Fail* (New York: Simon and Schuster, 1995), p. 26.

25 Greenberg, Jill, *End Times* (Alcobendas: TF Editores, 2006). See also Teicher, Jordan, 'Stunning Portraits of Crying Children that Brought the Photographer Hate Mail', *Slate* (4 August 2013).

26 IBB Solicitors, 'Grandparent Alienation: Taking Steps to Grant Greater Rights to Grandparents', (July 2019), published online: https://www.ibblaw.co.uk/wp-content/uploads/2019/10/mnid19280-IBB-Grandparent-Infographic-Report_v2-Single-Pages.pdf.

27 Quindlen, p. 92.

Chapter Two

1 Di Gessa, G. and Bordone, V., 'English Longitudinal Study of Aging', *Journal of Gerontology: Social Sciences* (3 October 2022).

2 Kahneman, D., Diener, E. and Schwartz, N., *Well-Being: The Foundations of Hedonic Psychology* (Russell Sage Foundation: 1999).

3 Apter, Terri, *Secret Paths: Women in the New Midlife* (New York: W.W. Norton, 1995).

4 Arpino, B., Pronzato, C.D. and Tavares, L.P., 'The Effect of Grandparents' Support on Mothers' Labour Market Participation: An Instrumental Variable Approach', *European Journal of Population* (2014), 30, pp. 369–390.

5 For a detailed discussion of this see Apter, Terri, 'Women at Work Report', The Female Lead (2021).

6 Huang, J. et al., *Women in the Workplace* (McKinsey/LeanIn, 2019).

7 Jones, L., 'Women's Progression in the Workplace', Government Equalities Office (October 2019); Lindley, Joanne Kathryn, 'Lousy pay with lousy conditions: the role of occupational desegregation in explaining the UK gender pay and work intensity gaps', *Oxford Economic Papers*, (2016), 68, pp. 152–173; Costa Dias, M., Joyce, R., Parodi, F., 'Wage progression and the gender wage gap: the causal impact of hours of work', Institute of Fiscal Studies (2018); Warren, T., Lyonette, C., 'Good, Bad and Very Bad Part-time Jobs for Women? Re-examining the Importance of Occupational Class for Job Quality Since the "Great Recession" in Britain', *Work, Employment and Society* (2018), 32(4), pp. 747–67, https://doi.org/10.1177/0950017018762289.

8 Cain Miller, C., 'The Upshot', *New York Times* (26 April 2019).

9 Apter, Terri, 'The Entitlement Gap: Women in the Workplace', The Female Lead (2021).

10 Quoted in Gifford, Charlotte, 'Childcare costs more than our mortgage – an extra 15 hours won't make a difference' *Daily Telegraph* (3 April 2024). A report published on 9 March 2023 by the charity Coram says that full-time nursery places for children under two costs £15,000 a year. As a percentage of full-time pay the average cost of full-time nursery for a child under two years is over 50 per cent in London and about 42 per cent in the north-west and Wales. See also, Buchanan, A. and Rotkirch, A., 'Twenty-First Century Grandparents: Global Perspectives on Changing Roles and Consequences', *Journal of the Academy of Social Sciences* (2018), 13(2), pp. 131–44.

11 'Looking after the grandchildren? Make sure it counts towards your State Pension', Department for Work and Pensions (26 July 2013).

12 UK Parliament, 'Written Evidence from Grandparents Plus' (IGF0058) (February 2016).

13 Estimate by SunLife Insurance, 29 August 2023. https://www.sunlife.co.uk/press-office/news/grandparents-childcare-salary/, retrieved 17 July 2024.

14 The UK government in some cases offers financial support to grandparents who regularly care for grandchildren either via child benefits or National Insurance credits, which contribute towards their state pension. But as the retirement age is raised throughout the UK and the EU, there is concern that the costs of providing childcare will also rise for grandparents or for parents: grandparents will either cut down on their paid employment before retirement, thereby reducing both current income and future pension income, or they will not provide childcare, thereby adding additional costs to the parents. See https://www.gov.uk/government/publications/national-insurance-credits-for-adults-who-care-for-a-child-under-12-fact-sheet/specified-adult-childcare-credits-fact-sheet.

15 Stahl, Lesley, *Becoming Grandma: The Joys and Science of the New Grandparenting* (New York: Blue Rider Press, 2016), pp. 20–1.

16 Livingston, G. and Parker, K., 'Since the Great Recession, More Children Raised by Grandparents', Pew Research Center (September 9, 2010).

17 Education sociologist Professor Madeleine Arnot lived in Portugal for several years and told me, 'I've seen grandmothers taken over by childcaring, the Latin [southern Europe way] way. Many younger women were determined that they were not going to do this.'

18 Crowley Jack, Dana, *Silencing the Self: Women and Depression* (Harvard: Harvard University Press, 1991); Crowley Jack, Dana, 'Silencing the self: Inner dialogues and outer realities' in Joiner, T. and Coyne, J. (ed.), *The Interactional Nature of Depression: Advances in Interpersonal Approaches* (American Psychological Association, 1999), pp. 221–46.

19 Vickers, Salley, *Grandmothers* (London: Penguin, 2020), p. 23.

20 White, Monica, 'Diary of a Supergran' in *Grandmothers* (*Ageing International*: 2001) 26: 3–4, pp. 34–43.

21 Livingston, G., 'Children Living with or Being Cared for by a Grandparent', Pew Research Center (4 September 2013).

22 Hayslip, B. et. al., 'Grandparents Raising Grandchildren: What We Have Learned in the Past Decade', *The Gerontologist* (2019), 59(3), pp. 152–63.

Chapter Three

1 Graham, Barbara, *Eye of My Heart* (New York: Harper, 2009), p. 201.

2 Gopnik, Alison, 'Why childhood and old age are key to our human capacities', *Aeon* (Washington DC: *American Psychological Association*, 9 November 2020), pp. 221–46.

3 Office for National Statistics (ONS),'How has life expectancy changed over time?' (Census 2021).

4 Porck, Thijs, 'Digging for early medieval grandmothers in Anglo-Saxon wills', *Early Medieval English in Nineteenth Century Europe* (23 January 2017), ERC Project.

5 Revedin, Anna et al., 'Thirty-Thousand-Year-Old Evidence of Plant Food Processing', *Proceedings of the National Academy of Sciences* (2010), 107(44), pp. 18815–19, cited in Gopnik, Alison, *The Gardener and the Carpenter* (New York: Vintage, 2017), p. 40.

6 Lary, Diana, *China's Grandmothers: Gender, Family, and Ageing from Late Qing to Twenty-First Century* (Cambridge: Cambridge University Press, 2022), p. 47.

7 Hawkes, Kristen, 'Grandmothers and the Evolution of Human Longevity', *American Journal of Human Biology* (2003), 15, pp. 380–400; Pavelka, M.S.M. and Fedigan, M. 'Menopause: A comparative life history perspective', *Yearbook of Physical Anthropology* (1991), 34, pp. 13–38; Austad, S.N., 'Postreproductive survival', in Wachter, K.W. and Finch, C.E., (ed.), *Between Zeus and the Salmon* (Washington DC: National Academy Press, 1997), pp. 161–74.

8 Binford, L.R., *Bones: Ancient Men and Modern Myths* (New York: Academic Press, 1981), pp. 35–86.

9 Hawkes, Kristen, 'Grandmothers and the Evolution of Human Longevity', *American Journal of Human Biology* (2003), 15, pp. 380–400.

10 Ibid. Here Hawkes presents but does not endorse the so-called 'hunting hypothesis'.

11 Kuzawa, Christopher W. et al., 'Metabolic costs and evolutionary implications of human brain development', *PNAS* (2014), 111(36), pp. 13010–15.

12 Bloch, Marc, *French Rural History* (London: Routledge, 1966), pp. 115–6.

13 Statham, June, 'Grandparents providing childcare: briefing paper', Childhood Wellbeing Research Centre (2011), Department for Education, Government Briefing Paper.

14 'Children Living with or Being Cared for by a Grandparent', Pew Research Center (4 September 2013).

15 Lary, Diana, *China's Grandmothers: Gender, Family, and Ageing from Late Qing to Twenty-First Century* (Cambridge: Cambridge University Press, 2022), p. 6.

16 Asis, M.M.B., 'Imagining the Future of Migration and Families in Asia', *Asian and Pacific Migration Journal* (2000), 9, pp. 255–72.

17 Botcheva, Luba B., 'Grandparents as family stabilizers during economic hardship in Bulgaria', *International Journal of Psychology* (2004), 39(3), pp. 157–68.

18 Duflo, Esther, 'Grandmothers and Granddaughters: Old Age Pensions and Intra-household Allocation in South Africa', *World Bank Economic Review* (2003), 17(1), pp. 1–25.

19 Botcheva, pp. 157–68.

20 Schulevitz, Judith, 'Why Do Grandmothers Exist?', *New Republic* (29 January 2013). See also, Angier, Natalie, 'Weighing the Grandma Factor: In Some Societies It's a Matter of Life and Death', *New York Times* (5 November 2002).

21 Thomas, P., Liu, H. and Umberson, D., 'Family Relationships and Wellbeing', *Innovation in Aging* (November 2017), 1(3), pp. 1–11.

22 2011 Census, cited in Agarwal, Bina, 'Long road ahead: From I-day speech to women's work', *Indian Express* (19 August 2022).

23 Pew Research Center Survey 2021. See also, 'Family Matters: Multigenerational Living is on the Rise and Here to Stay', Generations United (2021). www.gu.org/app/uploads/2021/04/21-MG-Family-Report-WEB.pdf.

24 Mooney, A., Stratham, J. and Simon, A., *The Pivot Generation: Informal Care and Work after Fifty* (Cambridge: UK: The Policy Press, 2002), table 3.8.

25 Mooney, A., Stratham, J. and Simon, A., p. 22.

26 Thomas, P., Liu, H. and Umberson, D., 1(3), pp. 1–11.

27 Erikson, Erik, *Childhood and Society* (New York: Norton, 1950), pp. 266–9.

28 Apter, Terri, 'Elder Care', paper presented at ASDO Conference on *Family-Friendly Practices in the UK and EU* (Rome: 3 June 2003).

29 Buchanan, A. and Rotkirch, A., 13(2), pp. 31–144.

30 Blaffer Hrdy, Sarah, *Mothers and Others* (Harvard: Harvard University Press, 2011).

31 Blaffer Hrdy, Sarah, *Father Time: A History of Men and Babies* (Princeton: Princeton University Press, 2024), pp. 8–26.

32 Martinez-Garcia, M., Paternina-Die, M., Cardenas, S., Vilarroya, O., Desco, M., Carmona, S. and Saxbe, D., 'First-time fathers show longitudinal gray matter cortical volume reductions: evidence of two international samples' *Cerebral Cortex* (April 2023), 33(7), pp. 4146–63.

33 Blaffer Hrdy, Sarah, *Father Time*, pp. 27–53.

34 Wolf, Martin, 'Coronavirus Diaries: Martin Wolf on the pain of family separation', *Financial Times* (7 April 2020).

35 Di Gessa, G., Bordone, V. and Arpino, B., 'Changes in Grandparental Childcare During the Pandemic and Mental Health: Evidence from England', *Journals of Gerontology Series B* (2023), 78(2), pp. 319–29.

36 Coall, D. et al., 'A new niche? The theory of grandfather involvement', in Buchanan, A. and Rotkirch, A. (ed.), *Grandfathers: Global Perspectives* (London: Palgrave Macmillan, 2016), pp. 21–44.

37 Wilton, Dr Virginia and Davy, Dr Judith A., 'Grandfathers – Their Changing Family Roles and Contributions', Blue Skies Report No 3/06. Families Commission's Blue Skies Fund, New Zealand Institute for Research on Aging (March 2006).

38 Raeburn, Paul, *Do Fathers Matter? What Science is Telling Us About the Parent We've Overlooked* (New York: Scientific American/Farrar, Straus and Giroux, 2014), p. 149.

39 Stahl, Lesley, p. 148.

40 Bates, J. and Taylor, A., 'Grandfather Involvement and Aging Men's Mental Health', *American Journal of Men's Health* (May 2012), 6(3), pp. 229–39.

41 Stahl, Lesley, p. 146.

42 Pipher, Mary, in Graham, Barbara (ed.), *Eye of My Heart*, (New York: Harper, 2009), p. 6.

43 Quindlen, Anna, p. 108.

44 Arber, S. and Attias-Donfut, C. (ed.), *The Myth of Generational Conflict: The Family and State in Aging Societies* (London: Routledge, 2007); Coall, D. and Hertwig, R., 'Grandparental investment: Past, present and future', *Behavioral and Brain Sciences*, (2010), 33, pp. 1–59; Szydlik, M., *Sharing Lives: Adult Children and Parents* (London: Routledge, 2016).

Chapter Four

1 The term 'borderwork' was originally used to describe gender boundaries in children's play and the ways in which interaction that usually reduces a strong sense of difference between people, can also be used to strengthen a sense of boundary. See Thorne, Barrie, *Gender Play: Girls and Boys in School* (New Brunswick, NJ: Rutgers University Press, 1993), pp. 63–91.

2 'Matrimoni, separazioni e divorzi: anno 2003', Italian National Statistics Institute (Rome: Istat, 2006).

3 Babies who are born without vision develop other means of response and are sensitive to nuances in touch and sound. Here I describe the most common route to attachment.

4 Meltzoff, A.N., 'Infants' causal learning: Intervention, observation, imitation', in Gopnik, A. and Schults, L. (eds.), *Causal Learning: Psychology, Philosophy, and Computation* (Oxford: Oxford University Press, 2007), pp. 37–47.

5 Gergely, Gyorgy, 'The social construction of the subjective self: the role of affect-mirroring, markedness, and ostensive communication in self-development', in Fonagy, P., Mayes, L. and Target, M. (eds.), *Developmental Science and Psychoanalysis* (London: Routledge, 2007), Chapter 2: pp. 45–82.

6 Byford, Annette, *Once a Mother, Always a Mother: On Life with Adult Children* (London: Ortus Press, 2022), p. 6.

7 Martinez-Garcia, M., Paternina-Die, M., Cardenas, S., Vilarroya, O., Desco, M., Carmona, S., Saxbe, D., pp. 4146–63.

8 Stern, Daniel, *The Interpersonal World of the Infant: A View from Psychoanalysis and Developmental Psychology* (New York: Basic Books, 1985), pp. 138–61.

9 Quindlen, Anna, p. 136.

10 Livingston, Gretchen, 'The rise of multiracial and multiethnic babies in the U.S.', Pew Research Center (6 June 2017).

11 'Population of England and Wales: Ethnicity Facts and Figures', Gov UK (22 December 2022, updated 4 April 2023).

12 Quindlen, Anna, p. 136.

13 Apter, Terri and Josselson, Ruthellen, *Best Friends: The Pleasures and Perils of Girls and Women's Friendship* (New York: Crown, 1998), pp. 46–79.

14 This example of competitive anxiety between grandparents came from a same-sex couple (both parents were men). My sample was too small to allow generalisation, but I saw no differences in grandparent dynamics between the same-sex couple and heterosexual ones.

15 See, for example, Bellah, R., Madsen, R., Sullivan, W., Swidler A. and Tipton, S. *Habits of the Heart: Individualism and Commitment in American Life* (Berkeley: California University Press, 1996), pp. 83, 142.

16 Young, Michael and Willmott, Peter, *Family and Kinship in East London* (London: Routledge, 1957), pp. 45, 76.

17 Young, Michael and Lemos, Gerard, 'Family and Kinship Revisited', *Prospect* (February 1998), p. 27.

18 Levine, Madeline, *Ready or Not: Preparing Our Kids to Thrive in an Uncertain and Rapidly Changing World* (New York: Harper, 2020); Fingerman, Karen, 'Millennials and their Parents', *Innovation in Aging* (November 2017), 1(3), pp. 1–16.

19 Coontz, Stephanie, *Marriage, A History: From Obedience to Intimacy or How Love Conquered Marriage* (New York: Viking, 2005), pp. 288–305; Cherlin, Andrew, *The Marriage Go-Round: The State of Marriage and the Family in America Today* (New York: Random House, 2010), pp. 140–44.

20 Harkness, S., Greg P. and Fernandez-Salagado, M., 'The Rise in Single-Mother Families and Children's Cognitive Development: Evidence from Three British Birth Cohorts', *Child Development* (2020), 91(5), pp. 1762–85.

21 Office for National Statistics (ONS) 'Childbearing for women born in different years, England and Wales: 2021 and 2022.' (Census 2021).

22 Ibid.

23 Harper, S. and Ruicheva, I., 'Grandmothers as Replacement Parents and Partners: The Role of the Grandmother in Single-Parent Families', *Journal of Intergenerational Relationships* (2010), 8, pp. 219–33.

24 Hill, K., Webber, R. and Hirsch, D., 'Staying Home and Getting On: Tackling the Challenges Facing Low to Middle Income Families Where Young Adults Live with Their Parents' (Loughborough University: Centre for Research in Social Policy, 2021).

25 Fry, R., Passel, J. and Cohn, D., 'A Majority of Young Adults in the U.S. Live with Their Parents for the First Time Since the Great Depression', Pew Research Center (4 September 2020).

26 Branson, Adam, 'Is Multi-Generational Living the Future of Housing?', (Modus, RICS, 1 March 2020); Joyce, Robert and Sturrock, David, 'Intergenerational Social Mobility in Britain', Institute for Fiscal Studies, Project No. 1013713; Office for National Statistics (ONS), 'Families and households in the UK: 2019, (Census 2021); Burgess, Gemma and Muir, Kathryn, 'The Increase in Multigenerational Households in the UK: The Motivations for and Experiences of Multigenerational Living', *Housing, Theory and Society* (2020), 37(3), pp. 322–38.

27 Merkel, Troy, 'Multigenerational Housing Accelerated by Pandemic Conditions', *Real Estate Industry Outlook*, RSM (2022).

28 Di Gessa, G., Bordone, V. and Arpino, B., 'Changes in Grandparental Care During the Pandemic and Mental Health: Evidence from England', *Journal of Gerontology* (2023), 78(2), pp. 319–29.

29 The National Association of Realtors has logged profiles of what they call 'multi generational home buyers' since 2012. Before 2012, grandparents searched for homes to accommodate adult children moving back with them. During the pandemic they searched for homes that would suit them together with the new parents.

30 Bowman, C.J., 'Holding Them Closer', *Hedgehog Review* (2013), 15(3), pp. 8–23.

31 'Matrimoni, separazioni e divorzi: anno 2003', Italian National Statistics Institute.

32 'EU.R.E.S. Un divorzio ogni quattro minuti', *Il Piccolo*, Italian National Statistics Institute (5 November 2003).

Chapter Five

1 Stahl, Lesley, p. 34.

2 Adcox, Susan, '6 Factors of Grandparent-Grandchild Closeness', Very Well Family (29 Novermber 2022), https://www.verywellfamily.com/grandparents-and-grandchildren-keeping-them-close-1695871.

3 Bakewell, Joan, 'Generation to Generation' in *Grandmothers* (*Ageing International*: 2001) 26, pp. 58–63.

4 Pittman, L., Brendle, C. and Ioffe, M. 'Quality and Quantity of Grandparent Contact: Associations with Late Adolescents' Psychological Adjustment', *Journal of Family Issues* (December 2023), 44(12), pp. 3059–88.

5 For a sound discussion about the relatively small effects of smart phones in contrast to the high-profile alarmist hype, see Odgers, Candace. 'Smartphones are bad for some teens, not all', *Nature* (2018), 554(7693), pp. 432–4; Orben, Amy and Przybylski, Andrew, 'Screens, Teens and Psychological Well-Being: Evidence from Three Time-Use-Diary Studies', *Psychological Science* (2019), 30(5), pp. 682–96.

6 Blakemore, Sarah-Jane, *Inventing Ourselves: The Secret Life of the Teenage Brain* (New York: Doubleday, 2018), p. 26.

7 For a discussion as to how Charles Cooley's concept of 'looking glass self' applies to teenagers see Apter, Terri, *The Teen Interpreter* (New York: W.W. Norton, 2022), pp. 16–18.

8 Zucker, K.J., 'Epidemiology of Gender Dysphoria and Transgender Identity', *Sexual Health* (14 October 2017), 14(50), pp. 404–11.

9 There were no trans people among the participating grandparents or parents – a deficit I hope other researchers can remedy.

10 It is not surprising that in a qualitative study the numbers are different from those in large groups. For thirteen of the grandchildren contributing to the research for *Grandparenting*, transitioning was a live issue and, of these, five said a grandfather was particularly supportive in terms of listening and accepting, while three felt a grandmother was the most supportive family member.

11 Buchanan, Ann and Rotkirch, Anna, 13(2), pp. 131–44; Wilton, Dr Virginia and Davy, Dr Judith A., 'Grandfathers – Their Changing Family Roles and Contributions'.

Chapter Six

1 Graham, Barbara, p. 202.

2 Coleman, Joshua, *Rules of Estrangement: Why Adult Children Cut Ties and How to Heal the Conflict* (London: Sheldon Press, 2021), p. 194.

3 Buchanan, A. and Rotkirch, A., 13(2), pp. 131–144.

4 Gilligan, M., Suitor, J., Pillemer, K., 'Estrangement Between Mothers and Adult Children: The Role of Norms and Values', *Journal of Marriage and Family* (August 2015), 77, pp. 908–20. For a more detailed look at grandparent alienation across the UK see IBB Solicitors, 'Grandparent Alienation: Taking Steps to Grant Greater Rights to Grandparents', (July 2019), Published online: https://www.ibblaw.co.uk/wp-content/uploads/2019/10/mnid19280-IBB-Grandparent-Infographic-Report_v2-Single-Pages.pdf.

5 Coleman, Joshua, p. 186.

6 Over 80 per cent of repeated domestic abuse victims are women. See Office for National Statistics (ONS), 'Domestic Abuse and the Criminal Justice System, England and Wales', (2020), Published online: ONS.

7 Myhill, A. 'Measuring Coercive Control: What Can We Learn from Population Surveys? Violence Against Women' (2015), 21(3), pp. 355–75; National Centre for Domestic Violence, 'Isolation Tactics: How Victims of Domestic Abuse Fall into the Trap', https://www.ncdv.org.uk/isolation-tactics-how-victims-of-domestic-abuse-fall-into-the-trap/, retrieved 12 July 2024.

8 Apter, Terri, *What Do You Want From Me? Learning to Get Along with In-Laws* (New York: W.W. Norton, 2009), pp.106–8.

9 Coleman, Joshua, p. 67 ff.

10 Coleman, Joshua, p. 133.

11 Way, Niobe, *Deep Secrets: Boys' Friendships and the Crisis of Connection* (Cambridge, MA: Harvard University Press, 2013), pp. 200–30.

12 Rabinowitz, F.E., *Deepening Group Psychotherapy with Men: Stories and Insights for the Journey* (American Medical Association, 2019), pp. 1–7.

13 Newberry, Laura, 'More than 1 in 7 Men Have No Close Friends: The Way We Socialise Boys is to Blame', *Los Angeles Times* (10 October 2023).

14 Coleman, Joshua, p. 133.

15 Ibid, p. 14.

16 Hanson, Pat, *Invisible Grandparenting: Leave a Legacy of Love Whether You Can Be There or Not* (Pacific Grove, California: Park Place Publications, 2013).

Chapter Seven

1 Benson, Harry, 'Sources of Family Breakdown in the UK', Marriage Foundation (2023) https://marriagefoundation.org.uk/wp-content/uploads/2023/07/MF-research-note-Source-of-family-breakdown.pdf.; University of London, Institute of Education, Centre for Longitudinal Studies (2023) *Millennium Cohort Study*. UK Data Service: Colchester, UK. http://doi.org/10.5255/UKDA-Series-2000031.

2 Bridges, L., Rose, A., Dunn, J. and O'Connor, T., 'Children's Perspectives on Their Relationships with Grandparents Following Parental Separation: A Longitudinal Study', *Social Development* (2007), 16(3), pp. 539–54.

3 Ibid.

4 King, V., Elder, G.H. and Conger, R.D., 'Wisdom of the Ages', in Elder, G.H. and Conger, R.D. (ed.), *Children of the Land: Adversity and Success in Rural America* (Chicago: University of Chicago Press, 2000), pp. 127–50.

5 Dunn, Judy et al., 'Parents' and Partners' Life Course and Family Experiences: Links With Parent-Child Relationships in Different Family Settings', *Journal of Child Psychology and Psychiatry* (2000), 41, pp. 955–68.

6 Bounds, Olivia and Mathewson, Mandy, 'Parental Alienating Behaviours Experienced by Alienated Grandparents', *Journal of Family Issues* (2022), pp. 3250–72.

7 Ibid.

8 Vitello, Paul, 'Parents of 9/11 Victims Torn from Grandchildren', *New York Times* (19 January 2007).

9 Ibid. See also, Droser, Veronica et al., 'Parent-child relationships following spousal/parental death: An application of relational turbulence', *Journal of Social and Personal Relationships* (January 2020), 37(1), pp. 3–26.

10 Femino, Jennifer, '9/11 "Gran" Slam', *New York Post* (17 October 2007).

11 Vitello, Paul, 'Parents of 9/11 Victims Torn from Grandchildren', *New York Times* (19 January 2007).

12 Avieli, Hila and Levy, Inna, '"I feel erased:" A Qualitative Analysis of Grandparents' Experiences of Parental Alienation', *Family Relations: Interdisciplinary Journal of Applied Family Sciences* (July 2023), 72(3), pp. 637–1396.

13 Amato, P.R., and Cheadle, J., 'The Long Reach of Divorce: Divorce and Child Well-being Across Three Generations', *Journal of Marriage and Family* (2005), 67(1), pp. 191–206; King, V., 'The Legacy of a Grandparent's Divorce: Consequences for Ties Between Grandparents and Grandchildren', *Journal of Marriage and Family* (2003), 65(10), pp. 170–83.

14 Scott Sibley, D., 'When Grandparents Divorce, Everyone Hurts', *Institute for Family Studies* (20 September 2018).

15 Hansard, HC Debate 2 May 2018, vol. 640, col 182WH.

16 Case title: A. Aashifa Begum v. Khader Beevi and M.A.A. Amanullah Khan (5 March 2024).

17 See, for example, Gransnet.com, StandAlone, The Grandparents Association, AgeUK, Grandparents Apart UK.

18 Wilton, Dr Virginia and Davy, Dr Judith A., 'Grandfathers – Their Changing Family Roles and Contributions'; Bridges, L., Rose, A., Dunn, J. and O'Connor, T., pp. 539–54.

Chapter Eight

1 For an extended discussion of this, see Golombok, Susan, *We Are Family: What Really Matters for Parents and Children* (London: Scribe, 2020), pp. 1–7.

2 Sanner, C. et al., 'Building Family Relationships with Inherited Stepgrandparents', *Family Relations* (2019), 68(4), pp. 484–99.

3 Dawkins, Richard, *The Selfish Gene* (Oxford: Oxford University Press, 1976), pp. 95–110. Dawkins makes it clear that 'the selfish gene' 'only means that genes are selfish. It doesn't mean that individual organisms are. On the contrary, one of the main messages of the selfish gene is that selfish genes can program altruistic behaviour in organisms.'

4 Statham, June, 'Grandparent's Plus Briefing Paper on Grandparent Childcare', Child Wellbeing Research Centre, (November 2011).

5 Anderson, L., Buck, C. and Hayward, G., 'Grandparents and Their Coresident Grandchildren', United States Census (26 February 2024).

6 'Family Support in Graying Societies', Pew Research Center (2015).

7 Office for National Statistics (ONS) 'Kinship care in England and Wales', (Census 2021).

8 Wang, Y., Chen, X., Wang, A., Peter Jordon, L. and Lu, S., 'Research Review: Grandparent Care and Child Mental Health – A Systematic Review and Meta-Analysis', *Journal of Child Psychology and Psychiatry* (2024), 65(4), pp. 568–86.

9 Scommengna, Paola, 'More U.S. Children Raised by Grandparents', Population Reference Bureau (March 2012); Livingston, Gretchen and Parker, Kim, 'Since the Start of the Great Recession, More Children Raised by Grandparents', Pew Research Center (9 September 2012), p. 2.

10 Glaser, K. et al., *Grandparenting in Europe: Family Policy and Grandparents' Role in Providing Childcare* (Grandparents Plus, 2013); Dolbin-MacNab, Megan, 'Just Like Raising Your Own? Grandmothers' Perceptions of Parenting a Second Time Around', *Family Relations* (2006), 55(5), pp. 564–75.

11 Chang, Leslie, *Factory Girls: From Village to City in a Changing China* (New York: Spiegel and Grau, 2008). See also, Lary, Diana, *China's Grandmothers: Gender, Family and Ageing from Late Qing to Twenty-First Century* (Cambridge: Cambridge University Press, 2022), pp. 68–70.

12 Stahl, Leslie, pp. 91–94.

13 Manlove, Jennifer, 'Teen Pregnancy Rates Have Declined Significantly', NPR Weekend Edition (8 January 2023); Office for National Statistics (ONS). Teenage Pregnancies: perception versus reality. (Census 2021).

14 For an extended discussion of this, see Apter, Terri, *The Myth of Maturity* (New York: Norton, 2001).

15 Livingston, Gretchen and Parker, Kim, 'Since the Start of the Great Recession, More Children Raised by Grandparents', Pew Research Center (9 September 2012), p. 2; Anderson, L., Buck, C. and Hayward, G., 'Grandparents and Their Coresident Grandchildren', United States Census (26 February 2024), pp. 20–588.

16 Hayslip, B., Fruhauf, C. and Dolbin-MacNab, M. 'Grandparents Raising Grandchildren: What Have We Learned Over the Past Decade?', *Gerontologist* (2019), 59(3), pp. 152–63.

17 Ibid.

Chapter Nine

1 Quindlen Anna, p. 120

2 Kalat, James, *Biological Psychology* (Santa Fe Springs, California: Wadsworth Publishing, 2009), pp. 391–93.

3 'Caregiving in the US: Research Report', AARP, National Alliance for Caregiving (May 2020).

4 See Apter, Terri, *Elder Care*, paper presented at ASDO Conference on *Family Friendly Practices in the UK and EU* (Rome: 3 June 2003). See also Mosse, Kate, *An Extra Pair of Hands: A Story of Caring, Ageing and Everyday Acts of Love* (London: Wellcome Collection, 2021).

5 Green, A., 'Grandparents, communicative memory and narrative identity', 47 Oral History 8 (2019). pp. 81–91. For a discussion of the importance of passing on family stories for children from ethnic minorities, see: Nandy, S. and Selwyn, J., *Spotlight on Kinships Care* (Bristol: University of Bristol, 2011), pp. 7–9.

6 Laland, K.N., Atton, N. and Webster, M.M., 'From Fish to Fashion: Experimental and Theoretical Insights into the Evolution of Culture', *Philosophical Transactions of the Royal Society B: Biological Sciences* (2011), 366(1567), pp. 958–68.

7 Dench, Geoff, 'Preface: Why Grandmothers?' in *Grandmothers* (*Ageing International*: 2001), 26: 3–4, pp. 5–12.

8 Gopnik, Alison, *The Gardener and the Carpenter*, p. 33.

9 Wiessner, Polly, 'Embers of Society: Firelight Talk among the Ju/'hoansi Bushmen', *Proceedings of the National Academy of Sciences* (2014), 111(39), pp. 14027–35.

10 Gopnik, Alison, *The Gardener and the Carpenter*, p. 124.

11 Ibid, p. 125.

12 Quindlen, Anna, p.120.

Bibliography

Adcox, Susan, '6 Factors of Grandparent-Grandchild Closeness', Very Well Family (29 November 2022), https://www.verywellfamily.com/grandparents-and-grandchildren-keeping-them-close-1695871.

Agarwal, Bina, 'Long road ahead: From I-Day speech to women's work', *Indian Express* (19 August 2022).

Amato, P.R., and Cheadle, J., 'The Long Reach of Divorce: Divorce and Child Well-being Across Three Generations', *Journal of Marriage and Family* (2005), 67 (1), pp. 191–206.

Anderson, L., Buck, C. and Hayward, G., 'Grandparents and Their Coresident Grandchildren', United States Census (26 February 2024).

Apter, Terri, *Secret Paths: Women in the New Midlife* (New York: W.W. Norton, 1995)

Apter, Terri, *Elder Care*. Paper presented at ASDO Conference on *Family Friendly Practices in the UK and EU* (Rome: 3 June 2003).

Apter, Terri, *You Don't Really Know Me: Why Mothers and Daughters Fight and How Both Can Win* (New York: W.W. Norton, 2004).

Apter, Terri, *What Do You Want from Me? Learning to Get Along with In-Laws* (New York: W.W. Norton, 2009).

Apter, Terri, 'Women at Work Report', The Female Lead (2021).

Apter, Terri, *The Teen Interpreter* (New York: W.W. Norton, 2022).

Apter, Terri and Josselson, Ruthellen, *Best Friends: The Pleasures and Perils of Girls and Women's Friendship* (New York: Crown, 1998).

Arpino, B., Pronzato, C.D. and Tavares, L.P., 'The Effect of Grandparental Support on Mothers' Labour Market Participation: An instrumental variable approach', *European Journal of Population* (2014), 30, pp. 369–90.

Arpino, B., Bordone, V. and Hank, K. 'The prevalence of grandparent childcare in Europe: A research update', *European Journal of Ageing* (December 2023), 20(1), p. 37.

Asis, M.M.B. 'Imagining the Future of Migration and Families in Asia', *Asian and Pacific Migration Journal.* (2000), 9(3), pp. 255–72.

Attias-Donfut, Claudine, 'The New Grandmother', *Grandmothers* (*Ageing International:* 2001), 26: 3–4, pp. 64–73.

Arber, S. and Attias-Donfut, C. (ed.), *The Myth of Generational Conflict: The Family and State in Aging Societies* (London: Routledge, 2007).

Austad, S.N. 'Postreproductive survival', in Wachter, K.W. and Finch, C.E., (ed.), *Between Zeus and the Salmon* (Washington DC: National Academy Press, 1997), pp. 161–174.

Avieli, Hila and Levy, Inna, '"I feel erased:" A Qualitative Analysis of Grandparents' Experiences of Parental Alienation', *Family Relations: Interdisciplinary Journal of Applied Family Sciences* (July 2023), 72(3), pp. 637–1396.

Bakewell, Joan, 'Generation to Generation', *Ageing International* (2001) 26, pp. 58–63.

Bates, J. and Taylor, A., 'Grandfather Involvement and Aging Men's Mental Health', *American Journal of Men's Health* (May 2012), 6(3), pp. 229–39.

Bellah, R., Madsen, R., Sullivan, W., Swidler A. and Tipton, S., *Habits of the Heart: Individualism and Commitment in American Life* (Berkeley: California University Press, 1996).

Binford, L.R., *Bones: Ancient Men and Modern Myths* (New York: Academic Press, 1981), pp. 35–86.

Blaffer Hrdy, Sarah, *Mothers and Others* (Harvard: Harvard University Press, 2011).

Blaffer Hrdy, Sarah, *Father Time: A Natural History of Men and Babies* (Princeton: Princeton University Press, 2024).

Blakemore, Sarah-Jayne, *Inventing Ourselves: The Secret Life of the Teenage Brain* (New York: Doubleday, 2018).

Bloch, Marc, *French Rural History* (London: Routledge, 1966).

Botcheva, Luba B., 'Grandparents as family stabilizers during economic hardship in Bulgaria', *International Journal of Psychology* (2004), 39(3), pp. 157–68.

Bowman, C.J., 'Holding Them Closer', *The Hedgehog Review* (2013), 15(3), pp. 8–23.

Bounds, Olivia and Mathewson, Mandy, 'Parental Alienating Behaviours Experienced by Alienated Grandparents', *Journal of Family Issues* (2022). pp. 3250–72.

Bridges, L., Rose, A., Dunn, J. and O'Connor, T., 'Children's Perspectives on Their Relationships with Grandparents Following Parental Separation: A Longitudinal Study', *Social Development* (2007), 16(3), pp. 539–54.

Buchanan, A. and Rotkirch, A., 'Twenty-First Century Grandparents: Global Perspectives on Changing Roles and Consequences', *Journal of the Academy of Social Sciences* (2018), 13(2), pp. 131–144.

Burgess, Gemma and Muir, Kathryn, 'The Increase in Multigenerational Households in the UK: The Motivations for and Experiences of Multigenerational Living', *Housing, Theory and Society* (2020), 37(3), pp. 322–38.

Burn, K.F., Henderson, V.W., Ames, D., Donnerstein, L. and Szoeke, C., 'Role of Grandparenting in Postmenopausal Women's Cognitive Health: Results from the Women's Healthy Aging Project', *Menopause*, (October 2014), 21(10), pp. 1069–74.

Byford, Annette, *Once a Mother, Always a Mother: On Life With Adult Children* (London: Ortus Press, 2022).

Capaldi, D., Three Generation Study (Oregon Social Learning Center, 2024).

Coall, D. and Hertwig, R., 'Grandparental investment: Past, present and future', *Behavioral and Brain Sciences* (2010), 33, pp. 1–59.

Coall, D. et al., 'A new niche? The theory of grandfather involvement', in Buchanan, A. and Rotkirch, A. (ed.), *Grandfathers: Global perspectives* (London: Palgrave Macmillan, 2016), pp. 21–44.

Cherlin, Andrew, *The Marriage Go-Round: The State of Marriage and the Family in America Today* (New York: Random House, 2010).

Coleman, Joshua, *Rules of Estrangement: Why Adult Children Cut Ties and How to Heal the Conflict* (London: Sheldon Press, 2021).

Coontz, Stephanie, *Marriage, A History: From Obedience to Intimacy or How Love Conquored Marriage* (New York: Viking, 2005).

Crowley Jack, Dana, *Silencing the Self: Women and Depression* (Harvard: Harvard University Press, 1991).

Crowley Jack, Dana, 'Silencing the Self: Inner dialogues and outer realities' in Joiner, T., and Coyne, J., (ed.), *The Interactional Nature of Depression: Advances in Interpersonal Approaches, American Psychological Association* (1999), pp. 221–246.

Dawkins, Richard, *The Selfish Gene* (Oxford: Oxford University Press, 1976).

Dench, Geoff, 'Preface: Why Grandmothers?', *Ageing International* (2001), 26: 3–4, pp. 5–12.

Di Gessa, G. and Bordone, V., 'English Longitudinal Study of Ageing, *Journal of Gerontology: Social Sciences* (3 October 2022).

Di Gessa, G., Bordone, V. and Arpino, B., 'Changes in Grandparental Care During the Pandemic and Mental Health: Evidence from England', *Journal of Gerontology* (2023), 78(2), pp. 319–29.

Duflo, Esther, 'Grandmothers and Granddaughters: Old Age pension and Intra-household Allocation in South Africa', *World Bank Economic Review* (2003), 17(1), pp. 1–25.

Dunn, Judy et al., 'Parents' and Partners' Life Course and Family Experiences: Links With Parent-Child Relationships in Different Family Settings', *Journal of Child Psychology and Psychiatry* (2000), 41, pp. 955–68.

Eaker, E.D. et al., 'Marital status, marital strain and the risk of coronary heart disease or total mortality: the Framlingham Offspring Study', *Psychosomatic Medicine*, (2007), 69, pp. 509–13.

Erikson, Erik, *Childhood and Society*, (New York: Norton, 1950).

European Commission, The Survey of Health, Ageing and Retirement in Europe (SHARE), 2004–2023.

Fingerman, K., 'The Role of Offspring and In-laws in Grandparents' Ties to their Grandchildren', *Journal of Family Issues* (2004), 25(8), pp. 1026–1049.

Fingerman, K. 'Millennials and their Parents', *Innovation in Aging* (November 2017), 1(3), pp. 1–16.

Forgatch, M. and Patterson, G., *Parents and Adolescents: Living Together Part 2* (Eugene Oregon: Castalia, 1989).

Gergely, G., 'The social construction of the subjective self: the role of affect-mirroring, markedness, and ostensive communication in self-development.' In Fonagy, P., Mayes, L. and Target, M. (eds.), *Developmental Science and Psychoanalysis* (London: Routledge, 2007), Chapter 2, pp. 45–82.

Gilligan, M., Suitor, J., Pillemer, K., 'Estrangement Between Mothers and Adult Children: The Role of Norms and Values', *Journal of Marriage and Family* (August 2015), 77, pp. 908–20.

Glaser, K. et al., *Grandparenting in Europe: Family Policy and Grandparents' Role in Providing Childcare* (Grandparents Plus, 2013); Dolbin-MacNab, Megan, 'Just Like Raising Your Own? Grandmothers' Perceptions of Parenting a Second Time Around', *Family Relations* (2006), 55(5), pp. 564–75.

Golombok, Susan, *We Are Family: What Really Matters for Parents and Children* (London: Scribe, 2020).

Goodwin, Marjorie, *He-Said-She-Said: Talk as Social Organisation Among Black Children* (Bloomington: Indiana University Press, 1991).

Gopnik, Alison, *The Philosophical Baby* (London: Bodley Head, 2009).

Gopnik, Alison, *The Gardener and the Carpenter* (London: Vintage, 2016).

Gopnik, Alison 'Why childhood and old age are key to our human capacities', *Aeon* (Washington DC: *American Psychological Association*, 9 November 2020). pp. 221–246.

Gottman, John, *Why Marriages Succeed or Fail* (New York: Simon and Schuster, 1995).

Gottman, John, *The Mathematics of Marriage* (Cambridge, MA: MIT Press, 2005).

Graham, Barbara (ed.), *Eye of My Heart* (New York & London: Harper, 2009).

Green, A., 'Grandparents, communicative memory and narrative identity', *Oral History* (2019), 47(1), pp. 81–91.

Hanson, Pat, *Invisible Grandparenting: Leave a Legacy of Love Whether You Can Be There Or Not* (Pacific Grove: California: Park Place Publications, 2013).

Harkness, S., Greg P. and Fernandez-Salagado, M., 'The Rise in Single-Mother Families and Children's Cognitive Development: Evidence from Three British Birth Cohorts', *Child Development* (2020), 91(5), pp. 1762–85.

Harper, S. and Ruicheva, I., 'Grandmothers as Replacement Parents and Partners: The Role of the Grandmother in Single Parent Families', *Journal of Intergenerational Relationships* (2010), 8, pp. 219–33.

Hawkes, Kristen, 'Grandmothers and the Evolution of Human Longevity', *American Journal of Human Biology* (2003), 15, pp. 380–400.

Hayslip, B., Fruhauf, C. and Dolbin-MacNab, M., 'Grandparents Raising Grandchildren: What Have We Learned Over the Past Decade?', *The Gerontologist* (2019), 59(3), pp. 152–63.

Hill, K., Webber, R. and Hirsch, D., 'Staying Home and Getting On: Tackling the Challenges Facing Low to Middle Income Families Where Young Adults Live with Their Parents' (Loughborough University: Centre for Research in Social Policy, 2021).

Jamieson, L., Ribe, E. and Warner, P., 'Outdated assumptions about Maternal Grandmothers? Gender and Lineage in Grandparent-Grandchild Relationships', *Contemporary Social Science* (2018),13(2), pp. 1–14.

Joyce, Robert and Sturrock, David, 'Intergenerational Social Mobility in Britain', Institute for Fiscal Studies, Project No. 1013713.

Kahneman, D., Diener, E., Schwartz, N., *Well-Being: The Foundations of Hedonic Psychology* (Russell Sage Foundation: 1999).

King, V., 'The Legacy of a Grandparent's Divorce: Consequences for Ties Between Grandparents and Grandchildren', *Journal of Marriage and Family* (2003), 65(10), pp. 170–83.

Kuzawa, Christopher W. et al., 'Metabolic costs and evolutionary implications of human brain development', *PNAS* (2014), 111(36), pp. 13010–15.

Laland, K.N., Atton, N. and Webster, M.M., 'From Fish to Fashion: Experimental and Theoretical Insights into the Evolution of Culture', *Philosophical Transactions of the Royal Society B: Biological Sciences* (2011), 366(1567), pp. 958–68.

Lary, Diana, *China's Grandmothers: Gender, Family, and Ageing from Late Qing to Twenty-First Century* (Cambridge: Cambridge University Press, 2022).

Levine, Madeline, *Ready or Not: Preparing out Kids to Thrive in an Uncertain and Rapidly Changing World* (New York: Harper, 2020).

Livingston, G. and Parker, K., 'Since the Great Recession, More Children Raised by Grandparents', Pew Research Center (September 9, 2010).

Livingston, G., 'Children Living with or Being Cared for by a Grandparent', Pew Research Center (4 September 2013).

Livingston, G., 'The rise of multiracial and multiethnic babies in the U.S.', Pew Research Center (6 June 2017).

Martinez-Garcia, M., Paternina-Die, M., Cardenas, S., Vilarroya, O., Desco, M., Carmona, S. and Saxbe, D, 'First-time fathers show longitudinal gray matter cortical volume reductions: evidence of two international samples' *Cerebral Cortex* (April 2023), 33(7), pp. 4146–63.

Meltzoff, A.N., 'Infants' causal learning: Intervention, observation, imitation. In Gopnik, A. and Schults, L. (eds.), *Causal Learning: Psychology, Philosophy, and Computation.* (Oxford: Oxford University Press, 2007), pp. 37–47.

Merkel, Troy, 'Multigenerational Housing Accelerated by Pandemic Conditions', *Real Estate Industry Outlook*, RSM (2022).

Mooney, A., Stratham, J. and Simon, A., *The Pivot Generation: Informal Care and Work after Fifty* (Cambridge:UK: The Policy Press, 2002).

Mosse, Kate, *An Extra Pair of Hands: A Story of Caring, Ageing and Everyday Acts of Love* (London: Wellcome Collection, 2021).

Myhill, A. 'Measuring Coercive Control: What Can We Learn from Population Surveys? Violence Against Women (2015), 21(3), pp. 355–75.

Nandy, S. and Selwyn, J., *Spotlight on Kinships Care*, (Bristol: University of Bristol, 2011), pp. 7–9.

Newberry, Laura. 'More than 1 in 7 Men Have No Close Friends: The Way We Socialise Boys is to Blame', *Los Angeles Times* (10 October 2023).

Odgers, Candace, 'Smartphones are bad for some teens, not all', *Nature* (2018), 554(7693), pp. 432–34.

Office for National Statistics (ONS), 'How has life expectancy changed over time?' (Census 2021).

Office for National Statistics (ONS), 'Childbearing for women born in different years, England and Wales: 2021 and 2022' (Census 2021).

Office for National Statistics (ONS), 'Families and households in the UK: 2019' (Census 2021).

Orben, Amy and Przybylski, Andrew, 'Screens, Teens and Psychological Well-Being: Evidence From Three Time-Use-Diary Studies', *Psychological Science* (2019), 30(5), pp. 682–96.

Pavelka, M.S.M. and Fedigan, M., 'Menopause: A comparative life history perspective', *Yearbook of Physical Anthropology* (1991), 34, pp. 13–38.

Pittman, L., Brendle, C. and Ioffe, M., 'Quality and Quantity of Grandparent Contact: Associations with Late Adolescents' Psychological Adjustment', *Journal of Family Issues* (December 2023), 44(12), pp. 3059–88.

Porck, Thijs, 'Digging for early medieval grandmothers in Anglo-Saxon wills', *Early Medieval English in Nineteenth Century Europe* (23 January 2017), ERC Project.

Quindlen, Anna, *Nanaville: Adventures in Grandparenting*, (New York: Random House, 2002).

Rabinowitz, F.E., *Deepening Group Psychotherapy With Men: Stories and Insights for the Journey* (American Medical Association, 2019), pp. 1–7.

Raeburn, Paul, *Do Fathers Matter? What Science is Telling Us about the Parent We've Overlooked* (New York: Scientific American/Farrar, Straus and Giroux, 2014).

Revedin, Anna et al., 'Thirty Thousand Year Old Evidence of Plant Food Processing', *Proceedings of the National Academy of Sciences* (2010), 107(44), pp. 18815–19.

Roiphe, Anne, 'Grandmothers Should Be Seen and Not Heard' in Graham, Barbara (ed.), *Eye of My Heart*, pp. 241–50.

Sadruddin, Aalyia F.A. et al., 'How do Grandparents Influence Child Health and Development? A Systematic Review', *Social Science and Medicine* (2019), 239, 112476.

Sanner, C. et al., 'Building Family Relationships with Inherited Stepgrandparents', *Family Relations* (2019), 68(4), pp. 484–99.

Schulevitz, Judith, 'Why do Grandmothers Exist?', *New Republic* (29 January 2013). See also, Angier, Natalie, 'Weighing the Grandma Factor: In some Societies it's a Matter of Life and Death', *New York Times* (5 November 2002).

Scommengna, Paola, 'More U.S. Children Raised by Grandparents', Population Reference Bureau (March 2012).

Scott Sibley, D., 'When Grandparents Divorce, Everyone Hurts', *Institute for Family Studies* (20 September 2018).

Scottish Government, *Growing Up in Scotland: The Involvement of Grandparents in Children's Lives* (Scottish Government, 2012).

Sheldon, Amy, 'Conflict Talk: Sociolinguistic Challenges to Self-Assertion and How Young Girls Meet Them', *Merrill Palmer Quarterly* 38(1992), pp. 95–117.

Silverstein, M. and Bengston, V.L., *Longitudinal Study of Generations, California, 1971, 1985, 1988, 1991, 1994, 1997, 2000, 2005* (Inter-university Consortium for Political and Social Research, 21 August 2019).

Smith, P., Smith and Drew, L., 'Grandparenthood', in Bornstein, Marc (ed.), *Handbook of Parenting* (Lawrence Erlbaum Associates, 2002), 3(1), pp. 141–72.

Stahl, Lesley, *Becoming Grandma: The Joys and Science of the New Grandparenting* (New York: Blue Rider Press, 2016).

Statham, June, 'Grandparents providing childcare: briefing paper', Childhood Wellbeing Research Centre (2011), Government Briefing Paper.

Stern, Daniel, *The Interpersonal World of the Infant: A View From Psychoanalysis and Developmental Psychology* (New York: Basic Books, 1985), pp. 138–61.

Szydlik, M., *Sharing Lives: Adult Children and Parents* (London: Routledge, 2016).

Tannen, Deborah, *You Just Don't Understand* (New York: Morrow, 1990).

Thomas, P., Liu, H. and Umberson, D., 'Family Relationships and Wellbeing', *Innovation in Aging* (November 2017), 1(3), pp. 1–11.

Thorne, Barrie, *Gender Play: Girls and Boys in School* (New Brunswick, NJ: Rutgers University Press, 1993).

Vickers, Salley, *Grandmothers* (London: Penguin, 2020).

Wang, Y., Chen, X., Wang, A., Peter Jordon, L. and Lu, S., 'Research Review: Grandparent Care and Child Mental Health – A Systematic Review and Meta-Analysis', *The Journal of Child Psychology and Psychiatry* (2024), 65(4), pp. 568–86.

Way, Niobe, *Deep Secrets: Boys' Friendships and the Crisis of Connection* (Cambridge, MA: Harvard University Press, 2013).

Wellard, Sarah, 'Doing it all? Grandparents, childcare and employment: An analysis of British Social Attitudes Survey Data from 1998 to 2009' (GrandparentsPlus: 2011, December).

White, Monica, *Diary of a Supergran* in 'Grandmothers', *Ageing International* (2001) 26: 3–4. pp. 34–43.

Wiessner, Polly, 'Embers of Society: Firelight Talk among the Ju/'hoansi Bushmen', *Proceedings of the National Academy of Sciences* (2014), 111(39) pp. 14027–35.

Wilton, Dr Virginia and Davy, Dr Judith A., 'Grandfathers – Their Changing Family Roles and Contributions', Blue Skies Report No 3/06. New Zealand Institute for Research on Aging (March 2006).

Wu, Katherine, 'Love Actually: The science behind lust, attraction and companionship' (14 February 2017), The Graduate School of Arts and Sciences, Harvard University; NIH (National Institute of Neurological Disorders and Stroke) Brain Basics.

Young, Michael and Willmott, Peter, *Family and Kinship in East London* (London: Routeledge, 1957).

Young, Michael and Lemos, Gerard, 'Family and Kinship Revisited', *Prospect Magazine* (February 20 1998), p. 27.

Zucker, K.J., 'Epidemiology of Gender Dysphoria and Transgender Identity', *Sexual Health* (14 October 2017), 14(50), pp. 404–11.

Acknowledgements

This book would not have been possible without the contributions of grandparents, parents and grandchildren who were willing to disclose intimate details of their attachments, confusions, conflicts and hopes. My main thanks, therefore, go to the families who contributed to this book, with their voices, their time, their diaries and their generous inclusion of me as observer of their family life. Nearly all participants asked to be anonymous, but they know who they are and I hope I have done their stories justice.

I also benefitted greatly from more general discussions about grandparenting and parenting adult children from a range of people. Madeleine Arnot brought a keen sociologist's eye to contemporary trends in grandparents' and parents' lives. Carol Gilligan and Jim Gilligan offered encouragement, assuring me of the importance of the project and provided me with access to some fantastic reflections about grandparents. Christina Hardyment alerted me to the long span of grandparenting, and assured me of the possibility of a settled, comfortable rhythm in a relationship that often seems under pressure of time and change. Melissa Hines's scientific rigour as a quantitative psychologist is always helpful as well as daunting, and I am grateful for her sympathetic support of my approach to this subject. Diana Lary gave generously of her time to introduce me to the intricacies and vast changes in grandparenting in China. Carolyn Swain and David Swain meticulously outlined the process involved in decisions about moving close to grandchildren. From the very start of my work on the book, Janet Reibstein's vast experience and brilliant insights into family relationships informed my understanding of my own data. Conversations with Joyce Wood delighted me as we shared grandparenting's passions, joys and dilemmas. My colleagues at Newnham College, Cambridge, along with the College's financial support for research, also supported this book.

The work I did with the education charity The Female Lead, alongside CEO Edwina Dunn and lead researcher Veryan Dexter on The Women at Work project, helped me understand the breadth of challenges facing mothers today and why the input of grandparents is increasing. Prior to all the research and writing, the book was the brainchild of Clare Bullock, while Emily Cary-Elwes generously suggested me as its possible author. And without the championship of my agent, Kay Peddle, the project would not have found its perfect home with Duckworth Books. Finally, I thank Finlay, Xanthe, Nina and Franklin, who are teaching me what it is to be a grandparent.

Index